JOHN SMAILES is a journalist, motorsport commentator, publicist and, until recently, proprietor of a specialised communications agency. He co-wrote *Climbing the Mountain*, the autobiography of Australian motorsport legend Allan Moffat OBE, and the sixtieth anniversary history of the Confederation of Australian Motor Sport. In 1968, as a young staff writer for the Sydney *Daily Telegraph*, he was assigned to cover and help organise the London–Sydney Marathon. With the *Telegraph*'s motoring writer David McKay he wrote a book on the adventure entitled *The Bright Eyes of Danger*. Fifty years on *Race across the World* is its sequel.

Race across the World

The incredible story of the world's greatest road race
– the 1968 London to Sydney Marathon

JOHN SMAILES

ALLEN&UNWIN

SYDNEY•MELBOURNE•AUCKLAND•LONDON

First published in 2018

Copyright © John Smailes 2018

Allen & Unwin
83 Alexander Street
Crows Nest NSW 2065
Australia
Phone: (61 2) 8425 0100
Email: info@allenandunwin.com
Web: www.allenandunwin.com

 A catalogue record for this
book is available from the
National Library of Australia

ISBN 978 1 76063 253 3

Maps courtesy of Daily Express/Express Syndication, UK
Index by Puddingburn
Set in 12/17.5 pt Minion Pro by Midland Typesetters, Australia
Printed and bound in Australia by Griffin Press

10 9 8 7 6 5 4 3 2 1

The paper in this book is FSC® certified.
FSC® promotes environmentally responsible,
socially beneficial and economically viable
management of the world's forests.

For

Tommy Sopwith, who invented the marathon

Andrew Cowan, Brian Coyle and Colin Malkin
and the 97 other crews who set out to race across the world

Jenny, who was there even then

Contents

PART 1

The Prologue

1

Sabotage

'THE CRASH WAS DELIBERATE.'

The small man, grey hair cut short, with eyes so piercing they drill you, was unwavering in his assertion.

'The car that hit us was deliberately there. The crash was not normal.'

We had met in a cafe in Marseille airport, a happy place decorated in the manner of the sixties.

Jean-Claude Ogier and his wife, Lucette, had driven up from their holiday home at Saintes-Maries-de-la-Mer, and I'd flown in from the UK on a tight schedule. They'd brought their nine-year-old granddaughter, Juliette.

Our meeting was to review their part in the greatest road race of modern times—the 1968 London–Sydney Marathon.

Ninety-eight crews raced across half the world in pursuit of a total prize purse of £22,650—a huge sum fifty years ago, equivalent to more than £275,000 or almost $500,000. But it was inconsequential compared to the glory of crossing the line first.

Ogier had almost won it.

Driving with Belgian ace Lucien Bianchi, winner of the Le Mans 24 Hour race only two months before, the Frenchman was in sight of victory. The pair had kept their lightweight Citroën DS 21, a real rocket, in touch with the lead all the time. They'd been third at Bombay and across Australia had kept their head as a firestorm of desperate competition burst out around them. Across 5600 kilometres of the worst roads and tracks Australia's rugged outback and alpine regions could throw up, they'd set a cracking, but not attacking, pace.

That tactic had delivered them outright first, but it was tenuous.

At midnight on the last day of competition, after more than 16,000 kilometres, just 12 points separated the top six competitors.

Bianchi and Ogier's gap on the field was only 2 minutes and each minute was worth a point. It was too close to call and there were 694 competitive kilometres remaining.

Bianchi, the lead driver, took the wheel.

He was tempted to go on maximum attack, as he was certain those chasing him would do. But that would be foolhardy. A slip off the road would spell disaster. He had everything to lose, nothing to gain.

But he could also not afford to back off. A last-minute lunge by any of the world's best long-distance race and rally drivers could eradicate his slim advantage. All he could do was drive the Citroën as hard as he knew how, with maybe a miniscule margin for error in reserve. There was sparse light from the waning crescent moon to give texture to the tall trees lining the undulating roller-coaster of a track.

Bianchi, Formula One driver, sports-car ace, rally expert, was masterful that night. Ogier, co-driver and nominal navigator although they had no pace notes, sat in awe as the slightly built, moustachioed professional guided—not flung—the Citroën towards the dawn.

When they reached Hindmarsh Station, the last competitive stage on the near 17,000-kilometre journey, they were 11 minutes ahead. Bianchi had massively consolidated his lead.

Behind them the field had broken down, blown up, crashed and changed position, but they'd not caught the Citroën. It had been a night of legend, a fitting climax to a glorious adventure. The marathon, conceived in the UK to showcase the ailing British motor industry, had instead humbled the best cars from both that nation and Australia.

A French car was en route to victory.

Just two stages remained, each of around 165 kilometres, one mostly on gravel from Hindmarsh Station up to Nowra near the south coast of New South Wales, and the other on the national highway to the Warwick Farm Grand Prix circuit outside Sydney where the final route card would be stamped. Both were time certain but neither required effort. They were essentially transport stages, capable of being cleared without loss of points, unless, of course, disaster struck. It was the expectation of all the crews that the real marathon had finished at Hindmarsh Station and that they would now cruise to the finish.

Their job was done; their positions were set.

Ogier took over the wheel, and a tired but extremely satisfied Bianchi settled down in the right-hand seat of their left-hand-drive car.

It was early morning, just coming up to 8 a.m., and they had 2 hours 1 minute to cover the distance to the time control outside Nowra, an average speed of less than 80 kilometres per hour. Up through Braidwood in southern New South Wales, the Turpentine Range offered a wonderful, undulating open dirt road. Just 22 kilometres was bitumen; the rest, as they approached the Nowra Road where the control was set on a rickety trestle table under a canvas tent, was loosely graded hard-packed dirt.

Seventeen kilometres back from the control was Tianjara Creek, the last obstacle on the course.

Media from the major newspapers had flown down from Sydney, landed at Nowra and driven in by taxi to shoot the cars splashing through. The afternoon *Sun* newspaper, a competitor of sponsor and morning paper *The Daily Telegraph*, was looking to scoop its rival. They were both there, jostling for position. Television crews were on the creek exit. The word had got around. Tianjara Creek was buzzing with spectators.

Ogier cleared the creek—not gently but with spray flying. It was an act of celebration.

Just moments before, a white Mini Cooper S, a 10-foot-long (3-metre-long) performance car they called a 'brick' for its almost square shape, drove unchallenged through the control point at Nowra with two young men on board.

Incredibly, it set off the wrong way, in the opposing direction to the oncoming competition cars. The marathon did not close roads. No permit was requested or granted from council to close this final shire road, just as no closure had occurred on the fastest and most testing of the marathon's special stages. But common sense was expected.

Incredibly, nobody at control stopped them.

Two kilometres down the road from the control, John Gowland, manager of the Australian Ford team, was waiting for his cars. They'd be running early, and he intended to stop them and have a chat to the crews before they checked into control.

'I heard, then saw, the Mini coming the other way,' Gowland said. 'It was wrong. They should have had the road closed, but it was 1968.

'I stepped out onto the road, waving my hands at him, but he swerved around me and kept going.'

Gowland saw and heard nothing more. 'Then Andrew Cowan [in a Hillman Hunter] came through followed by Paddy Hopkirk [Austin 1800].'

There was no Citroën.

Two kilometres after the water splash, Jean-Claude Ogier had been approaching a right-hand bend. It was a big sweeper with low-lying scrub and a few trees to either side but with room for two cars to squeak past each other.

'I was in the centre of the road,' Jean-Claude told me in Marseille—his memory of that moment and his attention to detail still intense. 'Then the Austin [Mini] jumped to our side.'

Ogier went for the brakes. He's a left-foot braker. 'It's important not to brake hard,' he said. 'They are very sensitive.'

Ogier is determined that he moved out of the path of the Mini, but it kept coming.

The crash was catastrophic.

The two vehicles hit in a classic oblique offset position, right-hand front to right-hand front.

With a massive tearing of metal and not much energy absorption, both cars folded back to their firewalls, trapping the right-hand occupants—in the case of the Citroën, Bianchi.

The Mini caught fire and the two wrecks were entwined, welded together by broken body parts. A shattered carburettor and a motor still pumping petrol make for the worst kind of fire. Ogier, stunned, leapt from the wreck, reaching for his onboard fire extinguisher.

No one saw the crash, and no one was in earshot.

But then British ace, the most famous driver in the event, Paddy Hopkirk arrived in his Austin 1800. He was running second on the road and, although he wasn't certain, third outright in the marathon. Co-drivers Tony Nash and Alec Poole leapt from the car and aimed their small extinguisher optimistically at the damaged under-bonnet region of the Mini. Miraculously, the fire went out.

Hopkirk quickly assessed the situation and, recognising the need for assistance, left his two teammates at the scene, turned and sped back to Tianjara Creek. Going the wrong way was a calculated risk, but experienced competition drivers had a better chance of avoiding each other than those in the crash that had just taken out the marathon's leader.

Only one vehicle at the creek was fitted with a two-way radio. It was the media's taxi, and they used that to call for help. A small army of people—media, spectators and a smattering of officials— rushed to the scene.

'I was struggling to get the seatbelts free on the drivers of the Austin [Mini],' Ogier said.

'They were wearing four-point harnesses. I'd never seen them before. In our car we had only a lap sash.'

Bianchi's legs had been crushed and his ankle badly broken. One Mini occupant had broken his leg, too, and his passenger was drifting in and out of consciousness. By contemporary standards what happened next was deplorable medical intervention. The injured were transferred to private cars that had been driven up from the creek. They were rushed to the end of the stage and then on to Shoalhaven Hospital. At the time, it was probably the most sensible thing to do.

An official of the Australian Sporting Car Club, known as Lead-Foot Lenny for his prosthetic throttle leg, lifted Bianchi into his arms and carried him from the wreck of the Citroën to a waiting Renault 16.

Even as the injured were moved, wise heads had also separated the two crashed cars that were blocking the road. By the time Andrew Cowan arrived, third on the road and second outright in his Hillman Hunter, a small path had been cleared between the two vehicles.

It all happened in such a small amount of time.

Cowan saw Bianchi still trapped in the vehicle, but there was no assistance he could render. He was waved on. As Cowan drove away, Hopkirk believed his position was at risk. Uncertain of how much time he'd spent at the scene and not sure of his potential for points loss if he arrived late at control, he took one more look at his fallen rival and friend, and leapt back into his car, with great relief arriving at Nowra control without loss of time or points.

* * *

Half a century on, Jean-Claude and Lucette, who was also in the marathon, co-driving for the works Ford team, are in no doubt.

'I think the Austin [Mini] went on the stage purposely to stop us,' he asserts.

Over fifty years, in his mind, he has turned theory into fact.

'Someone knew there was an accident due to happen,' he claims, handing me a handwritten document in support.

But why and how? Where's the evidence?

'Citroën is very small in the marketplace,' he offers. 'A win for it in the marathon would not be good for sales of the others.' He has a point—whether British Leyland or Rootes Group, owners of Hillman, won the marathon, they'd be able to do more with it in their home markets than Citroën. But less so on the Continent.

'People were betting on the cars. They did not want us to win.'

That could be true. Ladbrokes was running a legal book on the marathon and even sponsored the coveted Teams Prize. Any number of off-course bookmakers in Australia were likely taking bets on it as well.

Race favourite Roger Clark had started at 8 to 1. The Ford Falcon, which came third because of the Bianchi crash, was at 33 to 1, and its crew had taken an each-way bet on themselves in London that earned them more than the prize money. But to run a kamikaze attack and to persuade two local lads to put their lives at risk is implausible.

'They were wearing four-point harnesses,' Ogier repeats. It's as if he thinks they were rigged for the collision.

'There were so many media there. They must have been tipped off that something was going to happen.'

Yes they were. They were there to cover the stage end of the greatest road race on earth.

Rumours spread quickly from the scene—the one most repeated even fifty years on is that the Mini drivers were off-duty police-men, drunk as well. The counterpoint is the observation made by journalists at the scene.

By the strangest of coincidences, three of the Sydney news media who travelled down to Nowra that day went on to win Australia's highest accolade for journalistic excellence, the Walkley Award. Although young, they were already seasoned professionals with proven news judgement. Sabotage was unlikely to escape them.

Bob Bottom OAM became Australia's most renowned crime-fighting investigative journalist, appearing as a witness in fourteen royal commissions into organised crime. His recollection of that day in Nowra is now virtually nonexistent. He was, as usual, meticulous in his detail, the only journalist to call police and get the names, ages, addresses and condition of the Mini drivers. That story was a small sidebar to the main piece I and others in the coverage team wrote on the sensational marathon finish.

John Hartigan was there for *The Sun*. He subsequently became chairman of News Limited in Australia, right-hand man to Rupert Murdoch and has always been regarded as the journalists' journalist.

'I flew down just to write block lines [captions] for my photographer,' he said. 'There was no more to it than that. We were out to splash a picture across the afternoon paper [in a bid to unsettle *The Daily Telegraph* the next morning].' Instead, Hartigan got all of the front page and most of the next. 'HEAD-ON CRASH. RALLY LEADER'S AGONY IN WRECK. COWAN UNOFFICIAL WINNER' the late final extra of *The Sun* screamed.

Hartigan's photographer was the multi-award-winning Russell McPhedran, inducted during the fiftieth anniversary year of the marathon into the Australian Press Club's Hall of Fame.

'McPhedran had a feel for things,' Hartigan said. 'Things happened around him.' It's more than luck: it's intuition, news sense—call it what you will. Hartigan calls it being 'kissed on the arse by a rainbow'. McPhedran's credentials include on-the-spot pictures of the Palestinian terrorist group Black September as they invaded the 1972 Munich Olympics; the moment a huge department store building collapsed under fire in Sydney; and a close association with Great Train Robber Ronald Biggs that netted several exclusives.

McPhedran jumped out of the taxi shooting, even while his media colleagues rushed to the aid of Bianchi.

'I don't know about the occupants of the Mini,' Hartigan said. 'Not a lot of attention was paid to them.'

The news team quickly headed for the airport—photographers first. No one had brought a picturegram machine, in those days a cumbersome piece of equipment usually carried in a truck. It was more efficient to fly back to Sydney and process the film at the office. They could still make it in time for the last city edition. Hartigan stayed behind, dictating his story directly to a copy-taker via a payphone. He was joined by Ian Morton, a journalist from London's *Evening Standard*, sister to the *Daily Express* that was co-sponsoring the marathon. Because of the time difference in the UK, Morton realised that the *Express* should get the story for its morning edition. Selflessly he dictated the most sensational story of the event under the by-line of David Benson, the *Express*'s motoring writer. The two had travelled the entire marathon route, competitive where they could be but with the best interests of the Beaverbrook Group, which owned both papers, in mind.

Benson was at Warwick Farm with me. The night before, the small band of journalists who'd covered the entire event had argued about which location we should be at to report the marathon's end. Warwick Farm was the preferred choice. That's where the colour would be, the results would be tabulated and the stories would unfold.

How wrong we were.

But it was at Warwick Farm that we got the quote from Sir Max Aitken, chairman of the *Daily Express* and father of the marathon: 'Thank God,' he said when he learned the win would go to a British car. 'It would have been a disaster if it had been won by a Frog or a Kraut.' It's not a line that ever saw the light of day in a newspaper—but, widely repeated, it must have fuelled the fires of Jean-Claude Ogier's conspiracy theory.

*　*　*

Andrew Cowan, his brother-in-law Brian Coyle and British Rally Champion Colin Malkin, in a Hillman Hunter, won the greatest road race in history from Paddy Hopkirk, Alec Poole and Tony Nash in an Austin 1800 by a margin of just 6 minutes after 16,694 competitive kilometres in 10 days 7 minutes 9 seconds.

Left to their own devices, they could have been considerably faster.

The 1968 London–Sydney Marathon—conceived by brilliant minds befuddled by alcohol; funded with jingoistic optimism by a newspaper proprietor from a country on the brink of industrial decay; organised with naive innocence by a committee operating on the ragged edge of competence; and contested by adventurers, dreamers, chancers and some of the most professional drivers in the world—was and will always be the World's Greatest Road Race.

The marathon was preceded in its ambition and magnificence of spirit by only two events: the Peking to Paris in 1907 and the New York to Paris in 1908, both feats of endurance that will never be replicated but neither, truly, a race.

It was followed by a series of ultra-marathons, some of them for professionals, some contrived for amateur experience, but none of which captured the essence of pioneering adventure that came with a challenge to 'race across the world'.

By the nanny-state standards of today, it was foolhardy, dangerous, courting disaster and so unlikely to go ahead that organisers should not even have bothered to apply for the permit. What permit? There was no known precedent, no set of rules or boundaries that could be raised as objections by nay-sayers acting in the supposed public interest to prevent it from happening.

All that stood between the marathon and its objective of getting from London to Sydney was a world in the midst of seismic social and political change: the most serious economic crisis since the Great Depression; a gold standard in meltdown; bristling student unrest in cities such as Paris and Belgrade through which a great race must necessarily pass; an unwinnable but for-the-first-time-televised war in Vietnam presenting almost daily scenes of unspeakable atrocities; Russia's invasion of Czechoslovakia; eleven borders that needed to open to clear a path for a planned 100 high-speed competitors; and an earthquake in Perth just before the event started.

Compared to dealing with today's bureaucracy, it was relatively straightforward.

There was no known objection to the London–Sydney Marathon: no protestors in the street, no environmental concern, no noise abatement.

On the other hand, there was very little preparation to ensure basic safety, important even then. Crowd control standards varied enormously by country, service-park facilities likewise; and

14

oncoming traffic—the least of concerns in Australia despite the outcome—presented life-threatening hazards at every turn.

You could do 150 miles per hour (240 kilometres per hour) in a road-going affordable sports car in 1968. Jaguar had released their 3.8-litre E-Type at the beginning of the decade, raising the performance bar and creating a new standard for all performance cars of the future. But you wouldn't want to drive it in the marathon. People tried. All sorts of high-flyers were making assumptions about what it would take to get halfway across the world in style and at speed. As knowledge became clearer, it was obvious that if you wanted to win you needed something purpose-built. If you wanted simply to get there, a huge feat in itself, you still needed to bulletproof a standard car to go the distance.

Cars were different then. There were no electronic aids, no automation, no autonomy. Headlights were so poor they were like candles compared to today. Jaguar (again) had introduced the disc brake only fifteen years previously, but many of the marathon cars would do it on old-fashioned, hard-wearing drums. Anti-lock braking did not exist. That's why the performance-driving schools existed, to teach you to stop and steer simultaneously. Power steering was at best an option and, if you had it, you usually sacrificed feel for lightness. Air conditioning was definitely available, but it added weight, sapped engine power and increased complexity. Seatbelts? Absolutely, but the webbing was big and heavy, there was no such thing as pre-tensioning, and in most countries, while manufacturers were compelled to fit mounting points, there was no law that required the belts as well.

Planned crushability, the use of a car's body to dissipate crash energy and save lives, was not considered. Stronger was better.

Some teams, even the leading ones, would reject the concept of installing roll cages in favour of saving weight.

On the upside, the marathon cars were simple to maintain. Servicing was mechanical, not electronic, and a spanner would solve most problems. On the other hand, the cars were fragile. The motor car is a hostile environment, and breakdowns then were the rule, not the exception. There seems to be an unwritten understanding in competition: 'Most mechanical issues would happen in the opening stages.' Why? Well, that's when things came loose, overheated, snapped or proved incapable of the task.

To compare the marathon car of 1968 to even the most basic road-going vehicle of today is to compare Apollo 11 to a contemporary small personal jet. You needed Apollo 11 to get to the moon, as you needed a marathon car to get to Sydney, but the technology built into today's small car or jet is far superior in every aspect.

The London–Sydney Marathon would touch and influence the lives of many people. It became a national school project in two countries. In the UK and Australia, students were actively involved in tracking the countries through which it passed. There were no computers, no means of engaging electronically with teams, no GPS. It was done in the analog way. The newspapers published a map, ran a mail-in competition, offered the opportunity for school excursions. Participants produced posters and collectors' cards. In Australia, a marathon board game was invented so you could race across the world on your kitchen table.

The speed of the great race would be a challenge for media.

In 1968, there was no electronic uplift of information, no memory card, not even videotape. You processed film in chemical baths and waited for it to dry. You shot television interviews on 16-millimetre film (sometimes 8-millimetre, but that didn't have sound) and you recorded sound on magnetic or optical stripe. News vision travelled slowly. It came by airfreight. The marathon was crossing into Asia by the time television coverage of the start in London arrived in Sydney. Still pictures were faster, but still needed a big, cumbersome picturegram machine to make them happen.

The Nikon F SLR camera, introduced at the turn of the decade, was purpose-built for the Vietnam War, the US space program and, as it turned out, the marathon. It was compact, lightweight and robust, but it still used film that needed to be developed.

The compact audio cassette, an analog magnetic-tape recording format, was introduced only in 1963, just in time for the war and the marathon. With the race moving so fast, it was possible to equip entrants with recorders and swap over the fragile plastic containers holding two miniature magnetic spools so that journalists could transcribe the crews' thoughts on the run. It would prove to be good in theory, not so in practice, as the bumping and thumping of competing cars caused massive disruptions in recording.

The core media would fly ahead of the race, leapfrogging to major controls. A special charter flight from now defunct British United Airways, a large and luxurious Vickers Viscount with four propellers, was stripped and kitted for the task. A toilet was turned into a darkroom. Bunks were installed—no lie-flats—to multi-task: good for the media and also able to airlift competitor casualties.

On the ground, media were left largely to their own devices. If they wanted to get into the Khyber Pass, they could take a taxi.

Timing of the event was equally rudimentary. Sealed mechanical clocks set to Greenwich Mean Time, the official time of the event, would travel to each control, enabling crews to clock in and out. They were little more than well-calibrated timecard punching bundy clocks. The marathon would be timed to the minute with a point deducted for each minute late. Penalties would be compiled manually. Today's rally standards call for timing to the second, perhaps the tenth of a second, and in some motor-sport events the hundredth or thousandth. Back then, the technology did not exist for such sophistication.

Each competing car was fitted with a mechanical trip meter, running off the vehicle's speedometer cable. It was relatively recent technology. Released only ten years prior, the Tripmaster made it possible for a rally co-driver to add and subtract distances on the go and help the driver maintain a preset average speed. The later Twinmaster had two odometers: one to record cumulative distance and one to record stage times. It could even work in reverse, so if a crew took a wrong turn they could subtract mileage as they found their way back to the course.

Like the cassette recorder, the trip meter was working in a hostile environment. A bump could cause it to jump a cog. Do enough of that and crews would be out of sync with their route chart.

If there had been an ambition to run the London–Sydney Marathon ten years earlier, it could not have been achieved. The politics of half the world had briefly aligned to open borders that were later slammed shut. And all the technology needed to make it happen was either invented or perfected in its decade. The World's Greatest Road Race could not have occurred at any other time. Try it later—as some did—and it would have been homogenised, stripped of the spontaneity that gave this event its raw purity.

There was a real hunger for the 1968 London–Sydney Marathon. The best drivers in the world wanted the challenge. And the best challengers, thrillseekers all of them, in the world wanted the drive.

The window, for this one moment in time, was open.

2

Vision

IN THE CRISP, CLEAR SKY above the English Channel, 30-year-old Max Aitken, son of Lord Beaverbrook, a member of Winston Churchill's war cabinet, was fighting for his life.

It was the Battle of Britain, and Aitken, a talented and determined pilot, was one of Churchill's Few: 'Never in the field of human conflict was so much owed by so many to so few,' the pugnacious Churchill proclaimed in his landmark speech to the House of Commons on 20 August 1940 in the midst of the battle.

They became The Few for ever more.

Fewer than 3000 of them against the crushing might of Hitler's Luftwaffe, repelling time and time again the German air attacks over their own home soil, bailing out if their aircraft was crippled, crash landing on English turf—if they were fortunate—so they could immediately report back to their squadrons to fly again. Almost 1500 of them didn't make it.

Aitken could have chosen not to be there. With his father on cabinet duty, he could have opted to run the family's newspaper business. They owned the London *Daily Express*. But that was not for him. Apart from the sense of duty, the thrill, the unadulterated adrenalin rush of pushing your fighter aircraft—in his case the Hawker Hurricane—up to and past its limit was what made life worth living.

You had to be so sensational up there. While there was supposed to be structure to an air battle, a hierarchy that had someone always watching your back, it was often not so in practice. A dogfight could break out and it became very personal, both pilots pushing their airframes up to and past their limits to gain a minute advantage on the other.

If the enemy didn't get you, your own ambition could as you pitched your kite into impossible manoeuvres, sometimes with G-forces so great that you'd black out as the blood rushed from your brain. There were no electronics, no fail-safes, no fly-by-wires. Just you, riding and controlling a mechanical beast while someone was trying to kill you.

Lord Beaverbrook, appointed Minister of Aircraft Production, had ramped up assembly to keep planes under the survivors. With a chronic lack of raw materials, he called on the public to 'give up their pots and pans to build Spitfires'. Max, his cherished child, heir to the Beaverbrook media empire, was one of those he was trying to keep in the air.

Max Aitken, ruthlessly and with great determination, shot down eight enemy aircraft in the Battle of Britain to be officially proclaimed a fighter ace. He was awarded the Distinguished

Service Order and the Distinguished Flying Cross. By the end of the war, he would have sixteen kills to his credit in the European and Middle Eastern campaigns—and he had survived.

He'd come to the war in a way different from most.

It was usual for the pilots of the RAF to be drawn from the aristocracy—they were, after all, the right sort of chaps—but even within that tight-knit coterie a class system prevailed. The RAF's 601 Squadron was called the millionaires' squadron for good reason. It had been born not on some windy airfield or in the war ministry but in the drawing room of White's, London's oldest and still most exclusive gentleman's club. In later years Prince Charles, heir to the throne, held his stag night there before his marriage to Diana; the couple enrolled their first son, William, at birth.

Max Aitken, Cambridge graduate and a man to whom privilege was natural and expected, joined the 601.

Long before the outbreak of hostility, it was all a bit of a lark. The chaps were known to drive fast cars, play polo—sometimes on motorcycles—and in many cases owned their own aircraft parked alongside those of their RAF Reserve Squadron. But increasingly there was a serious edge. The threat of massive disruption and of betrayal of the determination that a Great War could never be repeated was upon them.

When the Nazis invaded Poland, Max Aitken went to war.

* * *

You don't easily replace a war.

When you're Group Captain Sir Max Aitken and there's no war to fight any more, you still go looking for action. Sir Max joined the family firm as a director, but the newspapers were strongly in his father's hands. Lord Beaverbrook was revered and feared as the first 'Baron of Fleet Street', one of the most powerful men in the UK, and he used his newspapers without compunction as a ruthless weapon. Max had grown up surrounded by the famous and infamous. His younger brother, Peter, had Rudyard Kipling as his godfather.

Restless, Aitken built fast boats, bought fast cars, entered parliament and had two unsuccessful marriages in quick succession before he wed Violet, daughter of Sir Humphrey de Trafford, with whom he remained married until his death 34 years later.

In 1954, Sir Max used the *Daily Express* to found the London International Boat Show at the Olympia exhibition grounds. While travelling with Violet, he attended the Miami–Nassau Offshore Powerboat Race; enthused, he used the *Express* to introduce a clone, between Cowes and Torquay. It was held for the first time in 1961 and still runs today.

In 1964, the first Baron Beaverbrook succumbed to cancer, aged 85. Sir Max Aitken ascended to the chairman's role at Beaverbrook Newspapers and for three days assumed by hereditary right his father's title—and then renounced it. 'There will be only one Lord Beaverbrook in my lifetime,' he said.

It was a fair call. His father had been a colossus, not necessarily a great newspaperman but a towering newspaper proprietor. He had built the broadsheet *Daily Express* into the biggest-selling newspaper in the world with a daily circulation above four million. He'd bought the *London Evening Standard*—stolen it, some people said—and he'd begun satellite newspapers across the country, especially in Scotland. In 1948, he told a British Royal Commission into the activities of the press, with more than a small amount of arrogance and pomposity, that he ran his papers purely for the purpose of making propaganda.

* * *

It wasn't going well for Sir Max.

Under attack from the new breed of tabloids, especially *The Sun*, soon to be owned by Rupert Murdoch, circulation was receding. Four million had become a stretch target rather than a firm foundation. London was liberated in the 1960s. It was the place to be as long as you came equipped with a new view. Mini was maxi: Mary Quant's miniskirt and Alec Issigonis's Mini Minor were attainable symbols of a new wave of conscious consumerism. The message was clear. 'New' was 'now'—and anything old or unchanging had better get out of the way.

It wasn't just the *Daily Express* that was staring downturn in the face. The British motor industry, for all the success of the Mini, was under threat.

After the war, the British had set out to protect their industries from the peril of imports. A common market had been created on the Continent, but the UK had slammed its doors on free trade.

Continental car makers set up subsidiaries in the UK as a means of getting around trade blockades so they could tap the lucrative British market. But it was a short-term fix. Everyone could see that.

Suddenly British Labour prime minister Harold Wilson was pushing for entry to Europe's Common Market, but France's Charles de Gaulle was opposing him. There was a lot of resentment between France and England.

Of all the influential British newspapers, the *Daily Express* stood firmly on the side of protectionism, even in the face of increasing turmoil in industry and the paper's own falling sales. Sir Max Aitken's entrenched position was understandable. As a war hero, he'd fought in the skies; he'd seen friends die to defend their homeland. Those memories don't diminish. His own experiences had to count.

But how to get the message across—that Britain could still be great?

Stolid defence was not enough. Max needed something more—a show of strength, a guiding light, a rallying cry for British industry.

It came in late 1967 with a knock on the door from a trusted colleague.

Tommy Sopwith had won Sir Max's first *Daily Express* Cowes–Torquay boatrace in a 25-foot (7.6-metre) twin Cadillac powered boat called *Thunderbolt*. The Cowes–Torquay was a savage race. Boats did not just fail: they sank without trace. The seas were huge, difficult to read and unrelenting if you got them wrong. To win you needed to be both brave and resourceful; Sopwith, 28 years of age when he won, was all of that. As a racing driver, he'd very nearly won the inaugural British Touring Car Championship in 1958. He'd developed his own race team—Equipe Endeavour—and it was in his red, white and predominately blue craft—the Union Jack—that he proudly competed.

The Sopwith name carried huge cachet. His father, also Thomas, had owned the Sopwith Aviation Company, and it was under him that Herbert Smith designed the Sopwith Camel, the best-known fighter aircraft of World War I. Camel pilots were credited with almost 1300 enemy kills.

The Camel was not easy to fly. The standing joke was that Camel pilots could qualify for one of three crosses: the Victoria Cross (valour), Red Cross (injury) or a wooden cross (death).

*　*　*

Sopwith was excited when he stepped into Aitken's suite of offices on Mahogany Row. He'd just had lunch, a very long one, with a media colleague, Jocelyn Stevens, and they were going to run the World's Greatest Road Race, a race around the globe. It was going to be the most magnificent spectacle ever staged, attract entries from global car makers and it would be won, of course, by a British brand, he said with breathless optimism. Sopwith had written no proposal, undertaken no feasibility study, done no costing. Good Lord, they'd only just come up with the idea. And yet, somehow, this was more than a blue-sky proposition. It had life from the moment it left his lips.

'Max didn't take a great deal of persuasion. He thought it was a capital idea and he told me to get on with it,' Sopwith recalled half a century later.

It was a moment in time like no other. Had Sopwith determined not to approach Aitken directly; if he'd taken it to the accountants, put it though channels, or simply tried to do it outside the newspaper, it could well have become another great idea that never got up.

But at that exact instant, a man who was looking for an idea was presented with one, and all his upbringing had instinctively programmed him to understand it. As well as being a pilot, a war hero, a boatracer and a man with vision and enough cash to back it, Max Aitken was also a car guy. He loved them. He'd owned one of the rare and expensive lightweight Aston Martin GT 4s, and he'd only recently onsold it to flamboyant London property developer Bobby Buchanan-Michaelson, who made a huge mess of it by having Aston coach build a special and extremely ugly body. Buchanan-Michaelson would become one of the first entrants in this madcap new venture.

Strangely, it was Jocelyn Stevens who needed a push. He was a massively successful entrepreneur in his own right. At just 25 years of age, he'd bought the British high-society magazine *The Queen*. Riding the wave of liberalism, he'd transformed it into *Queen*— quite a different emphasis—which defined the new Britain. That's how he and Sopwith got together. In July 1967, Stevens published a one-off called *Queen in Flight*, and it made sense to have it guest-edited by the man whose name epitomised the spirit of aviation. It went rather well, leading to the celebratory lunch. Stevens' style was aristocratic bordering on arrogant. He wasn't known for his subtlety. He could be charming or ruthless in equal proportions. *Private Eye* magazine dubbed him 'Piranha Teeth'—flashed in eager bonhomie to a prospective advertiser or bared to a colleague who crossed him.

But there was bad blood between Stevens' family, the Hultons, and the Aitkens, going back four decades. In the early 1920s, Jocelyn's grandfather, Sir Edward Hulton, the first baronet of Downside, sold his entire conglomerate of newspapers to Beaverbrook. The package fetched £6 million. It was a good price, but the sale denied future generations of Hultons their birthright. Worse, Beaverbrook asset stripped, selling off components for enough money that it seemed that the principle asset he retained, the *Evening Standard*, came free. Even two generations later in Stevens' case—one in Aitken's—that didn't sit well.

'I had to do a great deal of work to bring Jocelyn and Max together,' Sopwith recalled.

But it was to good effect. Shortly after, in a delicious irony, Aitken would contract Stevens to help him turn around the fortunes of the failing *Evening Standard*. Within another two years Stevens would become managing director of both the *Standard* and the *Express*.

*   *   *

It was August 1967, and if this race was going to work it needed to happen with speed. 'I needed specialist help. I couldn't do it on my own,' Tommy recalled. 'I had to explore the potential for us to race across the world while simultaneously enthusing automotive companies to back it.' Sopwith was also up to his neck in the organisation of Aitken's Boat Show and the Cowes race, as well as preparing one more grand attempt to win at Cowes in his own right.

'I turned to Jack Sears.'

They called him Gentleman Jack, the quietly spoken son of a shoemaker—with a national chain of shops—who won the British Touring Car Championship twice and who was said, erroneously it was claimed, to have incited road safety authorities to impose a 70-mile-per-hour (110-kilometre-per-hour) speed limit on the newly opened M1 motorway after reaching 180 miles per hour (290 kilometres per hour) while testing a Daytona Cobra on it.

Sears and Sopwith had become national heroes in 1958 when they fought out the inaugural British Touring Car Championship. Although in separate classes—Sears in an Austin Westminster and

Sopwith in his Equipe Endeavour Jaguar 3.4—they arrived at the final round at Brands Hatch tied on points.

Officials suggested the title should be decided on the toss of a coin. For these two and for the credibility of the title, it was a laughable proposition.

British Motor Corporation volunteered to bring two identical Riley 1.5 rally cars to the final round. Sears and Sopwith would compete in two five-lap races, swapping cars between each clash, the winner to be decided by the smallest aggregate time. It wasn't a lap dash but a race. All was fair: a spin-out, a punt-off into the scenery, a breakdown—anything could determine the outcome. They raced cleanly, never swapped paint. Sopwith won the first race by just 2.2 seconds. With the bit between his teeth, Sears inched away in the second to win by 3.8 seconds. The combined winning margin was 1.6 seconds in favour of Sears. The pair shook hands and remained friends.

In that title fight, 28-year-old John Sprinzel driving an Austin A 35 for his own Team Speedwell was third. Sprinzel would also contest the Great Road Race.

Sears was to win the title again in 1963, alternating between a Ford Cortina GT, a massive 7-litre Ford Galaxie and a recently released Lotus Cortina, beaten in the last round, unsurprisingly, by Formula One star Jim Clark. Team Lotus owner Colin Chapman used Clark and Sears to develop his assault on big-capacity sports-car racing. The car was the Lotus 30, and it was dangerous. The brave Clark won three races in it, but Chapman quickly moved on to build a sequel car: the Lotus 40. Racer Richie Ginther described it as 'a 30 with ten more problems'.

It was in the 40 at the high-speed Silverstone circuit that Sears suffered a huge, life-threatening shunt. Badly injured and needing a year for recovery, he retired to his farm in Norfolk and it was there Tommy Sopwith contacted him.

* * *

'The concept of London to Sydney just evolved,' Tommy recalled. 'It was to have been a race across the world, but that was proving impractical.'

For it to be successful, the Great Road Race had to be always on display. It should be able to move swiftly through borders and doctrines, and it couldn't—as a concept—take longer than a month. The challenges were immense—firstly choosing a route and then planning how to move this massive endeavour to far-flung regions. Before a wheel turned, Sopwith, Stevens and Sears did their paper recce.

It was a formidable task.

There was no route south.

The Suez Canal, the man-made lifeline between Europe and Asia, was again in conflict. Israel had attacked Egypt, and Egypt's President Nasser had shut the canal, denying access to cargo and particularly oil tankers, forcing them to go around the long way, south around the Cape of Good Hope. Rising oil prices and the threat of further blockades had brought the world to flashpoint. World governments knew and feared the consequences.

Nor was there a route north. The Russian bloc, the great divide between Western and Eastern Europe, the face of the so-called Cold War, was at its height, so there was no route across Germany.

But, they discovered, there might be a route through the middle. Taking advantage of the relaxation of strict border controls through communist-controlled Yugoslavia, they drew a line, on paper, across France and Italy to its frontier, then on to Bulgaria, Istanbul in Turkey and then, with great optimism, across Iran, Afghanistan and Pakistan to India.

Their goal was to stay high in the far north of India and head through Burma (Myanmar), and then out onto the Malay Peninsula to Singapore. From there it would be a quick hop to Australia, then on to the USA and home.

But not even Earl Mountbatten of Burma, uncle of Prince Philip, second cousin of Queen Elizabeth, could get the border of the former British protectorate to open to a car race—no matter how great its significance. Sopwith and Mountbatten talked but there was no route past India. So it would be south to Bombay and then on to Australia.

But how to get from India to Australia?

In 1968, aircraft offered no solution. The Boeing 747 jumbo had not been built and the Antonov An-124, the giant Russian freight carrier, had not been invented.

Sea travel was the only answer.

Sopwith pulled the *Daily Express* card and spoke at high level to P&O. 'It's amazing the doors that open when you call from the *Express*.'

Since World War II, the Peninsula and Oriental Steam Navigation Company had been building passenger vessels for the London to Australia route. Australia, big on space, small on people, had developed a postwar policy of 'Populate or Perish'. Just as Britons were surveying the devastation wrought on their homeland, Australia, a place with arguably a better climate and greater prospects, had begun an Assisted Passage Migration Scheme. For just £10 you could buy a ticket to Australia and start a new life. Children travelled free. By 1968, one million immigrants had become Australia's 'Ten Pound Poms'. But the scheme was drawing to an end. The promised jobs weren't there as they once had been.

P&O had built fifteen large passenger liners to carry its human cargo. Now, under increasing threat from the airlines—Qantas's 'Kangaroo Route' to and from Australia was becoming more popular, although still very expensive—it needed new uses for its vessels. Pleasure cruising was logical, and an involvement in a high-profile event like the Great Road Race would provide substantial publicity. P&O agreed to divert the SS *Chusan* to Bombay to pick up the racers and their cars and deposit them in a port to be determined in Australia.

But they could not go on to the USA—P&O simply didn't travel that way.

Sopwith, Stevens and Sears faced up to the inevitable. Even a back-of-the-envelope calculation made their event just under a month long if they started in the UK and terminated in Australia. It was not possible to consider a further voyage to the Americas and then another to return to the UK.

Initial discussions with manufacturers had already identified that budgets were tight. The further you travelled, the less likely you'd be to have participation—and Sopwith did want quite a few starters and at least a few finishers.

'I was quite convinced we could run the event on private participation alone,' Sopwith said. But that was not Sir Max Aitken's concept. This wasn't to be a jolly jaunt for wealthy amateurs, although they were certainly welcome. This was to be the ultimate showcase of the UK's engineering superiority. The Continentals were most welcome to turn up with their Citroëns, Simcas and Renaults, along with anything from Italy that would last the distance, but only because the British teams needed something to beat.

Four weeks had passed since the Knightsbridge lunch and, although the *Express* had made no public announcement, the word, and enthusiasm, was spreading fast. In Sydney, the motoring editor of *The Daily Telegraph*, Australia's first touring-car champion, David McKay (he'd won it in 1960 in a Jaguar 3.4), stormed into the office of his editor-in-chief, David McNicoll. He'd just been alerted by a colleague in London that a great road race could be on.

McNicoll was not a fan of car racing or for that matter overly of McKay, but he and his boss, Sir Frank Packer, were big-thinking entrepreneurs. McNicoll had spent World War II in the European theatre variously with the AIF (Australian Imperial Force) and as a highly respected war correspondent. He'd returned to Australia to run the editorial affairs of Sir Frank Packer's *Daily* and *Sunday Telegraph*s, but the boss, FP, was anything but an absentee proprietor. He turned up every day—latterly in one of the two Mercedes-Benz 600 Grossers he maintained: one for him and one for his dogs that needed space when they were being taken to exercise—and he would be on the telephone at any time of the day or night to discuss the most minute matters regarding his papers.

Like Aitken, he saw his publications as weapons of influence. He clashed with unions about his bias and his requirement for staff to not only toe but promote the current company line. He was, in short, everything a young journalist wanted in a proprietor. This wasn't management from afar. This was a family affair, and it was an exciting and astounding place to work.

McNicoll fired a telex off to the *Express* that same day. Before the Great Road Race even had a name, it had two equal shareholders:

the London *Daily Express* and Sydney's *The Daily Telegraph*. Importantly, also, it had a start and finish point. It was always going to start in London, but now, because Packer was in Sydney, that's where it would end.

But what would it be called? Its working title had been the Great Road Race. Even in the swinging sixties, that was a bit too challenging. You couldn't conjure up an image of maniacs racing wheel to wheel across the world—well, half of it anyway—mowing down all in their path.

It couldn't be a rally. That was a description already used by some of the world's great events. The Monte Carlo was the kingpin, and everyone in Europe knew the concept of cars competing across stages over several days but in relatively confined spaces.

In Australia, there'd been the groundbreaking trials of the 1950s where hundreds of competitors had battled each other and the sometimes almost-impenetrable outback in events that had, literally, opened up a continent. One trial winner, Jack Murray, had even carried explosives to clear roads where none existed and had become forever known as Gelignite Jack.

But this great road race was special. This needed a description of Olympic proportions. It needed to encapsulate the very extremes of endeavour for human beings and their machines. The Greek legend of Pheidippides sprang to mind—the courier who ran from the outpost of Marathon to Athens with news of a great victory: 'Joy to you, we've won,' he cried and then died. In 1896, the first of the modern Olympic Games was crowned with a new event—a marathon in honour of the legend. It had become a highlight of every Olympics since.

There could be no better name or allusion. The London–Sydney Marathon had been born.

3

Discovery

MISS AUSTRALIA, PHYLLIS VON ALWYN, was thrilled to be asked to flag away the greatest motoring adventure of modern times—a madcap dash from the UK to Australia.

It was 1927, 41 years before the London–Sydney Marathon, and the first-ever attempt to drive overland to Australia was about to begin.

Von Alwyn, soon to marry Australia's pin-up cricket hero Jack Gregory, stood on the steps of the imposing Australia House on the corner of Aldwych and the Strand and flagged Francis Birtles away on his great adventure.

It was 19 October, and Birtles, a 36-year-old photographer, film-maker, long-distance specialist and one of the toughest outback operators Australia had turned out, would become the first person ever to drive from England to Australia: London to Melbourne to be precise, passing through Sydney.

He'd intended to do the entire 26,000-kilometre drive solo, but he picked up a hitchhiker halfway; without him, he would never have made it. The journey took eight months.

It was a time for grand displays of skill and daring. Long-distance travel—on wheels, wings and water—was still in its infancy, and many of these pioneers were as revered as astronauts would later become, the aviators especially. Even as Birtles was preparing to get to Australia overland, Bert Hinkler was planning to be the first to fly the trip solo. Birtles and Hinkler had a £10 bet (that's around $1000 today) as to who'd get there first, or at all. There were no guarantees either way. Planes fell out of the sky. Cross-country adventurers disappeared without trace.

Hinkler and Birtles met in London when Birtles was preparing the 14-horsepower British-made four-cylinder Bean he'd christened *The Sundowner*. Hinkler would leave London long after Birtles and reach Australia long before him, taking just 15 days to reach Darwin in his Avro Avian. Five years later, he was dead. The airborne record to Australia had already tumbled to 8 days 20 hours; chasing that target, Hinkler flew into a Tuscan mountainside above Florence. He was buried with full military honours at the direct instruction of Italy's prime minister, Benito Mussolini.

Birtles' route was quite different to that of the marathon, but the obstacles were similar.

The ebb and flow of armed conflict, the massive disregard for human life and the ease with which it could be extinguished dictated the course of the marathon's route, and they were as evident for Birtles as they were in 1968.

Birtles battled through rudimentary road conditions, some-times none at all, in a vehicle that required constant repair. His encounters with bandits and his escape from wild dogs should be legend. In truth, by the time of the marathon, he was little more than a footnote in automotive history, although he did make it to Singapore:

> We notice that Mr Birtles proposes to do Calcutta–Rangoon section by road. Does he know there is no road? Information received tells this is an impossible feat for a well prepared party, let alone a man alone. Even in fine weather the jungle is impenetrable by car and the danger from wild animals and head hunting natives is extreme. He should reconsider.
>
> (telegram from the Automobile Association of Burma, now Myanmar)

It was on the road to Rangoon that Birtles picked up his hitch-hiker, young Canadian Percy Stollery, an adventurer like Birtles who'd been a year on the road before his bicycle and belongings were stolen.

They shot a monkey for food and a tiger for survival. They winched the Bean through jungles, stripped wheels off it and wrapped chains around the brake drums to reverse up mud slopes, scrambling for traction. They caught malaria.

In Darwin, the Bean was impounded. Its import papers had dissolved in the Burmese rain. It took a telegram from Birtles to Prime Minister Stanley Bruce to get it released. Birtles drove swiftly and triumphantly to Melbourne.

'Hustling Hinkler' (so called by media) took some of the gloss off Birtles' efforts. Birtles was no hustler. Despite his filmmaking and some of the grand cross-country adventures he'd enjoyed, he was not a natural self-promoter—but he was a hero. A crowd of 10,000 lined the streets to welcome him to the Melbourne General Post Office on 25 July 1928. Bizarrely, his greeting was interrupted by a policeman who warned him to move on or he'd be booked for obstructing traffic.

* * *

It's said that the first long-distance drive in a motor car occurred in August 1888 when Bertha Benz, the diminutive but feisty wife of the father of the automobile, Karl Benz, with her children, commandeered the third production version of the world's first car without Karl's consent and went home to mother, a distance of 104 kilometres.

Whether it was the result of an argument or whether, as Mercedes-Benz history now claims, it was a deliberate publicity stunt is lost in a confusion of corporate correctness. But Bertha created history. She bought fuel from a pharmacy, cleaned a fuel pipe with her hatpin and insulated a control line with her garter, and she got to mum's in a day.

Six years later, French newspaper *Le Petit Journal* ran the world's first motor race—120 kilometres from Paris to Rouen, not much longer than Bertha's drive. The winner was decided by commit-tee. The giant De Dion steam car that crossed the line first was relegated to second for serious infringements of the rules, includ-ing not carrying a stoker for the steam engine, and first prize was awarded jointly to Peugeot and Panhard.

Another ten years on, car races were crossing borders. Long-distance events—some more than 1000 kilometres—on public roads were proving the worth of the motor car, exciting crowds and potential buyers and putting everyone—participants and spectators—at mortal risk.

In 1903, the Paris to Madrid race was abandoned, still in France, when in just nine hours eight people, including Marcel Renault, scion of the house of Renault, were killed, each in separate acts of mayhem.

When the field reached Bordeaux, 544 kilometres from the start, drivers were told to shut down their motors. Their silent cars were towed by horses to the railway station to be returned to Paris. The Race of Death sparked a ban, and it would be the last city-to-city race to be sanctioned in Europe, except Italy, for more than 25 years.

In its place, Grand Prix was born.

Motor racing couldn't stop. It needed to flourish. Competition was the lifeblood of car makers. In 1906, the Automobile Club of France erected more than 60 kilometres of spectator barricades near the town of Le Mans and held the world's first closed-road Grand Prix, won by Renault, over 1200 kilometres in 12 hours 14 minutes 7 seconds at an average speed of 100 kilometres per hour.

But it wasn't enough. For the insatiable car makers and their equally enthusiastic supporters, there was a desire to do more than go around in circles.

What needs to be proved today is that as long as a man has a car he can do anything and go anywhere. Is there anyone who will undertake to travel this summer from Peking to Paris by automobile?

French newspaper *Le Matin* had been a massive supporter of motor racing since the turn of the century. Motor racing was dangerous, compelling and exciting. It was good for circulation and for advertising. Building cars was good for the nation. *Le Matin* was keen to satisfy both needs. Now it was time to do more.

On 31 January 1907, it published its audacious challenge, almost out of Jules Verne. This was the age of heroic discovery and, although Robert Falcon Scott had stood on the seventh continent, no one yet had been to the poles, north or south, and no one had conquered Everest. The moon was an age away.

So to propose a car race—a marathon—from Peking to Paris was unthinkable.

Four manufacturers took up the challenge, and just six months later five cars, two from De Dion and one each from Itala, Spijker and Contal, rolled out of Peking (Beijing) bound for France. There was no prize money, but glory beyond riches. A jeroboam of Mumm was awaiting the first to reach Paris.

Prince Luigi Marcantonio Francesco Rodolfo Scipione Borghese, 10th prince of Sulmona, known to his friends as 'Skip', won, covering 16,000 kilometres in exactly 60 days. The two De Dions and the Spijker were 21 days behind.

There was a lesson for the marathon in the way he went about it. The vastly wealthy Borghese had the Ceirano brothers, the founding family of the Italian automobile industry, build him a vehicle purposely designed for such a venture. Then, as now, you cannot rely on series production to have the strength to endure.

The most important component was not mechanical but human. Twenty-five-year-old Ettore Guizzardi, a loyal servant of the 36-year-old prince, would keep the Itala running and do most of the driving—but, of course, Skip would take the credit.

Local knowledge and contacts counted. The third crew member, journalist Luigi Barzini, was a war correspondent who had spent time in China during the Boxer Rebellion and the Russo–Japanese war. It was not a safe part of the world to be—the Chinese and the Russians were as wary of the car race as the racers were of them.

Barzini rode in a single rear seat between two fuel tanks carrying 300 litres of highly inflammable fluid. It was more comfortable, but arguably no more safe than the smallest car in the event—the single-cylinder two-stroke French-made Contal tricar. All up, with crew, it weighed just 700 kilograms. The driver sat on a cycle seat; the co-driver perched in front on a hard, wooden platform directly over the axle. The Contal failed in the first two weeks, and the car company, opened in 1907, closed in 1908.

Along the Great Wall of China, across the Gobi Desert, Borghese then bounced the sturdy Itala down the tracks of the Trans-Siberian railway, avoiding the deep mud alongside.

Meanwhile, in a technique that would be adopted by Russia's Moskvitch team in the marathon 60 years later, the De Dions never left each other's sight—working as a tag team in an all-for-one effort.

Borghese drove triumphantly into Paris on 10 August to a massive reception. *Le Matin* had achieved its goal—although a victory to the Italians and not the French was perhaps not in the grand plan.

The Peking to Paris race proved a point—if your economy is shaky, if your sales or circulation need a boost, if there's a looming crisis of confidence in your manufacturing system, then a huge statement, a big event, is the answer.

Two months later, in mid-October 1907, the New York Stock Exchange plummeted 50 per cent and its ramifications were felt around the world. Exports to the USA dropped more than 25 per cent—many of them cars. The industrial sector once more met with *Le Matin*. Another race was called for: tougher, longer, through America, and quickly before the enthusiasm for the Peking race had worn off.

On 12 February 1908, the world's second great race left New York's Times Square in front of a crowd of 50,000 with another alleged quarter of a million lining the New York streets, bound for Paris.

The route was outrageous. The race was to be held in mid-winter—the worst in ten years. Successful competitors, if one could succeed, would become the first ever to drive across America in winter. From San Francisco they'd sail to Alaska, where they'd drive up the frozen Yukon River—on ice. Then, the most fanciful idea of all: they'd cross the world's most impassable piece of ocean, 80 kilometres of the Bering Strait between Alaska and Russia. They would motor across a frozen icefloe or, if needs be, they could catch a freighter. Once they hit Siberia, it would be easy. Just follow the Peking to Paris route all the way home.

Little wonder just six cars started.

The New York Times had joined *Le Matin* as co-sponsor, a prelude to the *Express–Telegraph* marathon partnership, and, in the absence of any great enthusiasm from the US motor industry, including Henry Ford, it coerced at the eleventh hour an entry from the Thomas Motor Company.

E.R. Thomas was America's biggest motorcycle manufacturer. In 1905, its Thomas Auto-Bi had established a new record, crossing the USA, in summer, in 48 days. Thomas had branched into cars, and it was their very latest 1907 Model 35, the Thomas Flyer, that entered the New York–Paris race.

It was the Itala experience reborn. The Flyer would be the biggest, heaviest and most powerful car in the race. Like the Itala, it was powered by a relatively simple four-cylinder engine, but this one developed 50 per cent more power: 60 horsepower. Its strength would lie in its crew. George Schuster, Thomas' in-house test driver and troubleshooter, would be the backbone of a rotating team of drivers. George could carry the Flyer home on his back.

At the other end of the field was the seriously obsessive Auguste Pons, the driver of the non-finishing lightweight Contal in the Peking dash. Totally convinced that lightness was the key to success, and therefore at least half a century ahead of his time, he again entered the smallest car in the event: a single-cylinder French-built Sizaire-Naudin of just 12 horsepower. It didn't even make it out of New York State. Its drive axle snapped, and a despondent Pons finally called it quits on weight loss.

In between the extremes were a German, an Italian and two other French teams.

Rules were made up on the run. The Flyer was first into San Francisco—41 days 8 hours 15 minutes after the New York start—creating a new transcontinental record, 11 days ahead of the Germans. By the time the Germans made the west coast, the Americans had already reached Alaska, reporting by telegraph that any hope of driving up the Yukon was impossible.

Organisers scrambled, rerouted the event and ordered them to drive back to Seattle, to catch a freighter to Japan, where they'd cross into Russia.

The Germans put their car, a Protos, on a railcar and steamed up the track to Seattle to catch the ship. It would prove to be a fateful decision.

For the next four months, a titanic battle ensued between the two crews. Their cars were by far the strongest and the only serious contenders.

The French dropped out; the Italians clung gallantly to vain hope, but they were to finish third—and last—almost three weeks behind.

Thirty kilometres out of Vladivostok, the Americans discovered the Germans virtually irretrievably bogged. But Schuster braked to a halt, produced a tow rope and directed recovery of his rival. 'It's just a race, not war'; you could hear the words echo down from the marathon more than half a century later. Germany's Lieutenant Hans Koeppen cracked a champagne, carried on board, to recognise a 'gallant, comradely act'.

On 26 July 1908, it was the Protos that drove first into Paris to massive acclaim. The Thomas Flyer was five days behind.

But the race committee had made a determination. Because the Thomas Flyer had made the trip into Alaska and acted as a pioneer for the field, it was credited with 15 days of driving—enough to take the win. And just to make sure, the Protos, which had caught a train, definitely not in the spirit of the event, was debited an equal amount.

There was not to be another long-distance event in the first half of the century. Two world wars would intervene, and the Russian Revolution of 1917 would shut down the only intercontinental access known at the time.

* * *

Reg Shepheard, a rambunctious, ambitious, single-minded salesman of engine lubrication additives, desperately wanted to become the first person to open the last automotive frontier in the world.

Outback Australia, part desert, part near-impenetrable mountain ranges, part rainforest—hot beyond relief in its centre, wet to the point of saturation north of the Tropic of Capricorn in summer—had been an enigma to Europeans since they arrived.

Shepheard had arrived in Australia in 1949 with a young family and the national franchise for a British-made oil supplement called REDeX. Did it work? Reg thought so. But whether it did or not, it was up to him to give it a reputation of reliability. What better way than to hold a Reliability Trial?

The concept of a Round Australia Trial had been floated in the 1930s but was soon quashed by authorities on the grounds that it was too dangerous—and besides, there were no roads.

And they were right. Ninety per cent of Australia's population lived on 10 per cent of its landmass. Farming clung to the seaboard and did not venture too far beyond the Great Dividing Range. The great cattle drives from north to south through the Red Centre fuelled the aura of the outback, but they were exceptions upon which Australia's self-image was based. In the 1950s, explorers were still exploring and Australia held a cache of mineral wealth, yet undiscovered. Broken Hill Proprietary owned a giant gash of ore in a far-flung New South Wales hillside, teetering on the edge of the true outback, providing a tantalising hint of what could lie beyond.

Reg knew what he had to do. For the sake of the nation but mainly for the sake of his product, he had to open the outback. Against great odds and with the help of the Australian Sporting Car Club, he devised 'the world's longest and toughest car trial'. It ran not around Australia but around its eastern half, neatly divided by a line drawn from Darwin down to Adelaide.

The REDeX Trial captured the imagination of the nation. Australia's fledgling car makers, principally Holden, entered, although it would not be until 1979 that a Holden factory team finally won.

On 30 August 1953, 187 cars left the Sydney Cricket Ground—outside the ground, of course, because no car would be allowed on the hallowed turf—and 14 days later Maitland chemist Ken Tubman, later to win the London–Mexico World Cup Rally in a Citroën, would claim victory by just 15 seconds in a last-stage dash.

By the last day of competition, eleven crews had clean-sheeted ('cleaned') the 'world's toughest car trial', incurring no penalties, so officials had turned on a tie breaker in a muddy paddock south of Sydney. It was a contrived and demeaning way to end such a mammoth venture, and Shepheard pledged to do better.

In 1954, he staged the true Round Australia Trial, an event that to this day stands as a benchmark. It circumnavigated the country, adding 5000 kilometres to the previous trial's 10,000 kilometres and yet allowed only an additional two days to complete the journey. And it created legends.

Jack Murray was a Sydney garage proprietor and taxi-cab owner—and so much more. With his good mate 'Wild' Bill McLachlan, he'd pioneered waterski racing in Australia and they'd become widely known as the larrikins of Sydney. One day, Jack and Bill headed out to the Hawkesbury River for a spot of skiing, and they just kept going. Three months later, they returned from a spontaneous Top End adventure, full of stories of crocodiles, snakes and roads with potholes so deep you could disappear from sight.

Jack reckoned he could win the REDeX Trial. He had a 1948 Ford V8 purpose-built for the job. She was called the *Grey Ghost*. Most of the entrants in this marathon of an event were racing drivers, not used to the outback. Not that Jack wasn't a racing driver. He'd raced with great success and even come fifth in the first postwar Australian Grand Prix, driving a Ford V8-engined Bugatti. But Jack knew how impassable the outback could be. That's why he stashed a few sticks of gelignite in the *Ghost* to blast a way through the bush.

Almost 250 cars left Sydney. Fewer than 120 returned. It was an incredibly testing event. Organisers had imposed great entrapments on the trial—average speeds that had to be maintained and secret controls that could disqualify you from contention, all on top of a country so forbidding that it sapped your energy.

Exhausted crews were driving short shifts at a time, snatching sleep for minutes. No doubt they were popping pills—a practice so illegal today it can have you flung from the sport, but then so normal it was part of your routine.

Gelignite Jack Murray survived and won. His was the only crew to clean-sheet the event.

The REDeX Trial provided marathon organisers with the assurance that the grand finish of their event would be all they needed. Compared to the uncertainty of Asia, the Australian leg was in no doubt. It could be manipulated to be as challenging as the marathon demanded or as forgiving as was required. It could offer an easy route to Sydney for those who just wanted to finish or, for those in outright contention, it could turn on a finale of such ferocity that it would defy any special stage ever held anywhere in the world.

* * *

In 1955, an expedition team of six undergraduates from Oxford and Cambridge drove two Land Rovers from London to Singapore.

It took them six months and six days across 29,000 kilometres.

No less a person than David Attenborough, then a young BBC producer in charge of a two-person 'Travel and Expedition' film unit, funded the attempt.

It was a huge undertaking—along the lines of the great polar and mountain peak ventures. Only two years before, Edmund Hillary had become the first to summit Mount Everest, just north of the Oxcam route. Adventure—human endeavour—was alive and looking for opportunity.

But almost as the Oxcam team completed their venture, the window quickly slammed shut.

'The world has divided itself against itself,' Sir David Attenborough said in an introduction to their film. 'There are places where you are not allowed to cross frontiers. The journey could not be made today.'

His comments applied equally across the entire marathon route. Communism had taken a turn for the worse in Germany and Eastern Europe. The Berlin Wall had become more than a symbol of the divide. In the conflict, a total of 140 people died trying to cross or defend it. Just one week before the marathon started in fanfare from London's Crystal Palace motor-race circuit, an escapee and an East German guard both died in a shootout. The East Berlin city commander claimed 'the cowardly act of murder' of the guard had 'filled the workers of East Germany with an overwhelming hatred toward the imperialist henchmen and wire-pullers' of the West. Not a place for a marathon to visit.

Further east, Beirut, the Paris of the Middle East when the Oxcam team learned to waterski behind a stylish timber Riva-style speedboat, had within three years become the scene of a bloody civil war. Lebanon was a tinder box, inflamed finally in 1971.

The Indo–Pakistani war of 1965 had resulted in an uneasy ceasefire in late 1966. Despite infractions on both sides, it remained in place long enough for the marathon to pass through before reigniting in 1971.

There was no access to or through Burma, either. In 1962, General Ne Win staged a coup d'état, and as a result 100 students were gunned down at Rangoon University. Ne Win imposed an isolationist policy, effectively shutting down his country's economy. And shutting down any hope of the marathon gaining access.

Why persist?

Well, London to Bombay was still a great adventure, a romantic cavalcade through aeons of civilisation. And it was doable, against amazing odds.

You needed only to follow the hippie trail.

From the early 1950s, a flood of laidback, long-haired, bombed-out beatniks, soon to be known as hippies, had crossed the Bosphorus into Asia in search of peace, love and dope. There was plenty of each, although peace was forever fractious.

By the mid-1950s, there were bus tours—magic buses—that could uplift their passengers from place to place, experience to experience. It was the ultimate hop-on, hop-off service. Buy a ticket for around $200 and you could travel half the world, hooking up in hangouts like The Pudding Shop in Istanbul, the Amir Kabir hostel in Tehran and Sigi's Hotel and Restaurant (Good Food and Rice Pudding) in Kabul.

Or you could just drift, inevitably heading north to the poppy fields of Kathmandu or south to the beaches of Goa.

It was innocuous, a titillating bit of fun. The bus drivers—if that was your mode of transport—knew the drill, warning their passengers when to take their last toke and when to dispose of their stash before passing through an intolerant border control. (Today the same plantations have grown into a gigantic criminal venture, a worldwide threat. But not then.)

The Beatles went to India in 1968 in search of heightened spiritual awareness through transcendental meditation with their yogi, Maharishi Mahesh. If anything legitimised the hippie trail, that was it. The Fab Four not only promoted it, they also presented it to an entire generation, wreathed in intoxicating smoke to the twang of a sitar.

But they didn't travel by bus, and Ringo Starr, perhaps the most grounded of the four, described the guru's barbed wire-enclosed encampment as 'sort of a spiritual Butlins'. He was also highly critical of the food—a lesson for marathoners at the end of the year.

Just the same, if ever India was to be a go-to destination, 1968 was the year. You could feel the touch of master promoter Jocelyn Stevens all over it.

4

Best of British

THE LIGHTS WERE GOING OUT for the British motor industry.

The country that had invented the Industrial Revolution two centuries before was still trapped in its clutches, unable and pretty much unwilling to move forward.

To walk into its car plants was to step back in history. It wasn't unusual to find parts of the factory still on earthen floor, compressed by time and hermetically sealed in grime. The ultimate guarantee of panel fit came not with engineering excellence but with a hammer. All around the panel shop, you'd find mallets made of copper or rubber that could be liberally used to straighten up the recalcitrant bodywork of cars still under construction.

The British government came up with a brilliant solution to ensure its car industry remained competitive. It imposed draconian taxes on the sale of imports into the UK, effectively keeping the competition out of the country or at least so overpriced they couldn't compete.

Half a world away, Australia pretty much replicated the UK— and still tugged the forelock to its monarchy.

The country's longest-serving prime minister, Sir Robert Menzies, loved the empire. He had been made Lord Warden of the Cinque Ports by Her Majesty Queen Elizabeth II, a huge honour, on his retirement in 1966 and was forever lampooned for his mewling tribute to her: 'I did but see her passing by and yet I'll love her till I die.' It was a different era, and you can't say he was totally wrong. The UK and Australia were entwined.

But he had done Australian industry a massive and everlasting disservice by providing it with protection from global competition. Improvements—like the Japanese motor industry's *kaizen*, which demands constant, minute developments—come only from the world's best standards.

Instead, huge tariffs and artificially high local-content requirements provided a secure haven for overseas car makers to build substandard cars at huge profit—most of which disappeared offshore.

Menzies' policy, curiously, benefited not so much the UK as it did the USA.

Was Holden ever 'Australia's Own Car'? Only if you believe Detroit is a suburb of Port Melbourne. Australia's domestic motor industry was never anything more than a subsidiary of offshore parents, whether American, European or ultimately Japanese.

When the UK held back from joining the European Community, its reticence confounded the architects of the scheme: 'I never understood why the British did not join,' said Jean Monnet, one of the leaders of the European Coal and Steel Community. 'I came to the conclusion that it must have been because it was the price of [World War II] victory—the illusion that you could maintain what you had without change.'

When the UK woke up to its mistake and wanted in, French President Charles de Gaulle rebuffed it, accusing the island nation of a 'deep-seated hostility towards Europe'. Worse still, he said, its application for membership was nothing more than a Trojan horse for US infiltration of the region.

It was hard to argue the last point.

The 'Big Three' American car companies were buying into the UK to shore up their investments. Chrysler had just taken a majority share in the Rootes Group, Ford was forging ahead with its quaintly named English Line, and General Motors owned Vauxhall.

Only British Leyland Motor Corporation, an amalgamation of two car and truck makers in 1968, was truly British.

European brands that had opened British assembly lines as a way around the UK's tax laws were finding the going tough in an increasingly hostile environment. Citroën, which had been one of the biggest employers in Slough, just west of London, closed its doors in 1966.

In this environment, Sir Max Aitken contended that an event like the London–Sydney Marathon was purpose-built for a show of chest-puffing superiority.

Rootes Group was first in.

Successful retail car dealers Reginald and William Rootes had begun making their own vehicles in the late 1920s so they could control the supply chain from inception to sale.

By the 1960s, they had no fewer than six factories dotting England and Scotland, and another nine assembly plants around the world. They had great brands, too: Hillman, Humber, Sunbeam and the somewhat lesser-known Singer. But growth had left them underfunded, and the cost of developing new models to stay relevant in a fast-expanding competitive environment was crippling. The Rootes family turned to the USA for help.

Their white knight was Chrysler Corporation—soon to face its own crisis. Chrysler lusted after Europe, just as its Detroit rivals Ford and General Motors had done. On the Continent, it had already taken a stake in Simca. Now it took Rootes.

Initially, in 1964, it was a friendly 30 per cent share with Rootes holdings exceeding its own, ensuring family control. But that didn't last long. It took just two years for Chrysler to seize better than 65 per cent. By the end of the 1970 financial year, Rootes Motor Limited would become Chrysler UK Limited. Another proud name gone.

Compared to British Leyland and Ford, Rootes was a minnow. From the 1950s, it had relied on the relatively inexpensive promotional tool of motor sport for a lot of its brand image. Stirling Moss was one of its works drivers, winning three Coupes D'Or in the extremely tough snow-covered Alpine Rally that wound through Europe.

That provided a logical name for their new car, the Sunbeam Alpine.

The biggest rally of all was the Monte Carlo, still the opening event on the World Rally Championship calendar. Sunbeam won the Monte Carlo Rally in 1955 with the Talbot 90. It was, by today's standards, a snail, with a 0–100 kilometres per hour time of just over 20 seconds and a claimed top speed of 140 kilometres per hour. But vehicle reliability was suspect, and just to get to Monaco—the finish line of the Monte—was a huge achievement.

In the early 1960s, Sunbeam had shoehorned a 4.7-litre V8 into the Alpine and called it the Tiger. It became the mainstay of their competition program, but few could afford it.

Rootes sorely needed an answer to the British Leyland–owned Mini Minor, the front-engine, front-wheel-drive shoebox that was sweeping the world. In 1963, they introduced the rear-engine, rear-wheel-drive Hillman Imp. It was just 875 cc—right in Mini territory.

It took bravery to drive an Imp fast. Its rear wheels had so much camber they wanted to clap hands when you poured the power on. You were always one step from disaster. But a young Scotsman, Andrew Cowan, began flinging one around the forests. Cowan won the Scottish Rally, the Scottish Championship and, at the very beginning of 1968, took a class win in the Monte Carlo. The Imp would never be a Mini, but for Rootes it had become its volume champion.

'We'd just returned from the Monte when we heard about the marathon,' Cowan said. 'It was way beyond just the next level. It was the challenge of a lifetime.'

Half a century later, Cowan can still not put his finger on the trigger that sparked Rootes' participation. Was it a marketing decision—an extension of the belief that motor sport provided cost-effective aspirational promotion? Or was it the highly enthusiastic competitions department simply rising to the bait: the determination that a challenge like this must be answered? Either way, the Monte win had given credibility to their proposal to the board of directors.

They waited with great anxiety.

The board's response was good and bad. By all means enter—but there is no additional budget to fund it. The marathon could not become an incremental opportunity. If it were to happen, it would have to be funded out of existing allocation.

So the winners of their class in the Monte put their title defence on hold. They also decided not to enter the 1968 RAC Rally, England's premier event, nor a number of other scheduled rallies. If there'd been a whiteboard in the workshop (impossible because whiteboard markers hadn't yet been invented), they would have wiped it clean and replaced it with just one word: marathon.

They were on their way to Sydney. But in an Imp?

* * *

No one expected Sir Donald (soon to be Lord) Stokes to sign off on the London–Sydney Marathon.

'Stokes was a truck salesman,' said Paddy Hopkirk, British Motor Corporation's most successful race and rally driver.

Hopkirk was the man who could rightly claim to be 'Mr Mini'. In 1964, with co-driver Henry Liddon, he'd won the Monte Carlo Rally outright in a 1017-cc Cooper S, leading home a three-car team that included two Flying Finns, Timo Mäkinen and Rauno Aaltonen. The win made Paddy as big in Britain as the Beatles, and to this day a signed photograph from the Fab Four acknowledging his shared stardom hangs in the bathroom of his sixteenth-century country house above the loo.

Hopkirk was not being derisory in his description of Stokes. It was an accurate assessment of a leading British industrialist who'd just been handed a poisoned chalice by Labour prime minister Harold Wilson.

British Leyland Motor Corporation had been incorporated in the first half of 1968 as an amalgamation of British Leyland, the truck company that was making money, and British Motor Holdings, the car maker that was not. Stokes, from Leyland, was made its chief. The joint venture had been manipulated by the Wilson government's Industrial Reorganisation committee in the hope that it would create a British equivalent to General Motors.

Stokes had known no other life but Leyland. He joined them as a sixteen-year-old engineering apprentice, working on the factory floor, up to his armpits in oil, grease and heavy machinery, and he loved his trucks.

In World War II, he'd risen to Lieutenant Colonel in the Royal Electrical and Mechanical Engineers, and his obvious management skills carried him to the top of the truck company when the war was over. He'd learned about cars only comparatively later in life, when Leyland bought Standard-Triumph in 1960 and in 1967 when they picked up Rover as well. But suddenly in 1968 he found himself on top of a heap of car brands and models. They were being made in no fewer than 40 factories, most of them grossly inefficient and in urgent need of rationalisation.

For an organised man, he was horrified not only to discover from the car side that there was little in the way of a defined future product plan but also to learn that many of the company's still most popular models were well past their use-by date. The Morris Minor, born in 1948, was still coming off the production line in barely saleable quantities and would do so until he finally killed it off in 1971. In the order of his priorities, a car race halfway across the world did not rate highly. In fact, any form of competition was not a pressing imperative.

Yet tucked away in the corner of a town just outside Oxford, BLMC had become the reluctant custodian of one of the most successful racing divisions in all of motor sport. Its headquarters at

Abingdon had spawned heroic victories—from early MGs to later Minis, from race and rally winners to world-record breakers.

Abingdon wasn't state of the art—not then, not ever. It was strange and sad. They'd done so well and yet management seemed to care so very little for them, best summed up by the forlorn array of filthy racing relics rusting under tarpaulins ponding with storm-water in the backyard.

Abingdon was a metaphor for the malaise of the entire organisation.

Competitions manager Peter Browning could see the writing on the wall. Far from getting more budget, he knew the likelihood was for none at all. Termination was a real possibility. But the marathon was too good an opportunity to pass up without a fight.

Browning pulled the 'new car' card on Stokes. The Austin 1800, a full-sized family car, had been initially launched in 1965, and a mid-life upgrade, the MkII, was scheduled for June 1968. It would be the perfect car to help promote BLMC's fresh new image. Because it was also manufactured in Australia, Leyland's most successful non-domestic market, it could not only help sales there, but Australia could also participate in the cost of the exercise.

It was the right hand to play. Remarkably, Stokes' board said yes: incredibly, to such a degree that Leyland was able to build a comprehensive and professional assault, the equal of any works team in the event.

Board agreement came at a price. Even as the competitions department was gearing up for the marathon, Stokes' accountants were slashing their way through 'excess'. Two years later the fabled Abingdon, holy grail of motor sport, closed its doors forever.

* * *

Ford was always going to enter the marathon. The world's second-largest car maker may have been publicly listed, but it was still run by the Ford family and Henry II had determined that in the 1960s motor sport would be his point of difference. As a volume manufacturer, he was compelled to build plebeian cars in their hundreds of thousands—but that didn't mean he had to accept 'boring' as a cornerstone of his company's image. Henry II wanted to bring excitement back into his grandfather's company—and he had the will and the money to do it. Boy, did he have the money.

In 1963, he'd made a takeover bid for Ferrari. He wasn't after the Formula One cars. He wanted the sports cars. And that was his big mistake. Enzo Ferrari loved F1, and he was affronted by Henry's lack of respect for the spindly open wheelers. The Ford deal was rejected so late in the negotiation that the art department had even designed the merged company's logo.

As it turned out, Ferrari's refusal was Ford's spur to create one of the greatest decades of motor-sport success in the history of the automobile. In lightning-fast succession, Ford designed and built the Mustang (admittedly under development while Henry was romancing Enzo), launched the giant-killing Ford GT40 that won the Le Mans 24 Hour four times in succession from 1966, developed a road-car relationship with Lotus, and backed development of the Ford Cosworth DFV engine that ironically won a record 155 Formula One races.

Henry's brief to his very senior line managers was to develop a performance image to help promote car sales. 'Any time a wheel turns in competition,' he said, 'we have to be there.'

Ford was in the UK from 1909—only six years after Henry I built his first car in Michigan—and it assembled cars in Manchester from 1911. In 1913, the locally made Ford Model T became the country's biggest-selling car. Six thousand Model Ts comprised 30 per cent of the total British market.

When Tommy Sopwith proposed the marathon to Max Aitken, Ford was again UK market leader. Its newly launched MkII Cortina had eclipsed the badge-sharing Austin/Morris 1100-1500, claiming 165,000 British buyers in 1967 for 15 per cent total market share, 35,000 ahead of the BMC product.

Ford was also on mainland Europe in Cologne, in Australia, and in any outpost where car making could be made profitable, usually with the help of compliant governments trained to understand the importance of local manufacturing to their GDP, even if the profits didn't remain within their boundaries.

Of all the car makers, Ford was perhaps the most centralist in attitude. Walk into any Ford outpost and you'd most likely be greeted with a Dearborn drawl.

Strange, then, that they didn't get together and enter one super team in the marathon.

Instead, in seeming isolation, three Ford outposts independently discovered it and developed and entered teams, in the most part ignoring each other's efforts. Ford UK was the logical primary entrant, and they attacked it big time with no fewer than six cars. It wasn't so much a legitimate motor-sport entry as a massive PR push. Ford's Head of PR, Walter Hayes, had brought a whole new perspective to how to promote motor-racing success.

He'd masterminded successful assaults on Europe's most revered car competitions with devastating effect. More than that, he'd turned them into PR masterstrokes.

With the launch of the Cortina in 1962 and its subsequent race and rally victories, Hayes had organised a gigantic celebration at

Cortina d'Ampezzo, site of the 1956 Winter Olympic Games. The best Ford drivers in the world carved down the ice-packed high-walled Olympic bobsled run in Cortinas, creating a PR coup that lives to this day.

Hayes saw the marathon not just as a race to win but also as a means of creating a publicity blitz the like of which had never been achieved. Within his team he wanted a crew who could not only win but lead outright from the starting flag, seizing day-to-day publicity. He wanted to back them with at least one team who would be slower and steadier, there at the finish. He wanted to capture the women's market with an all-female team (who would have thought of that in 1968?) and a husband-and-wife team for the yet-to-be defined lifestyle market. In 1968, that wasn't even on anybody else's radar.

Hayes was stunning in his intellect. As it turned out, less so in his execution. But that was to come. The choice of car? The Ford Escort had just been launched, but the Cortina was still the hero. A difficult decision.

On the other side of the world in Melbourne, just down the road from Sydney, there was no such equivocation. Bill Bourke, a big-talking American salesman, had adopted Henry II's crash-or-crash-through philosophy as a means of reclaiming lost sales in the Australian market and perhaps even saving the Australian Ford plant from extinction. Horsepower was the key. Bourke had argued with Dearborn to let his locally made Falcon be endowed as a performance car. In all other markets, it was everything Henry didn't want—boring and utilitarian. But in Australia, Bourke had equipped it with a Mustang-derived V8, and Ford had won the Bathurst 500, the country's premier car race, on debut.

That was 1967. For 1968, Bourke figured he'd chase the double—a back-to-back win at Bathurst, and a tilt at the marathon. The two events were separated by less than two months, and a win in both would be a huge boost to the end-of-year sales push. How many Falcons should he enter? Well, three seemed like a nice number—one for each level on the podium.

And that was pretty much it—both bookends covered. A typically small, nimble and quick Cortina out of England, and a big lumbering, threatening V8—the most powerful car in the event—out of Australia.

But there was still more to come.

Just as Henry I had staked an early claim to British manufacture, he'd done likewise in Germany. In 1930, he'd established a full manufacturing plant in Cologne. In World War II, Ford-Werke was sequestered as enemy property, building trucks with slave labour for the Nazi war effort, then returned to Ford with a healthy subsidy from the US government to repair the bombing damage they'd wrought on the plant.

In 1967, Ford set up Ford of Europe as a foil against the financial upheaval of the UK's Common Market dysfunction. It was intended to merge the assets of Dagenham in Britain and Cologne—to spread the load and the risk.

But it did nothing to tone down the rivalry that existed between its still geographically separated entities.

In 1968, Ford Germany made a huge offer to one of their countrymen. Jochen Neerpasch had been born in Krefeld, just 60 kilometres north of Cologne. By the age of 28, he'd become a Porsche works driver. At the beginning of 1968, when the marathon was becoming a serious consideration, Jochen had no interest in it. In January, he was one of five Porsche pilots to win the Daytona

24 Hour race—the others gradually migrating to his car as theirs broke down. Five winners made the top step of the podium very crowded.

That year, Jochen guided the comparatively benign eight-cylinder Porsche 907/908 to second at Sebring and Monza and third at Le Mans. He might not have been the supremely fastest of the Porsche pilots—not like Jacky Ickx and Rolf Stommelen—but at 300 kilometres per hour down Mulsanne Straight, he was a safe pair of hands. But that was not fast enough for Porsche.

There was a power race on in sports-car racing, and mid-season Porsche had embarked on a program to develop a flat-twelve-cylinder long-tailed device called the 917. Hugely powerful and good for a nudge at 400 kilometres per hour down Mulsanne, it would go on to become one of the most iconic—but not revered—sports cars of all time. Initially, it was powerful beyond the ability of its chassis or its aerodynamics to cope, and it frightened its drivers.

'You can only win at Russian roulette for so long,' was Neerpasch's startling quote when he jumped to the Ford camp. 'I knew the move would mean the end of my driving, but I knew, also, it would be good for my career.'

Neerpasch inherited a Ford company determination to enter the marathon. It wasn't his idea—he had his eye on developing a touring car–based circuit race program. He intended to leave the rallying to the British. But he was directed to compete.

As part of his glimpse inside Ford's future, he'd been introduced to the new Capri coupe to be launched in early 1969. This was the car he'd turn into the giant-killing Cologne Capri—a car revered in touring and sports-car racing and which half a century after its introduction fetches more than $1 million on the enthusiast market. Launch timing prevented it doing the marathon, but why not the Ford Taunus—a coupe version of Ford's exclusive-to-Europe mid-sized V6? The Capri would use a V6, too, so maybe there'd be something to be learned from it.

Without a lot of coordination between their three national operations, the Ford works teams had covered the spectrum—the powerful but comparatively compact Taunus had become the each-way bet between the polarised opposites of the two other teams.

* * *

General Motors, the world's biggest car company, was never going to enter the marathon, and it was all because of its own success.

In 1962, GM held 53 per cent of the US domestic market and was heading perilously close to the definition of monopoly, something frowned upon by the US government. The Department of Justice had already acted against other conglomerates, forcing them to break up. GM had determined that by stopping motor racing it would be less visible, arguably less successful in the salesroom and would save a lot of money besides.

The decision hurt its divisions, which relied on the 'win on Sunday, sell on Monday' ethos for their brand equity. It wasn't the first time this had happened.

They'd withdrawn seven years earlier as a kneejerk reaction to the world's most horrendous motor-racing accident—the 1955 Le Mans Mercedes crash that killed more than 80 people. Although they weren't at all involved in that incident, America's motor manufacturers determined that a voluntary withdrawal from auto racing—a spot of self-regulation—would be prudent before the authorities came knocking. The early days of NASCAR racing in the States were wild and woolly, and any fool could see that the car makers were only one wrong turn of the wheel away from the same disaster that caught out Mercedes.

They all broke the agreement. Even GM went racing under a false flag to prop up its then ailing Plymouth division. But this time it was serious. GM had acted unilaterally to ban car racing across its entire network, and woe betide any profit centre that broke the rules.

No matter how hard Tommy Sopwith knocked on the door of their Luton headquarters, GM was not receptive. Max Aitken's vision of a marathon to promote the entire British motor industry had fallen short by one.

In Australia, GM's Holden division, a direct Detroit subsidiary, took advantage of what Professor Geoffrey Blainey termed 'the tyranny of distance' in his bestselling 1966 book of the same name. Distance from Detroit brought some secrecy, and in 1964 Holden was able to use its dealers to enter and win their class in the Bathurst 500 with the Vauxhall-developed but locally badged and manufactured Viva small car.

But the real sales race was at the high-performance end of the market. Ford had won Bathurst outright in 1967 with its locally developed Falcon GT, a free kick as Holden was forced to sit on its hands by head office's 'no motor sport' dictum.

By 1968, GM-H had had enough. They approached David McKay to run a fleet of its new Monaro coupes in the Bathurst race. Naturally, they would run under the banner of the Holden Dealer Team, a company name that McKay initially registered, and no money would directly change hands between Holden and the team.

On the day they raced, Holden's executives gathered around a black-and-white television in a Sydney hotel, 200 kilometres from the circuit—the closest they believed they could come without being seen to have their fingerprints on the venture.

And they lost. Well, their own team did. A privately entered Monaro with a brake modification that creatively avoided detection by the event's scrutineers was crowned victor. It's a quirk of corporate ego that the executives weren't happy with that. Although on the surface they owned nothing, they wanted 'their' team to win and they castigated McKay, who brought the works vehicles home second and third, for not protesting the winner off the podium.

'It was a big mistake,' McKay later conceded. 'I thought the General would be well pleased that a genuine privateer had won the event.'

Entering Bathurst made McKay's job harder when it came to the marathon.

McKay had convinced his newspaper proprietor, Sir Frank Packer, that it was essential not only to sponsor the event but to enter it. After all, that was his motivation. He wasn't much interested in the marathon unless he could be in it and win it.

Packer agreed, but he wasn't at all concerned with the Fiats or Audis or any of the other low-hanging fruit that McKay could readily bring to the table, even if, well prepared, they could win. As the owner of Australia's leading newspaper, Packer wanted Australia's Number One car brand as a racing partner.

Wasn't McKay running three Monaros in Bathurst, less than two months before the marathon? How hard would it be to take those cars to Britain to win the marathon, too?

Packer's proposition was naive, but he was applying extraordinary pressure.

You don't say no to Sir Frank Packer. McKay and David McNicoll both knew that. They toiled for six months, breaking down the Holden barriers, offering deals within the newspaper, finding ancillary sponsors to lessen the budget burden, until finally in April 1968 they achieved agreement. The cars, obviously, would not be official Holden entries. They would be entered by *The Daily Telegraph* and ostensibly be prepared by McKay. There was a fair amount of subterfuge involved. A skunkworks of Holden people would be involved and would more than occasionally argue with McKay on specification and configuration of the three cars. But compared to Ford Australia's commitment, which was up-front, official and highly involving of its key people including drivers, the Holden effort would hold back enough to handicap it before it even left the starting ramp.

With six months to go, both newspaper proprietors could congratulate each other on the job they—or their people—had done. Between them they'd secured works entries from the world's Big Three—Ford, General Motors and Chrysler—as well as BLMC. It was the most solid of foundations, and anything else that came along would be a bonus.

5

Route Recce

JACK SEARS WAS THE MAN who set the marathon route. Tommy Sopwith joined him in Sydney to seal the deal with Sir Frank Packer and sign off the Australian leg.

Time was so short, and the world, then, so big. You could waste an awful lot of productive energy blazing a trail. Sears needed a short cut. He found it in Michael Wood-Power, a tour bus operator who knew every nook and cranny of the route to India. Wood-Power owned Penn Overland, which, since 1959, had been offering 'Journeys of a Lifetime' from London to Ceylon in just 72 days.

Wood-Power had done his original recce in 1958 in a clapped-out Land Rover, and since then his business had become the gold standard of bus tours. It cost more than £1000 to ride with Penn Overland for two-and-a-half months while others were doing it on the cheap for a couple of hundred. Michael agreed to show Jack the way to Bombay.

Neither, really, could produce a map. That would be the task of the most intellectual rally co-driver in all of Europe.

Tony Ambrose was a quiet and refined man, yet he chose to ride with the most tearaway rally drivers of the time. He won the 1965 European Rally Championship with Rauno Aaltonen. They took victory in the RAC Rally in a works Mini Cooper, then Tony went back the next year with another Flying Finn, Simo Lampinen, and they comprehensively rolled the car, losing his rally notes, but continued anyway on memory and blind reckoning until BMC team manager Stuart Turner pulled them from the event.

When they were competing in the 1964 Liège–Sofia–Liège, the toughest four-day nonstop endurance event in the world, Tony took the wheel of the big Austin Healey 3000 he was sharing with Rauno and drove it 120 kilometres in just 77 minutes over cobblestones in the dead of night, dodging unlit traffic while Rauno slept happily. They topped 240 kilometres per hour.

Tony was a must-have on the marathon recce. The Oxford graduate not only knew how to construct a route chart, but he also understood firsthand the psychology of the drivers who would compete at the top end of the event. Aaltonen and Lampinen would be major players in the marathon, and Ambrose knew exactly how to build a rally to test their temperament.

The three pioneers pulled out of London on 22 January 1968 bound for Bombay. They were driving a Ford Cortina GT lent by Ford GB. It was just ten months to the start, and there were works crews lining up behind them to start their own recces. No one, except for the rank amateurs who'd comprise a part of the field, wanted to do this marathon unsighted.

It was important to make your notes, come to terms with the magnitude of the task and to plan fuel and mechanical dumps, rest stops and to test border controls. Within months, the entire route would be crowded with marathon crews making their own plans. But before then, it was necessary to get the basics right. Where was it going?

The only thing they knew was that it was time certain. The agreement with P&O had established a drop-dead deadline for the departure of the *Chusan* out of Bombay. It would wait for no marathon straggler. It was possible, maybe, to play with the start date in London—but much of the challenge of this ultra-marathon, as some were calling it, was to race against the clock.

The Sears expedition was under great pressure. Not only did it have to find a route, but it also had to guarantee it. While Penn Overland could take hours passing through a border control with one bus, the marathon—with an anticipated 100 cars plus support vehicles—needed free passage. Penn had the advantage of familiarity with officials. Those same authorities had to be educated on what the arrival of the marathon would look like and how it would impact on them. Things could turn terribly ugly if they didn't know the marathon was coming.

And yet Sears and his bosses chose not to give authorities too much warning. Their logic was that to ask for permission, formally in writing, could lead to wholesale refusal. Give bureaucrats too much thinking time and they'll find a reason to say no. So Sears, as well as choosing the route, had to become the negotiator. Part diplomat, part entrepreneur, part persuader, his task on this recce was to introduce the concept to authorities for the first time.

He was, surprisingly, successful. At the border of India and Pakistan, he even chaired a meeting of customs officials from both sides, breaking down a hostile détente into a spirit of mutual cooperation. The two countries even agreed to share electrical power at a specially established marathon clearing station. And although the phrase had not been invented, they determined KPIs for the speed of travel through their posts.

Penn Overland was to reap the benefits of the cooperative spirit for more than a decade after, until finally hostilities once more closed borders, especially in the Middle East. Travel became dangerous and forbidden—and Penn closed.

The recce team was moving at high speed. Their plan had been to complete London–Bombay in a month, and they were running ahead of time.

Europe, through the relatively recently completed Mont Blanc tunnel, across into Communist-held Yugoslavia and Bulgaria and south to Istanbul, the doorway to Asia, had been relatively straightforward, although hazards of increasingly poor roads and huge, aggressively driven trucks were presenting obstacles.

Sears had been keen to set the route in approximately the same climate as that which marathon competitors would face. No point in setting the route in summertime if the marathon would pass through in winter. He almost made it. Winter across the higher altitudes of Turkey and Afghanistan gets more challenging as the season rolls on, so in one respect he was experiencing the worst of winter, no bad thing to allow for a little latitude of mercy. But when the expedition made it to the Lataband Pass—the camel track out of Kabul that links Afghanistan to the gateway to Pakistan—they hit a dead end.

Lataband, in the romantically named and devastatingly rugged Hindu Kush, is the Highway to Hell. It had been used by the Mughals in the sixteenth century, and for centuries beyond it was the only link from Kabul to Jalalabad, the trading town to the east. Rising 2500 metres on flint stones so sharp they can vivisect a tyre, it feels when you balance on the precipice that you could fall that whole distance if you slipped off the edge.

Ambrose's plan had the marathon driving the Lataband in the mists of the early dawn, but he would never know the route he had set. The recce car was blocked by snow: totally impassable. Frustrated, the expedition team turned north on a 'safe' road that skirted the mountain.

It would be one of a few alternate routes they'd plot, providing marathoners with excruciating choice—to take the possibly longer and therefore slower way, or to chance their skill on direct passage.

Setting a rally route, any route, is no easy thing. It's a complex equation of time, speed and terrain. You want to test competitors, but you also want them to finish—or at least a reasonable percentage of them to do so. Sears already knew his required finishing ratio at the halfway point. One hundred cars could start in London but only 70 could be accommodated on the SS *Chusan*. So there was a need to accomplish a rally of planned attrition. Thirty cars would have to be deliberately excluded.

It was up to Ambrose to determine how punishing they should make the average speeds between controls to achieve their target. More haste meant more breakdowns and fewer finishers. What would be an acceptable number at Bombay? They reckoned fifty. If half the field dropped out halfway, it would most likely be the amateurs and there'd still be a strong professional contingent to have a red-hot go across Australia.

But make it too tough, and the Australian authorities would never let you start. They were known to be the most conscientious of all when it came to enforcing their precious road rules. If the marathon gained a reputation as a flat-out, car-breaking road race as it sped across Europe and Asia, that would be in no one's interests. A degree of subtlety was required.

Making their calculations on the run, Sears and Ambrose settled on eleven time controls across Europe and Asia. In 11,030 kilometres from Calais, when the first time control started, the highest required average speed would be just 109 kilometres per hour, and it would be across the hardest special stage; the lowest would be 56 kilometres per hour, and the average moving speed would be 86 kilometres per hour. It would take 7 days, 9 hours and 28 minutes to get from London to Bombay; 88 per cent on the move and the remainder, such as it was, resting. There would be no penalty for being faster than the required average, so it was possible to claw back some rest time, but there would be a 1-point-per-minute loss for late arrival and a 1440-point penalty for missing any of the controls.

On paper it looked challenging but achievable.

Sears, Ambrose and Wood-Power had seen things on the recce that made them confident of their goal of attrition. They'd happily tell you about them if you asked, but few among the rank and file of entrants did. The professionals wanted to see for themselves.

Surprisingly, the recce team returned to England from Bombay. They didn't go on to Australia. For three months, they fussed about in preparation. The vast nation continent of Australia, the ultimate proving ground where the outcome of the marathon would be determined, lay neglected until May, far too late.

Tommy Sopwith went to Australia with Jack Sears, and they picked up a local navigator, John McKittrick, to help them set the route. McKittrick was a surveyor, a member of Sydney's North Shore Sporting Car Club and a keen committee member on major rallies such as the Southern Cross that, in the 1960s, were drawing top international competition.

He was a good friend of David McKay's—in fact, a valued organiser in McKay's Scuderia Veloce, one of Australia's first truly professional race teams—and McKay in turn was well known to Tommy Sopwith. Nine years before, McKay had been hanging off the side of a French mountain, where he'd beached his Triumph TR3 in the 1958 Tour de France car rally, and it was Sopwith who had come to his rescue. There was trust between them. Tommy and Jack spent a day at the Warwick Farm Grand Prix track in Sydney, where David was running the magnificent P4 Ferrari sports car he'd secured from the Ferrari factory, a sister for his LM 250. These things mattered. If McKay said McKittrick was up to the job, then Sopwith willingly agreed.

The route they set in such a remarkably short space of time was superb. The character of the Australian roads was so different from that of the first leg. Although the sea voyage would be interminably long for most competitors, the SS *Chusan* would become a time and space capsule, teleporting them from northern to southern hemisphere, from winter to summer and from extreme congestion to vast emptiness.

McKittrick kept the Australian leg of the marathon geograph-ically south, well beneath the Tropic of Capricorn. North of it, summer rains would make roads and tracks impassable and—in the 1960s, when bitumen was a rarity in the outback—would leave travellers stranded until the Wet came to its own end, whenever that might be.

Down south, there was the ball-bearing gravel of Western Australia, a road surface so lacking in traction that, at speed, tyres scramble for grip. There was mallee scrub so tall that it was like driving unsighted through a wheat field, always with the constant threat of a summer scrub fire that could spark instantly if a red-hot exhaust lingered over a bushy outcrop.

The Nullarbor Plain is crossed by a 900-kilometre ribbon of road, enticing drivers to go flat out only to have under-bonnet engine heat build to a point where the motor blows. Even now, cars are designed with a view to regular throttle moderation to give the engine a chance to breathe and cool. Cars aren't built for hours of pedal to the metal. At the time of the marathon, before the sophistication of electronic control units, long-distance motorists carried waterbags to top up their radiators even in 'normal' outback conditions.

In 1968, the Nullarbor was dirt almost the whole way. It might have looked smooth, but ruts and dips could develop without warning. The number of wrecks at the side of the track was testament to the car-breaking conditions.

In South Australia, the mighty Flinders Ranges contain fossils so old and rare that, in 2004, an entire new geological era, the Ediacaran Period, was named for the Ediacara Hills in the northern part of the ranges. In 1968, neither McKittrick nor the marathon knew of such things. The Flinders, hinting at the Wet season just north of them, presented sensational third- and fourth-gear rally roads where drivers could tuck their elbows in and drive with marvellous fluidity. A special stage, perhaps event critical, would roar straight through the majestic Brachina Gorge, flint stones and potentially fossils flying. The yellow-footed rock wallaby, now rare and protected in its Flinders habitat, was then just another marathon hazard. Across Australia, the survey team had seen many 'kangaroos'. They didn't differentiate between species but noted they would be a big concern.

The marathon would be decided in the Australian Alps, of that Sears and Sopwith were certain. They'd never seen roads like this— never-ending switchback mountain tracks through trees so tall that they blocked out the sun; mountain creeks, dry at the time of the recce, would be running fast with the spring thaw of snow; morning fog captured by the foliage, filtering the first light and playing tricks with drivers' spatial awareness. All this in the last 24 hours of competition, before a gentle, escorted ceremonial run to the finish.

Australia would be far more intense than Europe and Asia. There would be 24 time controls across 5664 kilometres to be covered in 2 days 21 hours 41 minutes. The fastest stage average would be 102 kilometres per hour; the slowest, the run into Warwick Farm, just 51 kilometres. Total average speed was 84 kilometres per hour. All but 2 hours 21 minutes would be within allotted time—that's 96 per cent of the entire Australian leg. If drivers were faster, they'd be able to rest.

It was a challenge beyond anything that had ever been set.

Yet no one blinked. There was no outcry, no outrage. Nobody suggested the limits of human endurance were being unduly tested. Team managers across the UK, Europe and in Australia simply noted the requirement and set about meeting it. Where they'd been planning on two-person crews, they were now contemplating three—two to drive, one to rest. But it was a gamble. An extra person adds exponential weight, to be avoided if at all possible. If you take on 80 kilograms of human cargo, what can you jettison in compensation?

There was an alternative.

In the 1960s, there was no WADA. The World Anti-Doping Agency was another 30 years in the future, set up in 1999 to create a blockade against the use of drugs in all forms of sport. It was established at Olympic level, and one of the first organisations to buy in was the Federation Internationale de l'Automobile, the world governing body of motor sport and automotive mobility. The FIA oversees the welfare of all car drivers and road users worldwide. Drug taking has never been a big problem for motor sport. 'Performance enhancement' in other sports is 'performance destroying' in motor sport. At speed, you can't take a risk with your natural reactions.

Staying awake and alert is another issue entirely.

In his later years, Sir Stirling Moss confirmed that his 1955 Mille Miglia victory, perhaps the most famous and revered long-distance race win on record, had been achieved after he'd taken a 'magic pill' given to him by five-times world champion Juan Manuel Fangio. Fangio had secured the pills from a medical student in Argentina and, according to Moss, shared them only once.

Moss won the 1600-kilometre race in a record time of 10 hours 7 minutes 48 seconds at an average speed of 159 kilometres per hour. His concentration was intense. Yet after the race and victory celebration, he drove with his girlfriend, Sally Weston, 600 kilometres through the night to a lunch meeting with Daimler-Benz directors at their German Stuttgart headquarters the next day before arriving in Cologne, a further 370 kilometres away, at 9 p.m. He'd been awake for 40 hours, and driving at intense speed for most of it.

'To this day, I've no idea if whatever that pill contained would be legal or illegal, accepted for sport or a banned substance,' Moss told an interview with the respected *British Motor Sport* magazine. 'But at the time, it was no issue. Dexedrine and Benzedrine were commonly used in rallies where you might have to drive for 36 hours. The object simply was to stay awake, just like wartime bomber crews. Anyway, I took mine and we finished. That night I noted in my diary that "Fangio's pills are fantastic".

There's no doubt that wakey-wakey pills were around at the time of the marathon. Former top navigator, BMC team manager and member of the marathon organising committee Stuart Turner confirmed in his book: 'Pills were legal and doctors gave prescriptions quite readily. A tablet taken at 10 p.m. kept you alert through to a greasy breakfast the next morning.'

Stimulants come with a downside. They can make the heart race, cause headaches and nausea and, with prolonged use, can promote tiredness.

Now, with enlightenment, no one is likely to admit they used bennies in the marathon. What was once accepted has become shameful. Only Moss, well into his eighties, has had the confidence to make the admission.

Moss was offered at least two drives in the marathon. Still in recovery from his near-fatal crash at Goodwood six years before, he prudently declined.

* * *

Sopwith and Sears announced the official marathon route just five months before the start. It would leave Crystal Palace, an inner London motor-race track that was a hangover from the 1930s, on 24 November 1968 and would arrive at Warwick Farm, a Sydney motor-race track on the edge of the city's suburbia on 17 December. There was barely enough time to prepare. Suddenly there was a mini traffic jam on the route as teams, mainly the factory entries, sought to discover what the road looked like and what facilities were available.

Tyre dumps, fuel caches, mechanical workshops and tow trucks became urgent considerations. The marathon was making few plans on their behalf. Every team was on its own. If they got caught in customs because their documentation was not complete, then that was the team's error. If they were stranded on a mountaintop, there would be no sweep car to pick them up. At best their absence would be noted at the next time control.

Castrol, a major sponsor of the teams, decided to take matters into its own hands. Route charts were not well known at the time. Pace noting, pioneered by Stirling Moss's co-driver, Denis Jenkinson, in the 1955 Mille Miglia when he used large rolls of paper, unwinding, to call upcoming speeds and distances, was still largely a black art. Virtually no one called corner to corner as they do now.

Tulip symbols, the schematic drawing of the road ahead from a bulb at the base of the diagram, had been invented for, naturally, Holland's Tulip Rally in the 1950s—but even into the 1960s, they were not a standard description.

Castrol could see trouble looming—and opportunity. In just twenty weeks, not a lot of reconnaissance was going to be achieved by competitors. Stuart Turner, working for Castrol and on the marathon committee, mounted a recce mission. Turner knew what he was doing. He was one of the new breed of high-speed 'office managers'—part co-driver, part tour guide—who'd grown up in the new wave of professional rallying. He'd won the UK's RAC Rally with Erik Carlsson in 1960. He was too busy to go himself, but he knew the person he could send. He came to an arrangement with Ford.

Bill Barnett, Ford's competitions manager, was keen to see for himself. Sweden's Gunnar Palm, who had won the 1963 Monte Carlo

Rally with Carlsson, had secured a place in Barnett's Lotus Cortina team, and he could be relied on for navigation notes, undertaking a vital dual role for the event and the team. The wild card in the recce car would be John Davenport, a freelance Ford co-driver and also a highly credentialled journalist who, the previous year, had come second in the Monte alongside Ove Andersson. Davenport had already accepted a Porsche ride and would not compete in the Ford team. Their goal was to produce a set of notes that would be available to all Castrol competitors. They were so successful that their notes became the unofficial route chart, highly prized and sought by those who didn't get them directly from Castrol.

But they weren't perfect.

'We've done our best to note what we saw, but it is up to you to be alert for changes,' the recce team said in their preliminary disclaimer.

There are a lot of road junctions that you will come to which do not appear in the notes and in those cases a very simple rule applies. If there is no signpost, then follow the road that you are on because if you were intended to have turned off, we would have told you to turn off.

At many places when we arrived on recce, there were road-works involving diversions which have been entered in the notes. Despite the slow pace of road repairs and construction the world over, some of these could be finished by the time the rally takes place. Alternatively, someone may have dug up the road in a new place.

Don't forget to keep your sense of direction should you take an unscheduled diversion or you may never find your way onto the route again.

SAROBI ᵗₒ DEHLI

No SP ⟋⤴   0.00
   PETROL

(ROADWORKS)   ↯⤴   1.04

         ⟨̣⤴ !!   1.41

      BAD   DIP !   8.00

AND 100yards DIP!

      BAD   DIP !   16.60

TOLL   PAY 30 Af   36.07
(THIS IS DIFFICULT TO SEE)

      No SP ⟊   41.45

AND 200yards TOLL - GIVE UP PAPER

(! NARROW BRIDGE) ⌐⟋   43.50

(ROADWORKS) ⟅⟆   46.10

Pace notes for part of the route from Sarobi to Delhi.

Davenport had learned to read and draw 'tulips' a few years before when he was introduced to them by rival competitor Henry Liddon, who would be co-driving in the marathon for British Leyland. Properly used, tulips can add substantially to a crew's confidence and speed, but they depend on accurate mileages. And the Castrol notes did not guarantee that: 'Everything is measured in miles so if you have your trip set in kilometres you are in for some arithmetical nightmares,' the road book said.

'From London to Bombay we used a Lotus Cortina whose trip was set very, very accurately over a measured mile, but in Australia, two other cars were used and the mileages there may not be quite perfect.'

The Castrol team would not recce the Australian route until three weeks before the marathon began. People were forgetting Australia. The daunting nature of the task of getting to Bombay was consuming them.

'It was a big mistake on my part,' said Rootes driver Andrew Cowan. 'We were short on budget and time. I drove the route from London to Bombay but then relied on co-driver Brian Coyle to go to Australia to do our notes. It cost me time and confidence. You get a feel for a place when you see it. You understand and remember, for example, a line of telegraph poles and what's beneath them. You connect with the road surface—and you don't forget. So when you get there in the event you're more familiar and more comfortable.'

Cowan's concerns could well have been echoed by the entire top end of the field. Some did not recce at all, relying on assigned note takers to do the legwork. In the marathon itself, they'd be hiring cars, even taxis, to charge ahead on the critical stages and get back to the start in time.

Cowan's recce was more strategic than most. Working on a very limited budget, Rootes built a recce car that would also become the team's spare-parts vehicle in Bombay. Cowan and Coyle would leave it there. It was also, even at this late stage, a prototype. As well as noting and understanding the route, they also wanted to test the car to breaking point. They began the recce in September, surely too late, and well behind the other works teams.

And they broke the car too early—a half shaft that robbed the car of all drive snapped in Bulgaria, and the nearest repair was in Turkey. For two days, Cowan and Coyle cajoled tow trucks and flat-bed trucks to take them to the border with Turkey, where they pushed the car between the border posts of the two countries. Parts flown from England took four days to clear Turkish customs.

It was a chilling indication of what was in store for the marathon.

'We ran into problems all the way across,' Cowan said. 'Customs held us up and officialdom even more so.' But they got to see what they wanted.

Back at base, Cowan filled in a comprehensive questionnaire detailing everything from the lubricants and tyres they estimated they would use through to the time they thought they would lose on the stages that could not be clean-sheeted without time penalty.

There was a great deal of conjecture about time loss. No one was expecting to clean-sheet the marathon. The winner would be the crew who lost the least amount of time and kept their car together the whole way. At various, critical, points of the marathon, crews would be presented with choices of alternative routes. Some would be faster than others but with greater danger.

They were flying blind.

Place names that no one had ever heard of took on immense importance, the roads between them even more so.

Cowan and Coyle found the southernmost route between Sivas and Erzincan in Turkey virtually impassable. To them, the longer northern route seemed safer, even if, in their estimation, it would cost them half an hour of late time.

'When we did the survey, half an hour seemed a reasonable amount to give up,' Cowan said. 'There were expectations that time loss in Australia would be measured in several hours, so, fractionally, the loss in Turkey did not seem so great.'

Brian Coyle flew on to Australia while Cowan returned to the UK, and he was amazed. The Australian route was nowhere near as treacherous as anticipated. It was hard, yes, and driving skill would be paramount, but the bush tracks were not necessarily car killers.

Coyle was dissatisfied with his Australian survey. Chrysler had organised a station wagon in Adelaide so he could see the Flinders Ranges and the Alps. His guide would be a local journalist, Chris de Fraga, a fast and reliable driver but not a top-flight rally competitor. Then he would fly back to Perth to see the mallee scrub sections, but he'd not drive the Nullarbor Plain.

An incomplete survey is cause for concern. But it was all they had.

Cowan, a Scot who defines the term 'frugal', was convinced he'd miscalculated in Turkey. If Australia was not to be the horror section he thought, then he could not plan to give away so much time between Sivas and Erzincan. Against all his fiscal concern, he hopped on a plane, this time with co-driver Colin Malkin, and went to force a way through the southern route.

Contemporary convention dictates that recces are never conducted at competitive speed. Teams in the World Rally Championship have special 'gravel' cars that simulate the feel of the rally machine, but it's up to the driver to estimate corner speeds as they pass over the course. Not so the marathon. Cowan attacked the Sivas stage, a rough, undulating, mountainous track seldom used by any vehicle. In a rental car, they were 46 minutes faster than the northern route in the recce car. Their decision was made.

British Leyland's survey was the most comprehensive of all. It resulted in more secret and 'exclusive' roads than anyone else in the event had found or imagined.

The survey was headed by Henry Liddon, one of the most credentialled rally co-drivers of all time. Liddon would lose his life nineteen years after the marathon in Africa's Ivory Coast Rally when the light plane in which he was travelling crashed on take-off.

Liddon, along with drivers Tony Fall and Brian Culcheth, took an Austin 1800 rally prototype from London to Bombay, spending a great deal of time prospecting in Iran, convinced there was a better way than either route nominated by organisers from Tehran to Taybad near the border with Afghanistan—and they found one.

British Leyland's third road would be their closely held secret. But it came with a challenge. Not clearing the massive traffic jams of Tehran to get to it could negate any advantage on it. They would need a guide.

British Leyland's Australian crew—Evan Green, Jack Murray and George Shepheard—were instrumental in the second part of the survey. Green and Murray were round-Australia specialists, and they knew more about the outback than almost anyone. But Shepheard, son of the man who conceived the REDeX Trial, had also competed in the 1964 Round Australia Trial with a young driver called Colin Bond, who would go on to become the only person to win the Australian Touring Car Championship, the Australian Rally Championship and the Bathurst 1000. Shepheard had a few tricks of his own.

The Australian trio surveyed from Perth to Sydney, then Shepheard took an Austin 1800 back to Perth and brought Liddon across to see and confirm their findings. One track, exclusive to them, would shave minutes off the run through the Flinders Ranges.

Liddon was well pleased, even more so when he was introduced to British Leyland competitions manager Alan Kemp and marathon manager Gus Staunton, who had galvanised a huge volunteer army of supporters across the continent to man gates and provide backup.

Green, Murray and Shepheard flew to Bombay to pick up the Liddon recce car and drive it back to London. Although they were travelling in the opposite direction, they were getting a feel for the terrain; on the special stages, they'd stop and practise. It was almost their undoing.

'We drove the Lataband Pass four times,' Shepheard said. 'It was in terrible condition, and Evan was driving it like a champion. The road, if you can call it that, was populated with people and animals so you had to be careful. Way up above us we could see riflemen. Stopping was not something you'd choose to do.'

George needed a toilet break, so they stopped.

'I was standing there looking out over the entire Hindu Kush unchanged for millions of years, when I heard a noise.

'"That's strange," I thought. "It doesn't sound like either Evan or Jack."

'When I walked back up to the road, there's Evan and Jack being held up by a group of young bandits wearing bandoliers and brandishing rifles.

'"We're in a spot of trouble here," Evan said quietly.

'Jack—that's Gelignite Jack—was keen to barter his way out.

'"Give them your cigarettes," he said. I was the only one of us who smoked.

'Then as I handed the cigarettes across, Jack invited them to light up using a huge Ronson Variflame lighter he carried to boil coffee on the run.

'When the flame shot out it caught one bloke by surprise and his beard was singed. He stepped back and instead of dropping his rifle he handed it to Jack while he beat out the flames. The others burst out laughing.

'After that, with no language, we jollied our way out of there—even giving them a look through the telephoto lens of my camera to see the Kush like they'd never imagined it.'

It was a scary moment, and it could have gone terribly wrong.

David McKay persuaded General Motors to send a V8 Holden Premier to London so he could survey back to Bombay. With friend and sometime rallyist David Lewin, an expat Australian with a thriving dental practice in the UK, they set out to retrace a route David had completed fifteen years before. McKay had driven—in fact, been one of the first—on the Hippie Trail. If ever there was a person less likely to embrace alternative lifestyles it was David, but with his wife, Betty, he'd driven a very early VW Kombi all the way from Bombay to Wolfsburg and on to London. It was an epic journey over two months, and now he was keen to do it in reverse in less than a week.

Jack Sears had also given him a special task: to map and secure exact mileages over the Lataband Pass. The route the organisers had been unable to survey would now be recorded by a competitor.

Lewin was on for a Holden seat in the marathon. The survey convinced him otherwise.

'My thoughts are now a kaleidoscope,' he wrote. 'I recall the dreadfully dangerous road from Istanbul to Ankara on the fast bitumen with the roadside littered with burnt-out and mangled wrecks of cars and trucks. Might is right in this part of the world as far as the rule of the road goes anyway. I would try to doze on these frightening sections but my companion would ask me to give him the average speed, fuel consumption etc, at the oddest moments, perhaps with a view to keeping me awake so that I could keep him awake.'

Carburettor trouble and broken gear selectors made the recce testing, but Lewin produced an impeccable set of pace notes—far more comprehensive than the Castrol ones. Half a century later, the crew of another of the *Telegraph* Holdens claimed they were never shared. The Australian Ford Falcon team, while part of Ford's three-country approach, never saw the Lotus Cortina team's notes, either.

The last recce was done by Ford. Almost as an afterthought and perhaps prompted by the fact that no one else had done it, Bill Barnett and Gunnar Palm flew to Perth in early November to chart the route to Sydney. So rushed was the trip that the official works team didn't have a car available; they rented one. Twenty-four hours later in the middle of the outback, they tore off one side of the suspension. Using fencing wire, they improvised a solution but the car was capable of being driven only in reverse. And that's what Palm did for 70 kilometres until they found civilisation.

6

The Continentals

IN 1966, THE FRENCH ORGANISERS of the world's most famous and important rally—the Monte Carlo—contrived to disqualify the British winners from the podium. They sparked an outrage that threatened the event, the sport and British–Continental relations.

The snub—and it was much worse than that—elevated in intensity to become a symbol of the discontent and disrespect that existed between the UK and France.

The world's greatest sprint rally drivers—Timo Mäkinen, Rauno Aaltonen and Paddy Hopkirk in Mini Coopers, and Roger Clark in a Ford Cortina Lotus—had raced into the first four places in the Monte. Sixth-placed Rosemary Smith (Hillman Imp) had won the Coupe des Dames.

It was a British rout.

And then they were gone.

The brilliant little Mini Coopers had won in 1964 and 1965 as well. It had been five years since a French-made car had won.

The disqualifications elevated fifth-placed Pauli Toivonen and co-driver Ensio Mikander to victory in a Citroën DS21 from a brace of Italian Lancia Fulvias.

Scrutineers had stripped the British cars to pieces looking for fault. They'd found nothing until they stumbled on a wiring path, outside the strict letter of the regulations, which meant that the headlamps could only be dipped in conjunction with the driving lights, not independently.

The French were technically correct, although their interpretation was open to dispute. BMC and Ford fired in protests that were, predictably, dismissed.

The British boycotted the prize giving and, it's said, so did Prince Rainier, ruler of Monaco.

The following year, with the heat barely out of the controversy, BMC extracted ice-cold revenge. Rauno Aaltonen and Henry Liddon won again for Mini.

It was with this background that René Cotton, former driver, private team owner and in charge of Citroën's competitions program, gave great consideration to the London–Sydney Marathon.

Cotton and Citroën had made the decision to shift their focus to long-distance rallies. The Minis and emerging threats from even more purposeful cars like the Porsche 911, Alpine-Renault and Lancia Fulvia had made the Monte unsuitable for the larger Citroëns. The marathon, on the other hand, was built for the Citroën. Cotton had only to convince his board.

Organisers had not expected a big entry from Europe, certainly not from the works teams. Tommy Sopwith had been to Mercedes-Benz and Peugeot, the obvious candidates, and been politely refused. He'd sought an audience with Karl Kling, the veteran motor-sports manager of Mercedes-Benz. Kling was a former Formula One driver for the Silver Arrows, finishing second by less than a second in the French Grand Prix to the great Juan Manuel Fangio. He'd been handed the most difficult of tasks— appointed motor-sports manager after the 1955 Le Mans 24 Hour disaster when a Mercedes car speared into the crowd. The German company withdrew from motor sport, and its eponymous motor-sport boss Alfred Neubauer retired. But there was still a need to service the motor-sport endeavours of the raft of private entrants, and that's the role Kling was given. Over several years, he had gradually eased the company back into competition, winning the 1961 Algiers–Cape Town Trans Africa Rally himself, at the wheel of a Mercedes-Benz 220SE.

Kling told Sopwith that the cost of mounting a full effort with total support was not something his board would countenance. If the regulations were written differently, banning external service and support crews so that each car needed to be self-contained, then he might reconsider. Mercedes-Benz was doing very well in Europe at the time. Its annual growth was exceeding 8 per cent. There wasn't much incentive to go chasing a prize that might be elusive and expensive.

Sopwith did not hold high hopes. BMW had only a few years before been on the verge of bankruptcy, even courting Mercedes-Benz for a possible merger. Money was tight, and BMW's motor-sport involvement was focused on affordable touring-car racing. Porsche's competitions manager, Baron Fritz Huschke von Hanstein, formerly a BMW works driver and winner of the 1940 Mille Miglia, shared the common Teutonic view. Although

Porsche had won the 1967 European Rally Championship with Polish driver Sobieslaw Zasada and was celebrating its maiden victory in the 1968 Monte Carlo with British driver 'Quick' Vic Elford in a 911 T, there was no appetite to spend a lot of money on a one-off event. It would be different, of course, if there was a need to support a private entry. Porsche was big on customer support. Some of its customers' teams were achieving well above the works' effort.

* * *

French maker Simca came to the marathon through its parent, Chrysler. When Rootes Group made its decision to enter, it wisely called a meeting of all members of the Chrysler family. Increasingly, entrants were realising the real cost of participation lay in the logistical support that had to be laid down across eleven countries.

Rootes reasoned that if they could entice their parent to enter from the USA and their French sibling to field a team, then the cost of support could be shared.

American entry was never really a proposition. The US makers had a huge and lucrative domestic market, and the marathon was running nowhere near their doors. In the end, just one US entry would start, carrying a CBS news camera operator who would make the marathon visible across the USA.

Simca, though, was on. The company—which had been founded by Fiat, had absorbed Ford of France only a few years before and was then bought by Chrysler—had recently launched a new front-wheel-drive 1100 sedan, the volume model in its sporting range, and the marathon would provide ideal promotion.

Simca was some car.

The sports models offered four-wheel disc brakes, performance conversions by Abarth and styling by Italian masters Bertone and Giugiaro. Their competitions manager was Pierre Boucher, an enthusiastic rally driver with four Monte Carlos to his credit. He readily accepted the challenge of entering the new 1100 in the marathon. It wasn't likely to win, but with marathon promotion it would become for a time the biggest-selling car in Europe.

* * *

Fiat wasn't interested in the marathon. It was the biggest-selling brand in Europe, and it held better than 18 per cent of a crowded market. Cecil Gavuzzi, its PR manager, told journalists with his tongue firmly in his cheek that Fiat was happy fielding its second-string car. Fiat had recently purchased a strategic 20 per cent of Citroën.

DAF—van Doorne Automobiel Fabriek—on the other hand was independent, run by the Dutch van Doorne brothers, Hubert and Willem.

Hub van Doorne was an inventor, and DAF had perfected his continuously variable transmission (CVT). Hub's CVT is among the great automotive inventions of the twentieth century. A belt driven on a series of pulleys, CVT has become the staple transmission of hybrid and electric vehicles. Without it, the advancement of green technology in cars would have been severely curtailed.

In 1968, CVT still needed to be proven. The van Doornes were truck and bus makers. In 1958, they had designed a small car around their CVT system, and for the next eighteen years a succession of DAFs came to market but the car brand wasn't to make it to its twentieth birthday. It was folded into Volvo, and DAF went back to being a highly respected truck brand.

The marathon provided DAF with a huge opportunity to prove and promote CVT. It employed two of the best race and rally experts in the Netherlands—one of them, Rob Slotemaker, was so good on ice and low-grip surfaces that he taught Paddy Hopkirk and the BMC team to drive. DAF would mount a huge effort, even chartering a KLM (Dutch Airlines) DC3 to fly in support the entire way. They entered themselves as the Dutch National Team.

* * *

In Russia, the Iron Curtain was being raised from the inside.

Eleven car makers within the USSR turned out two million vehicles—cars and trucks combined—each year, but less than 50 per cent of local demand was being met. Fiat was gearing up to build a Russian facility. It had effectively won a tender fought against VW, Ford, Peugeot and Renault to become a partner of the state and build a people's car based on their 124.

Even as the Russians were inviting Fiat in, they were also becoming exporters. Their Moskvitch, a knock-off of the Opel Kadett, was in big demand in nearby Norway and Finland, and also, strangely, in France.

A trading company, Avtoexport, set up in the 1950s to promote sales of Russian products, would export cars and simultaneously import engines and essential equipment that could not be made locally. By 1968, Avtoexport was selling 55 per cent of all Moskvitch production outside the USSR and much of that beyond the Iron Curtain. They'd even begun eyeing the main markets, including the UK. What better way to promote their Moskvitch than to enter it in Britain's bold event?

Avtoexport entered four of their popular 408 model, taking marathon organisers by surprise, and announced plans to acquire dealerships in the UK at the end of the race. The marathon would prove the reliability of the Moskvitch. By decree: four Moskvitches would start, and four would finish.

*　*　*

Volvo broke the dam wall of German resistance to the marathon. The Swedish manufacturer had made its name for safety—seizing the ascendancy even from Mercedes-Benz. Its most important invention was the three-point lap-sash seatbelt. It was so earth shattering in its contribution to occupant safety that Volvo magnanimously, but with the certainty of a global blaze of publicity, gave its patent to the world.

The marathon appealed strongly to Volvo's competitions manager, Gunnar Andersson. He was a gun, winner of the 1958 and 1963 European Rally Championship and of the 1961 Mille Miglia in a Ferrari 250 GT Berlinetta.

With encouragement from its Australian distributor, Volvo opened its competitions department to private entrants who wanted to contest the marathon.

The Germans sat up and took notice. Here was a middle ground—an opportunity to put a toe in the marathon water by providing factory support but not entering a works team. They could have some say over the integrity of the cars that were being entered without having to spend a fortune. If any of those vehicles looked like they were going to be in contention towards the closing stages, it would be relatively inexpensive to swoop in and shepherd them home.

Karl Kling set up a special workshop. He had already determined the best specification for the marathon. The four-door 280 S was his choice—and he recommended the still-new fuel-injection model—the E—because injection, he felt, would be able to cope better than carburettors with the variations in fuel quality that competitors would encounter.

It worked this way.

Customers bought their own cars through their own dealership network, then Kling would take them off the production line straight to the workshop, perhaps after he had driven them several hundred kilometres to settle them in. In the workshop they'd dismantle and rebuild them.

Engine and gearbox blueprinting was all the rage in series production racing. A car's horsepower could be significantly increased and its reliability better assured through the simple process of going to the spare-parts bin with a micrometer. By matching every engine component to ensure each was at maximum factory tolerance, it was like making a Stradivarius out of an off-the-shelf violin.

The cars were strengthened, especially around the suspension mountings. Stronger springs and dampers were fitted, and ride height was increased by the simple method of fitting bigger wheels—15 inches up from 14 inches.

Underbody protection was essential. Sump and gearbox guards were added, including a special guard to protect the clutch cylinder, which was exposed. Any external piping, like the brake and fuel lines, was insulated with webbing to offer protection.

Kling had thought his way through driver fatigue. Whether it was to be a two-, three- or even four-person crew, he reasoned that a well-upholstered and relatively silent interior would be a boon to the occupants. While some marathon cars would front the starter with gutted interiors and lightweight window glass, all in the interests of weight saving, Kling kept his cars close to standard. He devised a special seat, stretched over standard seat frames. The goal was to keep the driver and passengers well contained and supported in high-G-force motoring. There's a difference between being comfortable at road speed and at competition levels of cornering force.

The conversion of three cars and the modification of another two each took about six weeks, done concurrently. It was no small task, but it was by no means a works effort. Compromises were made sometimes to meet strict engineering standards.

Bigger fuel tanks were needed, and for the Mercedes-Benz factory this was a big problem. Rules got in the way. Kling was able to blow out the existing tank to a degree but not replace it. The solution was to carry jerry cans in the boot. And that meant stopping to refuel.

The threat of kangaroo strike in Australia had been considered. To protect the radiator, Kling placed it, effectively, in a cage, with bars from the chassis frame to the bodywork covered in wire mesh, which had the added advantage of catching loose rocks and twigs. This single modification would prove to be Mercedes' downfall.

Now caught up in marathon fever themselves, Mercedes arranged to put a mechanical service point at Belgrade—the last point of Western 'civilisation' before the marathon headed off into uncharted territory. Kling strongly hinted that if any of the crews made it to Australia they might expect to see another factory mechanical team there.

* * *

Porsche, like Mercedes, had determined that building cars for its customers was better than letting them do it themselves. It took a visit to Ferdinand 'Ferry' Porsche by Polish rally champion Marek Wachowski to make it happen.

Wachowski and his driving partner, Sobieslaw Zasada, were Polish heroes. They'd twice won the European Championship from behind the Iron Curtain, each time with the active support of their country's premier, who had opened doors and helped them achieve visas and carnets. Wachowski considered himself blessed. In the Warsaw uprising of 1944, he and his mother had escaped death when the Nazis went from door to door pulling citizens into the street and executing them in brutal reprisal: 'I was an aircraft enthusiast and my copies of *Der Adler*, a German plane magazine, were spread all over the floor,' he said. 'The soldier sent to shoot us turned out to be a fan, too, and he stayed to talk, not kill.'

When the pair decided to enter the marathon, Wachowski went to Stuttgart to talk to Huschke von Hanstein. 'He said no, so I asked for a meeting with Ferry Porsche. Surprisingly, he gave me fifteen minutes. I spoke of the marathon but not once did I request money. He asked me why not and I replied, "If I had I would not have had the privilege of meeting you." The next day he instructed von Hanstein to support us.'

Three Porsches would be prepared at the factory. All three cars—a new 911 S and two 911s that had already been used in competition—were stripped to the metal and reinforced with bronze welding on all seams. Special modifications were made to the flat six 2.0-litre air-cooled engine. Compression ratio was reduced to 8.6:1, detuning the car from its standard 130 kW to 120 kW to better accommodate expected low-octane fuel supplies.

Wachowski and Zasada did a full recce. In Australia, they hit a kangaroo, severely damaging their rental car.

Porsche mechanics visited Berlin Zoo to observe and measure Australia's largest marsupial for themselves. The solution they came up with was to build a tubular and mesh cage inside which was a Porsche. It was theoretically effective, although no one would ever know since no one hit a roo.

Four spare tyres were mounted to the roof of the cage along with external fuel and oil tanks, which were plumbed into the car to provide replenishment on tap. There was a lot of weight riding high above the Porsche's normal centre of gravity.

Porsches sit low on the ground, and technicians were concerned that a deep creek crossing could be the end of their drivers' marathons if water sucked into the engine through the exhaust. They devised an ingenious snorkel that wound from the exhausts up onto the roof, forming part of the external roll cage.

Porsche had been using magnesium wheels on its early short-wheelbase 911 road cars. It opted for steel wheels on the marathon cars, perhaps not as strong on-road but more durable in the expected conditions. Steel, though, adds more weight and does so in a critical area.

A Porsche that started out weighing 1030 kilograms, a good, nimble, fighting weight, had ended up tipping the scales—with its crew—at 1450 kilograms.

Like Mercedes, Porsche was banking on its cars making it to Australia. If they did, then Huschke von Hanstein himself would bring three mechanics.

* * *

Citroën received board approval incredibly late. It wasn't whole-hearted backing, but there were limited funds for a two-car team and the Automobile Club of France would pay for a third.

It was a time of incredible turmoil for Citroën. Much of its shareholding had been sold to Fiat, and traditional management channels had broken down. Tyre manufacturer Michelin, which had been the principal investor in Citroën since it bailed it from bankruptcy in 1935, was losing its influence. The infraction was causing ructions in government. President de Gaulle was not pleased.

Taking that bigger picture into account, René Cotton and Citroën PR director Jacques Wolgensinger considered themselves fortunate to get anything up at all.

Cotton was a team manager in the mould of Kling and von Hanstein. These three were not mere bureaucrats but dyed-in-the-wool motor-sport legends in their own right. The spirit of competition flowed through their veins. Motor sport then, as now, existed on passion. Leave a decision whether to go motor racing to a keen young executive to review against other ways to spend company funds, and there's a strong chance racing won't be the first choice. Motor sport exists on President's Prerogative. Someone on high has to love it.

Cotton was a seasoned racing veteran with six Mille Miglias to his credit. He drove a Mercedes 300 SL in the ill-fated 1957 race in which Count Alfonso de Portago crashed his Ferrari 355 S, killing himself, his co-driver and ten spectators. It was a disaster almost as big in its consequence as the 1955 Le Mans.

Cotton had raced in five Le Mans 24 Hour races and won the Spa 24 Hour twice. In 1958, aged 44, he'd taken over management of l'Ecurie-Paris-Ile-de-France, a racing team servicing private

Citroën entrants when the troubled Citroën factory had officially withdrawn from the sport.

One year later, Paul Coltelloni, a long-time Citroën supporter, used his wife's ID 19 to win the Monte Carlo Rally. It was a most important victory for Citroën and would be its last at Monte Carlo until the controversial 1966 event. Coltelloni was a hero.

Not many drivers were paid back then—certainly not Citroën drivers. Instead, in a glittering victory ceremony at the Hotel Ritz, Citroën presented Coltelloni's wife with a magnificent Blancpain platinum-and-diamond lady's jewel watch, a symbol of their appreciation. They presented Cotton with the opportunity to come in out of the cold and run their reconstituted competitions department.

Under Cotton's control and assisted by his wife, Marlène, who would take over the department after René's death from cancer in 1971, Citroën stormed to victories in rallies across Europe. The Cottons had met in Biarritz at the prize giving for the 1960 Tour de France Automobile. Marlène became René's assistant, and they married in 1962.

The big, ungainly front-wheel-drive DS 21 was purpose-built for a long-distance event like the marathon. It was a perfectly balanced car. Its hydro-pneumatic self-levelling suspension, a system superior to that of the Austin 1800, was well suited to all terrains. Unlike the Austins, which ran a transverse motor across their front axle, the Citroën's 2.2-litre four-cylinder engine was longitudinal, mounted back from the front axle with the gearbox in front of it, providing better weight distribution and power transference. It was almost, by technical description, a mid-engine car.

Cotton and Marlène set off on a quick route survey from Paris to Bombay. There was no time to get to Australia. They'd cover that off if their cars got that far. There was no time to match the British in the depth of their survey; no looking for alternative routes. But they had a plan.

Citroën had a growing network across the Middle East and Asia. In Tehran, a central marathon service point, Alfred Aysseh had begun local assembly of Citroëns. Aysseh had already offered service facilities to the Holden team, but for sound commercial reasons was happy to help his own factory, too. That would become the hub of Citroën's operations.

The Cottons planned a complex service regime, suited to their budget. It looked good on paper, but for their small band of service technicians it was physically punishing, more so than competing.

Led by chief racing mechanic Michel Parot, Citroën would have a team of six mechanics placed in strategic positions across the first leg to Bombay. One team of two would use commercial aircraft to fly to Istanbul, Tehran and Kabul. Two teams of two mechanics would drive ID 19 shooting brakes—big station wagons—to Istanbul, where one team would wait for the marathon to arrive. The other, including Parot, would drive on to the Afghanistan border, surveying the southern route that Cotton had not had time to see. Then they'd phone back to him in Tehran and he would make the decision which way the competing cars would go.

In the Cotton plan, the first service team by then would have sped ahead of the marathon, and both service crews would greet the competing cars when they exited the long, punishing Iranian desert.

At that point, Team One would turn and drive back to France. Team Two would pick up a third mechanic and follow the marathon at race pace. It would dog the rally cars through Kabul, skirt the special stage Lataband Pass and be in Sarobi at the other end in time to service the competition cars when they came off the Pass. Then they would simply keep going all the way to Delhi and Bombay, 2500 kilometres nonstop.

The 'Brake' was not a competition car, not specially prepared. It had a bench front seat, and the rear was given over to spares. 'It was a long way, nonstop, three men on the front seat, without eating or sleeping except in the car,' Parot recalled fifty years later. 'It was an interesting experience: five days' abstinence for me.'

Citroën went to its parts warehouse and built a composite car that would be as easy as possible to keep on the road. They would be using the new 2.2-litre 1969 model DS 21, but it would be fitted with body panels from the 1967 car. The reasoning was simple. They needed to be able to change the headlight bulbs easily. The 1969 car had more intricate, fully recessed lights, and they would take too long to service.

René Cotton calculated that the additions he wanted to make to the marathon car would add around 100 kilograms—so he set about stripping that much weight out of it first.

Citroëns were already relatively lightweight, ahead of their time, with alloy bonnets and a glass fibre roof. The weight-loss program entailed stripping out the interior trim right down to window winders on the back doors. All sound-proofing material was removed. The rear seats were discarded and the bumper bars unbolted. Heavy window glass came out, replaced by perspex.

And then weight went back on. Skid plates were placed under the engine, gearbox and exhausts. Citroën wanted to give its cars a range of 1000 kilometres, so three new fuel tanks were installed. It was an ingenious system. Each was interconnected, so crews could switch between the tanks to mix their own octane brew on the run. If they got a bad dose of substandard fuel in one location, they could create a hybrid octane mix from another tank. A completely separate fuel system was set up, ready should there be any pump trouble. There was a duplicate electrical system, too, adding minute but important weight.

Cotton left out a roll cage. Roll cages provide structural rigidity as well as protecting occupants. But the weight was thought to be too punitive. Crew safety, important as it turned out on the last day of the marathon, was not a compelling concern. The Citroën teams did not use helmets, either.

Without the weight of a cage, Citroën was able to sling a spare lightweight perspex windscreen beneath the roof and even stack aluminium mud ramps under the seats in case of bogging.

All up, the big Citroën weighed not much more than its show-room mass of 1200 kilograms.

The 2.2-litre engine remained standard, not detuned. Fed by a single twin-choke down-draught Weber carburettor, it put out 85 kW at 5750 rpm. Citroën played with the final drive on the four-speed manual gearbox, lowering the gearing slightly for greater acceleration. Speed in the gears was approximately 50, 100, 140 and 170 kilometres per hour. Maximum speed could be increased by maybe 10 kilometres per hour by fitting higher-profile tyres for the long straight sections.

The manual gearshift was where it always was on the steering column. The steering was power assisted.

Partner Michelin was instrumental in developing tyre strategy. The works cars would use Michelin XAS on the road sections but would then switch to a lower-profile rally tyre, codenamed NORA, for the special stages. They were very special, not available for public sale, and they howled like hounds on the road. The Citroëns would carry their tyres not on the roof or in the front compart-ment over the axle but in the boot.

The neat thing about the Citroën was its hydro-pneumatic suspension. It was independent on all four wheels, unusual for the time. It came with an automatic ride leveller regardless of load, but ride height could also be manually adjusted in increments from 171 millimetres up to 292 millimetres using a lever inside the car. The clearance adjustment could be used to jack up the car for a wheel change. Because of the system, Citroëns could be driven on three wheels.

There was a lot of optimism around Citroën. The car's specification wasn't exactly a model of simplicity, but the package was a blueprint for long-distance, high-speed competition. Many of the highly favoured works teams were looking closely at this last-minute entry. If it could hold together, the Citroën, they reasoned, could be a real contender.

7

Playing the Field

KEITH SCHELLENBERG was like Toad of Toad Hall, a larger-than-life character, leaping with joy from one adventure to the next with a comet-size trail of publicity blazing behind him.

An Olympic tobogganist, Yorkshire rugby captain, powerboat racer, owner of his own island off the coast of Scotland, and entrant in the London–Sydney Marathon of a 1930 Bentley tourer, he was imagined by some to be the spirit of the event.

While the works teams were supported with service aircraft, fuel and parts dumps, strategically placed mechanics and even pop-up rest areas, Schellenberg and his crew of two were having none of it—going it alone in a vehicle almost 40 years past its use-by date, 35 years older than any other car in the race.

'I just don't think it's right,' Schellenberg said, referring to the works teams as he attempted with theatrical flourish to affix his racing numbers to the deep-green Bentley. 'It's difficult—it has no doors, you see.'

Nor did it have windows, just thin plastic to guard its three occupants—Schellenberg and chums Norman Barclay and the Hon. Patrick Lindsay—from either alpine cold or desert sand, should they get that far. The Bentley had six cylinders sharing its massive eight litres, so each cylinder had more cubic capacity than one of the works Simcas. Snakes of exhaust pipes emerged from the left-hand side and converged on a totally inadequate muffler sitting quite close to the ear of the rear-seat occupant.

Schellenberg was always regarded as colourful. He quite liked the 'Toad' reference but only when his daughters used it. He saw himself as perhaps a little more responsible than the *Wind in the Willows* character. But only just. It was not too big a stretch to cast Lindsay and Barclay in the *Willows* roles of Rat and Mole.

But that's where the analogy ended. The Bentley, the oldest, largest, heaviest vehicle in the event, captured the imagination of many, but it by no means represented the ambitions, standard of preparation or even the investment of the 60 amateur entrants selected from the 155 who had originally entered expressions of interest.

For the amateurs, it was first necessary to fall in love with the idea of traversing the world for the sheer pleasure of the challenge. Once you'd caught the spirit, the rest was relatively straight-forward. It was different for the works teams. For them there was commercial imperative involved. Success would bring the factories great riches. Even Francis Birtles had driven for the fiscal future of Bean.

With the best will in the world, a privateer couldn't enter the London–Sydney Marathon with a view to winning. A works team would always have a massive edge. If there were enough works teams, then the odds of an outsider getting up became commensurately less.

For the private entrants, it was never about the money.

First prize outright was £10,000—or, as the *Daily Express* put it, 'a pound a mile'. For the outright victors, that purse fifty years on is equivalent to £120,000 or more than $200,000. First prize for the best private entrant was £500 (the equivalent of around £6000 or a little over $10,000).

And yet they came from everywhere. Ten countries and nineteen different makes of vehicles. There were more than 40 models within the makes. There was no such thing as a marathon-spec car, one that would carry its occupants safely to Sydney. Where's the adventure in that? Everyone had an idea of what would be best for the task.

English brothers Pat and Tony Downs spent more to enter the marathon than they did on their VW 1200. The entry fee was £550 ($1300) and that included the boat fare. Most spent a lot more. Many, hovering on the threshold of professionalism, approached the car factories for help to prepare and semi-fund their private entry. And that caused confusion.

Defining a private entry confounded the organisers. They never got it right. The waters were muddy from the start. If you were entered by a sponsor, no matter how small, did that mean you were no longer self-entered and therefore not private? If you were self-entered but you'd managed to secure factory assistance, however slight, did that disqualify you from private classification? They were questions put regularly to the committee, and they never successfully answered them.

Andre Welinski epitomised the problem. The tearaway Polish-born solicitor had immigrated to Australia after the war and done very well. He had a waterfront home at Sydney's Seaforth overlooking the Spit Bridge. Andre's yacht was at the bottom of his garden. He was Schellenberg-esque, the fastest and most convincing salesman you'd ever meet. Andre drove Volvos, and his mechanic, Gerry Lister, brother of Volvo dealer Tony, had become the first person to win a race in Australia in a Volvo. When the American Oil Company (AMOCO) fortuitously embarked on massive expansion in more than 30 countries, including Australia, Andre was on to them. In a trice, it seemed, he had a car, a sponsor, his media and his driver all lined up.

But it was a one-off effort—depending on how you viewed AMOCO, a private entry. Max Winkless, the managing director of the still fledgling Volvo Australia and a top racing driver, proposed much more. He approached the Volvo factory and found them willing to build special marathon cars for private entrants.

There would be one for Welinski, who would share with Lister, and another for Winkless, who would drive with John Keran, his winning class co-driver in the 1966 Surfers Paradise 12 Hour in a Volvo P 1800. There was an entry from Western Australian television for inaugural Round Australia Trial winner Ken Tubman driving with motorcycle ace Jack Forrest, after whom Forrest's Elbow at Australia's Mount Panorama circuit is named. And Bob Holden, the winner of the 1965 Bathurst 500 with Rauno Aaltonen in a Mini Cooper S, had emerged as a Volvo driver for the marathon. He was proposing to drive his 142 S from Sydney to London to recce the route, then drive it back in the event.

Suddenly AMOCO, which had signed on for a little, had got a lot. And they were up for it.

A private entry had grown into a works effort—except it wasn't really a factory team, was it? Just a bunch of likely lads from Australia who'd gotten together to meet the marathon challenge. It kept growing. AMOCO hired a cameraman, Rob McAuley, to travel with Bob on his recce and shoot a documentary to pre-promote the event. Then they hired an aircraft, a state-of-the-art twin-engine ten-seat Piper Navajo, the best you could get in those pre-private-jet times, and loaded it with parts and people, including Mike Kable, the first motoring journalist on Rupert Murdoch's relatively recently established national newspaper *The Australian*. So heavy on take-off that it took the full length of Sydney's Kingsford Smith main runway to struggle into flight, it would perform an aerial survey of the route, flying through—not over—the Khyber Pass.

When Bob Holden made it to Gothenburg, his rally car was broken. Stress cracks had started in the windscreen and moved to the chassis in several places. Volvo was delighted. This was the sort of feedback they wanted. They gave Bob a new car and reverse engineered his to discover what needed to be strengthened in the marathon cars they were building. Legitimately, they saw this as destruction testing for future road models as well. But a works effort? Perhaps the balance was tipped when they hired their own plane for the return journey across Europe and Asia, laying down service dumps and putting service mechanics on the road as well.

Elsie Gadd was a beneficiary of the Volvo effort. Ms Gadd (never Elsie) was a 47-year-old London surveyor and part-time property developer who just happened to drive a Volvo. Customer service was important then as now. Volvo offered a pick-up and drop-off service, and when her car was returned to her, the young delivery driver, Anthea Castell, mentioned the marathon. Pretty soon

Castell was working for Ms Gadd, they'd found two female part-time racing drivers—Jennifer Tudor-Owen and Sheila Kemp—and Volvo's non-works department in Gothenburg was preparing a 145 S station wagon. There was a Ladies' Prize (£200) and not too many entrants. For Volvo, it must have seemed an investment worth making.

Two other Volvos were entered, too: one for William Chesson, owner of Lydden Hill Race Circuit in Kent, the venue two years before of the world's first Rallycross event. Another was for John Tallis, who had secured the services of Paul Coltelloni, by then approaching fifty. Coltelloni was a colourful character. In the same year he won the Monte Carlo, he won the European Championship when winner Erik Carlsson was docked 25 points for having an incorrect door rondel. When it was pointed out that 25 points was not enough to tip the balance of the championship in Coltelloni's favour, Carlsson was fined another 25 for the other door.

* * *

Like Volvo, were the factory-prepared Mercedes-Benzes works cars or privateers?

The most prominent of the Benz teams—former Formula One drivers Innes Ireland and Michael Taylor along with Olympic bobsledder (another one), long-distance driver and powerboat racer Andrew Hedges—all felt like professionals but in a very amateur way. They'd grown up in a different environment from the high-pressure professionalism of today and, while their intentions were honourable, they were really in the marathon for the sport.

Ireland had raced over six seasons, including three for the works Lotus team. Taylor had had just two Formula One races.

His career ended in the second at the high-speed Spa circuit in 1960 when he scythed through the trees without anyone noticing and disappeared from sight. It was Lucien Bianchi, driving for Cooper, who glimpsed debris in the forest, stopped and ran into the undergrowth. He found Taylor near death, stabilised him and then rushed back to his car and sped for help. Taylor christened his son Lucien.

Ireland and Taylor both had a reputation for being *bon vivants*. Hedges set an even higher bar. All three of them had intended to pick up the Mercedes from the factory and drive it to Istanbul in a trial of car and crew. But they never quite found the time. If this was a professional effort, it wasn't one for the textbooks.

Bobby Buchanan-Michaelson was another to receive assistance from Mercedes. A man who could out *bon vivant* any of Ireland's crew, Buchanan-Michaelson, 43, lived large when the money was available. He'd banked on having Stirling Moss in the car. When Stirling declined, Bobby secured David Seigle-Morris, an accomplished rally driver and navigator, once a member of the BMC team, as well as Australian Max Stahl, a journalist and fortunately an excellent bush mechanic. Stahl flew to London expecting to work on the car. Instead, he joined Buchanan-Michaelson in a series of late-night parties and escapades. The marathon, by comparison, would be a relief.

Two Australians took advantage of the Mercedes-Benz customer delivery service. Victorian transport company owner Desmo Praznovsky, with friends Stan Zovko and Ian Inglis, would guide home a 200 D. High-profile Sydney surgeon Alec Gorshenin would drive the sports version, the 280 SL, with Ian Bryson. Gorshenin, of Russian descent, was best known as the husband of Gold Logie–winning entertainer and actress Lorrae Desmond. Their marriage was not to endure. It may have come as some discomfort to Gorshenin when he realised one of the cars against which he was competing was sponsored by British actor Terry-Thomas, who had been his wife's lover before her marriage to Gorshenin for almost a decade when she was working in London in the 1950s. Gap-toothed Terry-Thomas specialised in playing the archetypical British cad.

Driving the marathon's smallest car, an MG Midget, John Sprinzel definitely qualified as a private entrant. Sprinzel had won the British Rally Championship in a Sprite, the badge-engineered sister car to the Midget. He was a Sprite/Midget expert—he'd even written textbooks on their tuning—so it seemed logical to enter the marathon. It was a tight squeeze. The auxiliary fuel tank went on the roof, directly above the heads of Sprinzel and his co-driver, 1966 British Rally Champion Roy Fidler. They raised sponsorship by crowdfunding.

Slightly larger, but only just, was the MGB of London PR supremo Jean Denton, a persuasive powerhouse. In later years, Prime Minister John Major anointed her Baroness Denton of Wakefield, and she served in parliament as party whip and a minister. Denton enjoyed motor racing for what it did for her business. She was a self-promoter. While brilliant engineer Tom Boyce (who would later design and build the ill-fated Amon Formula One car with New Zealand's Chris Amon) worked with British Leyland to build a very special 'B', complete with hydrolastic suspension like that of the Austin 1800s, Denton secured naming rights sponsorship from *Nova* magazine and lashings of publicity. Boyce would co-drive with her in the marathon.

In Australia, two journalists—Eileen Westley, editor of the women's section of *The Daily Telegraph*, and Marion 'Minny' Macdonald, the paper's columnist under the by-line 'Society

Spy'—were determined not to be left out. They'd arranged to borrow a car from British Leyland in Australia. The previous year, it had been used in a promotion—the Tortoise and Hare Race—in which Evan Green and Gelignite Jack Murray had circumnavigated Australia in the Morris 1100, 'racing' a light aircraft that marginally won. Sir Frank Packer was particularly protective of his female staff, in a gruff paternal way—nothing untoward—and he took some persuasion. Part of his deal was that they'd take driving lessons. The driving instructor was Peter Wherrett, who'd soon become Australia's first television motoring personality, with an ABC program called *Torque*. Wherrett lost control of the women. They assaulted the heavy timber safety fence on the main straight of the Warwick Farm racecourse, destroying the *Tortoise*. Embarrassed, British Leyland rolled out another one also christened *Tortoise* as a subterfuge, and it became their marathon car. They were joined by Westley's friend, Jenny Gates, because by then they'd realised that two drivers weren't enough.

* * *

The UK provided the majority of the private entrants. Forty teams came from the marathon's starting point and twelve from Australia. There were two from Switzerland and one each from Italy, the USA, Germany, India, Ireland and Japan. It was a logical ratio. It was a long way to ship a car from your home country to the start and logistically difficult when there was no ready place in London to undertake final preparations. The marathon had not been kind in that regard. There wasn't a lot done in the way of specific pre-event mechanical support. It was a different matter at the opposite end. Jack Sears and Tommy Sopwith went to pains to ensure that import regulations in Australia would allow ready sale of a used marathon car without tax penalty. A marathon car that made it to Australia did not have to be taken home again, a substantial freight-cost saving.

The Ford Cortina, in its various forms, was the privateer vehicle of choice. Thirteen Cortinas would face the starter alongside the works cars. The Austin 1800 was next most popular. Six of them had been chosen, but there was also a Morris 1100, an Austin 1300 and two MGs from the same marque. For the factories, the popularity of their cars was flattering, but it also imposed responsibility. It was simply impossible to leave customers stranded. Even as the works teams were planning their own service strategies, they were giving some—not a lot—of thought to others in their camp. If you were serious about the marathon, there was always a door slightly ajar at the factory.

Duncan Bray, Simon Sladen and Peter Sugden, all under 25, did it the right way around. They didn't approach their car maker until they had something to offer.

They bought a second-hand Lotus Cortina rally car, then found sponsorship. Model car makers were earning substantial money from miniature competition replicas even then (now the business is huge), and Dinky Toys were the biggest. They agreed to fund the effort totally, in return for the rights to produce a model of the car. The boys took it to Ford, which agreed. Ford would also assist with preparation, either in their own overworked shop or at specialist tuner Alan Mann Racing. It was a fully professional cash-and-kind arrangement. Then Dinky had a management change and reneged. Ford and Alan Mann honoured their end of the deal regardless.

Bill Bengry, a multi-franchised car dealer from Hereford, near the Welsh border, was used to doing it his own way. Bengry had won the British Rally Championship twice pretty close to its inception, both times with VWs from his own dealerships, and he'd parlayed that into drives in the great Continental rallies and even Africa, where he'd proved resilient and a stayer. While others crashed out around him, Bill was invariably there at the end. He had won his class three times in the Liège–Sofia–Liège rally. He regarded his chances in the marathon quite highly.

Bengry built a very special Cortina GT in his own workshop. He'd had a look at Ford's plan to run the twin overhead camshaft Lotus Cortina, and he'd put a big question mark over longevity. The pushrod GT may not have delivered as much power, he reasoned, but it would be reliable. It was a good strategy, almost prescient. There was no money and no time to do a recce. In fact, very few of the private entrants would see the rally road until the competition. But Bengry was prepared for the worst. He built an exhaust system like nothing anyone had seen. It curled up out of the bonnet and over the roof, well clear of any obstacles beneath the vehicle. Bengry would be co-driven by local farmer Arthur Brick and pharmacist John Preddy.

*   *   *

Connections are everything. Graham White was in the secretariat of the Royal Automobile Club of Great Britain. David Dunnell was the stepson of British motor-sports commentator and former racing driver John Bolster, and John Jeffcoat worked at a construction equipment company that agreed to sponsor their entire effort. Visas—no problem. Publicity—assured. Funding—amazingly, even should something go wrong, seemed strong, like a great big insurance policy. They chose an Austin 1800, had it prepared externally at a speed shop of renown—Janspeed—and went for a long-distance drive to Scotland to work on crew compatibility. They remain one of the few crews to own up to making Benzedrine part of their travelling kit.

* * *

Australia was soon to enjoy a share-market boom. Within a year, a stock called Poseidon would create a mineral market bubble unlike anything the industry had seen. The only BMW to start in the marathon was sponsored by the Pan Australian Unit Trust, a company associated with its driver, Colin Forsyth. Forsyth and co-drivers Robbie Uniacke and James Rich were typical of the adventurous spirit of the marathon—professionals in fields well separated from the motor industry who were drawn by the challenge. Within that same year, the Pan Australian Unit Trust was being hailed as one of the British industry's high performers.

In India, Bomsi Wadia was an entrepreneur of a different kind. One of the country's most in-demand gynaecologists, he'd invented and marketed surgical instruments to make his speciality more streamlined. Wadia was a true enthusiast. When Bob Holden's Volvo arrived in Bombay by ship en route to its cross-world recce, it was Wadia who was directing the off-loading. The most valuable hands in Bombay were wearing workman's gloves and driving a crane. 'I'd heard about you coming and wanted to see and help for myself,' he said. Wadia had entered a Lotus Cortina in the marathon, beginning a lifetime's obsession with long-distance competition.

The biggest rally in North America was the Shell 4000, stretching from Calgary, Alberta, to Halifax, Nova Scotia. Maryland enthusiast Sid Dickson went along to watch. Although Paddy Hopkirk and Tony Fall were both competing, the rally was dominated by big American cars. That convinced Sid. He bought one of the works Rambler Americans on the spot (it's always good to get them at the end of a competition, before the good bits disappear). With co-driver John Saladin, he secured CBS cameraman Jerry Sims to accompany them and make a documentary. There was plenty of room for Jerry and his gear. They even cut a turret into the roof, like in an army tank, for Jerry to use for shooting.

* * *

The biggest surprise in the marathon is that Italy did not embrace it. If ever there was an event purpose-built for car-mad Italians, it was this one. It took two Formula One drivers to wave the flag.

Giancarlo Baghetti became, briefly, a national hero when he won his first-ever Formula One world championship race on debut in a shark-nose Ferrari 156. It was the French Grand Prix at Reims, and all three of the works team had retired, but he still had to race and pass Dan Gurney's Porsche—it was a worthy effort. He'd won his first two non-championship races immediately before as well, carving a place in history as the only person to win his first three Formula One races in succession.

Giorgio Bassi, eleven months Giancarlo's senior, had driven in just one Formula One race, the 1965 Italian Grand Prix in a Scuderia Centro Sud BRM, and he'd retired before the flag.

They both moved on to race touring cars and sports cars with mixed success and, in 1968, both passionate enthusiasts, they seized on the marathon. To suggest they were not well organised is to criticise the work ethic of a nation. They built up a Lancia Fulvia 1.3 HF, a car that was coming into its own in European rallies—but in a marathon? Armed with optimism, they headed for the start.

* * *

In South Australia, Stewart McLeod, a canny, deep-thinking, highly organised rally competitor and burgeoning event promoter (he'd run the 1979 Round Australia rally), had determined that the most efficient car for the conditions would be an Alfa Romeo. It ran a twin overhead camshaft engine like the Lotus Cortina. It was as powerful and perhaps better configured. McLeod rationalised that Alfa service would get the car back to Australia, and he could take it from there. He and co-drivers Jack Lock and Tony Theiler knew Australia well, especially the area north of Adelaide in the Flinders Ranges. They'd even carved a secret way that would give them a substantial edge. They built the Alfa in Adelaide, perfectly to their specifications, then they shipped it off to Milan to await their arrival. They'd use the drive up through the Mont Blanc tunnel and France to run it in and familiarise themselves with the roads.

When they got to Milan, they found their car was in pieces. Alfa had decided to help them, pulling it down and building it again. But the Italians were working to their own schedule. With the marathon just days away, the Australians, frustrated and annoyed, set to work to rebuild it as best they could. They may have left a few pieces out.

* * *

Three other Australian crews arrived in the UK in better shape. Motoring journalist Clyde Hodgins had teamed with technical college teachers Don Wait and Brian Lawler to support a school project in which students built up an Australian Survival Car to showcase technology. It had sixteen non-standard safety features built into it, including a padded dashboard. The New South Wales Minister for Transport, Milton Morris, launched it. 'I am confident competitors will observe high standards of safety,' he said. 'I am proud to see Australia well represented in the marathon.' Hodgins and Wait shipped the car to Bombay and drove it to London to survey the route.

Former Victorian trials champion Reg Lunn turned up with a Ford Falcon GT similar to the works cars but without some of their modifications. He chose not to accept works advice.

Round Australia expert Jack 'Milko' Murray from Maitland—a different person to Gelignite Jack Murray—went with Bert Madden and one of Australia's first true rally professionals, John Bryson, in a four-door version of the Holden team's Monaro. It is unlikely factory advice was offered.

* * *

There were no Japanese cars in the marathon, even though by the 1960s most Japanese makers were adopting motor racing as a legitimate way to improve and promote their product. The marathon was a giant leap too far.

Nobuo Koga, already a Japanese racing veteran with a best-placed eighteenth outright in a Honda S 800 in the Nürburgring 84 Hour, took matters into his own hands. He entered a Vauxhall Viva GT and invited young Yojiro Terada to join him. Terada would go on to become a Mazda factory driver and would compete in 29 Le Mans 24 Hour races, scoring class victories for the company's revolutionary rotary engine cars.

* * *

The marathon was all things to all people. Another two Australians were using it to find a quick and relatively inexpensive way home. Ian Mackelden, a young advertising executive on the almost-obligatory UK working holiday, responded to an advertisement placed by driving instructor Peter Wilson for 'co-drivers anxious to share expenses on an exciting trip to Australia'. David Walker, an Australian racing driver, had gone to England to seek his fortune. At the end of 1968, his career was faltering and he found a ride in a Vauxhall Ventora sponsored by his employer, the Jim Russell Driving School. Happily, he returned to the UK, where he won the 1969 British Formula Ford series and drove Formula One for Team Lotus.

* * *

The smartest thing the London–Sydney Marathon did was hook up with the military.

Ford, British Leyland and Rootes each directly assisted a military entry. In return, they received logistical support, help with transportation, cartography, even fitness training. It was a good deal.

The British military had resources, budget and time. They also had enthusiasm. The RAF and the army had motoring associations, prepared to pay their entry fees if the case was strong enough and the competitor could prove capability.

Eight armed forces entries started.

Ford signed up one of three cars from the British Army Motoring Association. Captain David Harrison and Lieutenant Martin Proudlock of the army's Junior Leaders' Regiment put a proposition to Ford: they could become the company's sixth official car, giving it two teams in the team's prize. It made sense.

The two officers were gifted the Lotus Cortina that Roger Clark had used in the 1967 RAC rally, along with all the components necessary to bring it up to full marathon specification. They had limited access to the Boreham workshop, and they would be full Ford team members with their own service plan equal to that of Ford's outright contenders.

In return, the army provided access to its training ground in Northamptonshire and its endurance course in the Welsh mountains. The army subjected Ford team members to simulations of survival in the extremes of heat and cold. It gave them practical instruction on how to divine water when none existed and how to avoid frostbite. They were taught to treat snake bite.

Nutrition was an abstract concept in 1968, except for the military. It wasn't just about avoiding Delhi Belly by not drinking the local water. It was learning what sustenance to take en route that would provide optimum energy for minimum waste. And it was getting your body in the best possible physical shape to be able to deal with the stresses of high-speed travel and perhaps even the G-forces of sudden impact.

Looking to win the PR stakes, British Leyland signed up the Red Arrows.

Broadcaster Raymond Baxter was the conduit. He did PR work for British Leyland and the Red Arrows, where he was the on-ground voice of their in-air display. It was such a good fit.

The RAF's close-formation display team radiated skill and bravery. Every boy (and many girls—although the first female Red Arrow would not be appointed for another 30 years) wanted to be a Red Arrow.

Flight lieutenants Terry Kingsley, Derek Bell and Peter Evans were also members of the RAF's Motor Sports Association, but the BLMC association was directly with the Red Arrows. It would prove to be a major distinction. In 1968, the Red Arrows inaugurated the Diamond Nine pattern that became its trademark. While they were learning to fly that, British Leyland took them to their test facility at Bagshot, a tank-proving ground—and they rolled. That achieved some publicity.

British Leyland committed fully to its pilots. They built the entire car, then they built another one for the navy. Commander Philip Stearns and captains James Hans Hamilton and Ian Lees-Spalding would skipper the Royal Navy Austin 1800.

The RAF had a lot of logistical expertise and freight capacity. It offered it all up to British Leyland and, as budgets began to stretch tight, it was accepted. RAF Transport Command provided British Leyland's stand-by facility. If their supplies were at the RAF base, boxed and ready to go, they would be loaded on the first aircraft headed for the intended location that had surplus space.

Rootes Group directly sponsored the RAF's Motor Sports Association. Squadron Leader Tony King and flight lieutenants David Carrington and John Jones were assigned the second Hillman Hunter in what was, compared to Ford and British Leyland, a very modest assault on the World's Greatest Road Race. 'With what resources we had, we were better off concentrating on one lead car—mine,' Andrew Cowan said. 'But we also needed a second car for backup. The air force had helped us out on other rallies, so we thought they'd be good. We rang them just as they were about to ring us.'

Rootes identified cartography and meteorology as two major concerns. Who better than the air force to forecast weather conditions?

And then war broke out. In Tehran, two factory representatives—one from British Leyland and one from Rootes—were waiting for an RAF freighter to arrive. When it unloaded, there were only boxes labelled British Leyland on board, although some contained Rootes parts. The mistake drew attention to the military assistance, and repercussions went all the way back to the British Ministry of Defence. Questions were asked. Hasty assurances were given. But the ministry made a strong point to the Red Arrows team. Only Rootes would be the official representative of the RAF.

The RAF had also privately entered a Ford Cortina—a GT, not a Lotus—for flight lieutenants Allan Dalgleish and Sean Maloney and First Officer Nigel Coleman. There seemed to be no connection with the works teams.

The motto of the 17/21st Lancers, a proud and distinguished cavalry regiment, was 'Death or Glory', slightly extreme even for the marathon.

Lieutenant Gavin Thompson applied to his regiment for permission to enter. His entry fee was paid, and he was authorised to draw down a Land Rover from ordnance. The marathon allowed only vehicles powered by two driven wheels, so the four-wheel drive of the Land Rover was permanently disabled. The regiment imposed one demand. While Thompson could share the drive with another officer—Lieutenant C.J. Marriott—he was required to take four personnel and the other two must be drawn from the ranks. The two officers called for volunteers. They received 800 applications and took the top 200 on a driving test to determine the two who'd participate.

The Royal Green Jackets was a tactical response infantry regiment of the British Army with the apt motto 'Swift and Bold'. They were used as shock troops and marksmen. Their proud claim was that, while the rest of the army marched at 120 paces a minute, they marched at 140. George Yannaghas and, at the last moment, Lieutenant Jack Dill chose to drive a Porsche 911 T.

Rover, a division of BLMC, sold a lot of cars and commercial vehicles to the British armed forces. Part of the job description of Rover salesmen was to stay tight with the decision-makers. The British Army Motoring Association offered common ground, and two 1965 Rover 2000 TC rally cars provided opportunity. Major John Hemsley, Warrant Officer Frank Webber and majors Mike Bailey and Freddie Preston were already rallying in Rovers through their association, and they were the logical choice. Rover assigned a technician to the army's School of Electrical and Mechanical Engineering to prepare the cars with stronger springs, higher ground clearance and auxiliary fuel tanks.

Every member of the 'military division' had only one concern. They'd received their visas and were cleared by their organisations to go. But they would be driving into Eastern Bloc countries. It seemed inconceivable, but would they be allowed through?

8

The Works Teams

'BUILD A CAR TO FINISH FIRST' was Ford's goal.

'Build a car to finish last' was the Rootes Group response.

Both were right. The works teams were certain that the car that finished the marathon was going to win.

Small cars, really small cars, would not cut it.

'We made up our minds very early that the Hillman Imp was not built for the marathon,' Andrew Cowan said. 'It was too small to carry the load and too vulnerable in the conditions, most of which were unknown. At the back of the workshop there was a Hillman Hunter which had been used in one event. On paper it looked okay.'

Rootes built performance out of its engine for the race across Europe and Asia, and then cunningly devised a new engine system for the run home across Australia. Ford built a rocket ship to go fast from the start.

Rootes looked at the demands on its crew and decided, reluctantly, to run three people in the still-cramped cockpit of its Hillman Hunter. Ford decided that the additional weight, along with the psychological constraint ('the third person is always the odd one out'), warranted only two people.

They were flying blind. No one had ever raced in marathon conditions, never mind the total 16,700 kilometres—equivalent to more than three Le Mans 24 Hour races. One stage alone covered 2500 kilometres through high altitude and desert, on punishing surfaces, and required an average speed of at least 107 kilometres per hour.

The same car had to deal with the mountains of Europe and Asia and the gibber deserts of Australia; endure temperatures from below zero to more than 40 degrees Celsius; cruise, faultlessly, at high speeds to avoid time penalties; and be tractable to deal with the extremes of deep bogs and slippery low-traction gravel. The same engine would be required to remain reliable when delivering peak performance on premium fuel or on an octane rating not much better than paraffin from fuel picked up in Asia.

Sir Max Aitken's challenge energised the motor industry. To find a way of getting from London to Sydney required testing, ingenuity and determination that far outstripped contemporary design parameters. No one undertook pre-production testing the way the marathon cars were thrashed. They do now, but not then.

The marathon had everyone spooked.

It had become a battle of team managers as much as of drivers. Rootes had recently employed Des O'Dell, eight years Cowan's senior, who had worked on the Le Mans–winning Ford GT40 program, Ford's answer to Ferrari, and before that on Aston Martin's DB4 racing efforts. 'He was a motor-racing man, and he brought a lot of that knowledge to the marathon because it was more than a rally. It was a race as well,' Cowan said. O'Dell answered to Marcus Chambers, the Rootes competitions manager, and formerly manager of British Leyland competitions when it was BMC.

'Marcus was old school—a thoroughly lovely English gentleman, once a racing driver, whose forte was administration. You could trust him—send him to Bulgaria with tyres and fuel and know he'd be there.' But O'Dell was the man. He even fabricated an Aston Martin rear-axle housing especially for the Hunter.

Across at Ford, they were stared down by rally manager Bill Barnett and competitions manager Henry Taylor. Taylor was a former Formula One driver before a career-ending crash and yet another member of the British bobsled team. Barnett was so enthusiastic, he volunteered to help prepare the Castrol route survey across the entire marathon.

Peter Browning was the competitions manager at British Leyland. Like his predecessor, Stuart Turner, who was part of the marathon's organising committee, Browning was an ex-PR, not a credentialled motor-sport competitor, but his office was at Abingdon and he was cocooned in a workshop of knowledge.

All three teams headed to tank-testing courses around the UK in an attempt to break their cars. 'It was only by driving them to absolute destruction that we could find out what might break in the marathon and prepare for it,' Cowan said.

Chassis strength needed major improvement, especially around the roof pillars, which would carry roof-mounted wheel and tyre assemblies. Four tyres and wheels could weigh up to 50 kilograms— a lot of mass to put at the highest point of the car.

Innovation abounded. Rootes went to the British Motor Industry Research Association (MIRA) test track and rushed around with tanks full of low-octane petrol to discover at what point they would burn out a piston. 'We came up with a three-tank solution so we could mix our octane on the run,' Cowan said. 'If we had no choice but to accept a low-octane fill in Asia, we could supplement it with higher octane from one of our other tanks.' It was a solution the works teams all arrived at.

Altering the fuel mixture to deal with octane and altitude became an art form. British Leyland had a simple cable, like a hand throttle, to advance and retard the engine on the move. Rootes couldn't get the auto-system right. Instead, they built a special spanner. The crew would go under the bonnet and alter the timing to predetermined settings. They practised so often they had the change down to seconds.

Dual electrical circuits were wired through the cars and, for essential items such as fuel pumps and alternators, a third was packed in the spares box.

Routing all pipes and hoses from front to rear was a major task. The British Leyland team devised a special conduit to move the hydrolastic fluid of the Austin 1800s around the car without exposing it to underbody damage. Brake lines were treated the same way.

Bonnets were lightened, and window glass was replaced with lightweight plastic. Magnesium wheels could reduce unsprung weight, a major factor in making racing cars handle better, but when Andrew Cowan broke a Dunlop mag wheel at the Bagshot tank-testing course, Rootes used heavier Minilite mags, accepting the weight penalty. *Evening Standard* journalist Ian Morton was there that day. 'They broke the sump guard, too,' he observed. The problem with magnesium was that it could easily be penetrated by a pepper shot of rocks. It was combustible, too. A magnesium-fuelled fire could quickly burn your marathon car to the ground.

Each of the three British cars from which the winner was expected to come was powered by four-cylinder engines. The Lotus Cortina had the least capacity but the most power of all. It was 1600 cc, but with its then revolutionary twin-camshaft cylinder head—standard fitment these days on family cars—it turned out a claimed 81 kW. Its opposition believed the marathon Lotus Cortina was making a lot more, somewhere in the region of 112 kW, which is consistent with the track-racing versions that needed to be 130 kW or more to be competitive. Rootes utilised a 1725-cc Sunbeam Rapier engine for its Hunter, developing around 80 kW for the first phase across Europe and Asia. This engine used a lower compression ratio, all the better to accept lower-grade fuel. In Bombay, it would receive a higher-compression cylinder head built by specialist tuner Holbay, which would provide it with parity with the Fords. Both the Lotus Cortina and Hillman Hunter used a conventional longitudinal engine layout driving the rear wheels. Cowan fought hard for the ability to use an electric overdrive on second and top. The overdrive manufacturer at first pushed back but then found a way; he got it on all four gears, providing him with greater options to reduce the load on his engine and to make better use of its torque.

British Leyland was less conventional. Its 1798-cc engine was mounted latitudinally—east–west—across the car, powering the front wheels. Conventional wisdom of 1968 said that front-wheel drive in a car the size of a Mini Minor was okay. But FF—front-wheel drive and front-wheel steer—put too much pressure on the system of a larger car. The Austin 1800 was marginally the largest of the three and the least powerful. Published power figures for the Mk II were only 64 kW but, like the others, that was just the starting point.

In Australia, there was a lot more power in play.

Ford's GT Falcon was developing a claimed 171.5 kW and a stump-pulling 420 Nm of torque. It would flash from 0 to 100 kilometres per hour in 8.5 seconds, underwhelming by today's standards but whiplash-producing for its time. Holden's Monaro was producing 186 kW. The two approaches on how to win a marathon were totally opposing. The British were scientific.

Ken Harper, a homegrown genius rally mechanic, built two of Ford Australia's three Falcon GTs in a large shed in the backyard of his home in East Malvern, a Melbourne suburb. Harry Firth, lead driver of the Ford team, built his car in his own workshop. Firth devised a system of water-cooling the big Ford's brakes before they became red hot. Another team member, Ford engineer Ian Vaughan, 'wasn't game to use the system in case it made the brakes explode'.

David McKay drove the London to Bombay section to lay down supplies and survey the driving conditions while *The Daily Telegraph*'s Holden Monaros were built at General Motors' Melbourne plant. There was not a great deal of communication between McKay and the factory. The Holdens' innovation was a lockable safe under the parcel shelf to hold the crews' currency and passports. McKay specified air conditioning and three-speed automatic for his Monaro. Both were sensible requests. Driver fatigue—whether two crew members or three—would be a big factor.

The US space program (Neil Armstrong would set foot on the moon seven months later) was scientific in its choice of crew compatibility, the marathon less so. The problem was huge. For most of the marathon cars, not so the Australian V8s, adding a third person would contribute more than 5 per cent of the vehicle's total mass. Extra weight would sap horsepower and use fuel. It would affect handling and attack component longevity. It was everything you didn't want in a competition car.

The split of two- or three-person crews among the works teams was almost half and half. Of the 32 factory-entered crews, including Simca, Moskvitch and Citroën, 17 would be crewed by two people and 15 by three. Ford UK and Germany, along with Citroën, would run with two.

For Ford, the choice was based on proven performance.

Swedes Bengt Söderström and Gunnar Palm had together won the 1967 European Championship for Ford. They seemed mismatched: Söderström, big, bluff and 110 kilograms, was the opposite to his more compact co-driver, Palm, but they'd proved themselves over medium distances.

Eric Jackson and Ken Chambers were also a known pairing. Jackson, a Ford dealer from Barnsley in the UK, had worked with Chambers since the early 1960s to smash long-distance records for Ford. They'd driven around the world in 42 days. They'd set a new London to Cape Town record of 13 days 8 hours 48 minutes, beating the previous record by just 18 minutes. And, in a superstunt for Ford, they'd raced and beaten a ship, the *Windsor Castle*, from Cape Town to Southampton. Neither was the fastest rally driver in the Ford team, but they could be relied on to keep the car together—as it turned out, to their own detriment.

Nick and Jenny Brittan were a great human-interest story. Nick was a racing driver, in a Ford Anglia called the *Green Bean*, and promoter of the English Formula Ford series. Jenny, an Australian model, was formerly the wife of Doug Blain, the founding editor of the UK's *Small Car* magazine. Nick and Jenny were a high-profile power couple with a finely tuned sense of promotion.

Rosemary Smith and Lucette Pointet were the odd couple, more so than the Swedes, yet on paper they shouldn't have been. Ford wanted a women's team. Both were highly credentialled drivers, at the top of their craft. Smith, outgoing to the point of being brash but sensational company to be around, had won The Netherland's Tulip Rally outright. Both women's careers mirrored each other—Pointet on the Continent for Citroën, Smith in the UK for Rootes then Ford. Pointet's partner, Jean-Claude Ogier, was also in the marathon, co-driving for Citroën with Lucien Bianchi. But Smith had been controversially disqualified from victory in the Coupe des Dames in the 1966 Monte Carlo Rally as part of the great lockout of British teams. Pointet, for Citroën, had inherited that win. That might have given Ford a clue to compatibility.

Ford's big hope lay with its star sprinter, Roger Clark, and Sweden's Ove Andersson. Ford wanted a dream team, a pairing capable of winning the marathon from the front. Clark had by then won the first of his four British Rally Championships. He was a wild man. He liked to drive more sideways than the Scandinavians: 'As long as I'm not actually looking out the back window at the time, I should be able to get it back,' he used to joke. Andersson, the Swedish rally champion and second in the previous year's Monte Carlo, was capable of carrying the car home on his back if it failed. Clark was happy to have Andersson as a partner. 'With Ove in the car with me, I don't have to beat him.'

Paddy Hopkirk, acknowledged master of the 360-degree spin in a Mini, was British Leyland's Clark equivalent. Tony Nash had become his co-driver only the year before, and they were beginning to understand each other as a team. Alec Poole was a racing

Marathon men in Sydney. Left to right: Jack Sears, honorary secretary and in charge of route-setting; Tony Ambrose, one of the world's best rally navigators; and Tommy Sopwith, chairman of the organising committee, in a publicity photograph taken on Bennelong Point.

Gelignite Jack Murray warned competitors about car-sized holes dug by the mythical yowie. He wasn't far wrong: on his own recce (pictured), he found washaways big enough to swallow his BMC Austin 1800.

Sobieslaw Zasada and Marek Wachowski, from Poland, surveyed Australia in a rented Ford only weeks before the start of the race.

In the former goldmining region of Western Australia, Sobieslaw Zasada and Marek Wachowski grappled with directional signs where there were no roads and sometimes no towns.

Evan Green, Gelignite Jack Murray and George Shepheard surveyed the European and Asian route in reverse, dressing their car for publicity shots. Green drove the Lataband Pass at speed four times.

Lucien Bianchi (right) and Jean-Claude Ogier and Lucette Pointet (soon to be Mrs Ogier) were alpine specialists. Lucien and Jean-Claude almost won the marathon for Citroën. Lucette drove for Ford.

The newly formed British Leyland Motor Corporation built all their marathon cars in their Abingdon workshop, the mecca of UK motor sport, outside Oxford.

In Sydney, Evan Green, Gelignite Jack Murray and George Shepheard set up a publicity shot in British Leyland's race workshop to display the modifications that needed to be made to a marathon car.

Porsche technicians went to Berlin Zoo to measure a kangaroo, then built comprehensive 'roo cages' to fit their cars. Not one hit a kangaroo.

Ford UK's 'inner' works team, left to right: the long-distance specialists, Ken Chambers and Eric Jackson; the women's team, Rosemary Smith and Lucette Pointet; the 'hares', Roger Clark and Ove Andersson; and the 'second hares', Gunnar Palm and Bengt Söderström.

Ford also entered power couple Jenny and Nick Brittan. They generated amazing lifestyle publicity, but were eliminated after a series of shocking crashes. They went on to run ultra-marathon events of their own.

The 'General's Army'. *The Daily Telegraph* airfreighted GM's three Holden Monaros to the UK, where their crews joined them. Left to right: David Liddle, David McKay and George Reynolds (car 36); Barry Ferguson, Doug Chivas and David Johnson (car 76); and Doug Whiteford, Eddie Perkins and (missing from the shot) Jim Hawker (car 68).

Flying Finn Rauno Aaltonen, on the front left bonnet of the BMC Austin 1800, brought multinationalism to an essentially all-Australian and UK British Leyland team, among them Paddy Hopkirk and Gelignite Jack Murray (both on the roof) and Tony Fall (front right bonnet).

The three Australian Ford Falcon GTs looked huge in London. Left to right: team manager John Gowland with Bruce Hodgson and Doug Rutherford (car 29); Bob Forsyth, Jack Ellis and Ian Vaughan (car 24); and Harry Firth, Gary Chapman and Graham Hoinville (car 2).

The police were called when Gelignite Jack Murray captured media attention by waterskiing on the Thames outside the Houses of Parliament.

Miss World, Australian Penny Plummer, met the eventual winners, from left to right, Colin Malkin, Brian Coyle and Andrew Cowan, before flagging away the marathon.

Keith Schellenberg's majestic 1930 eight-litre Bentley stayed with the marathon for three days. It then rolled down an embankment when the ground gave way beneath its weight.

The start crowd was huge. Bill Bengry, Arthur Brick and John Preddy were first away in their Ford Cortina GT. On the starting ramp are Sir Max Aitken (light-coloured jacket) and world Formula One champion Graham Hill.

The sign said it all: the exact distance was 16,694 kilometres. No one had ever competed over that immense distance before.

London provided an evocative backdrop for the marathon's departure. The Red Arrows team of flight lieutenants Derek Bell, Terry Kingsley and Peter Evans flew past Big Ben.

The docks at Dover and Calais were a mass of people and colour as the marathon crossed the Channel en masse in the *Maid of Kent*. By the time the marathon reached Le Bourget airport, there would be confusion.

The back roads of France were wet and snow-covered in November, and many teams became lost. Lucien Bianchi kept his Citroën on a straight line to the first stop-control outside Paris.

Travelling through the Mont Blanc tunnel into Italy was like going from night into day. Nick Brittan passes the BMC Austin 1800 of Tony Wilson. Both cars would stop to mask their numbers to avoid being pulled over by police.

The big Australian V8s were able to stretch their legs on the autoroutes and autostradas of Europe. Doug Whiteford, who'd done a season of sports-car racing in Europe, wound out his Monaro.

One of the marathon's favourites, Rauno Aaltonen, with Henry Liddon (waving) and Paul Easter, who is about to take his turn at sleeping in the rear. The bank of lights at the front of the car was essential for night vision at high speeds.

Crowds suddenly appeared wherever the marathon went. The Ford UK entry for the British Army Motoring Association, driven by Captain David Harrison and Lieutenant Martin Proudlock—shown here in Turkey—made it to Sydney in outright 30th place.

Andrew Cowan set out to travel light but at the last moment discovered equipment that needed to be brought along. He discarded one of his four roof-mounted spare tyres and replaced it with a toolbox. Here he enters the Khyber Pass.

Road conditions varied immensely. Bruce Hodgson (Ford Falcon GT) opted for stiff-blocked off-road tyres when the road started to break up.

Nick and Jenny Brittan were left shell-shocked by a series of crashes and were finally eliminated in Iran when they hit the truck shown in the top right of this picture.

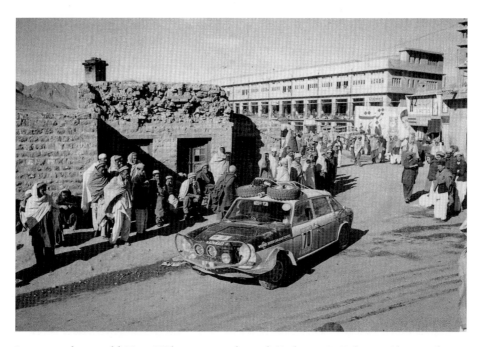

It was another world. Tony Wilson passes through Peshawar in Pakistan, close to the eastern end of the Khyber Pass.

driver from Ireland, just like Paddy. He'd raced an Austin Healey Sprite to fifteenth outright in the just-completed 1968 Le Mans 24 Hour race, two places behind Jean-Claude Ogier. Son of a British Leyland concessionaire, he was an excellent mechanic and an ideal third man. He'd become British touring-car champion the next year.

Rauno Aaltonen was every bit as good as Hopkirk—both as a rally and racing driver. He was one of the original Flying Finns, and his co-driver, Henry Liddon, was the best of the best of high-speed office managers. Liddon had won rallies with Aaltonen, Hopkirk and Tony Fall—but the others now had regular co-drivers. Liddon would go with Aaltonen. The third man would be Paul Easter, Timo Mäkinen's regular co-driver. The pair had been disqualified from victory in the 1966 Monte Carlo.

Tony Fall's was the 'safety' car—the equivalent to Jackson and Chambers. With regular co-driver Mike Wood and young up-and-comer Brian Culcheth, the all-British team was highly regarded by British Leyland management.

From Australia, Evan Green (British Leyland's PR director), George Shepheard and Gelignite Jack Murray had been elevated to full team status. Their car was built in Abingdon.

Rootes had just one car until the magnitude of the task presented a real requirement to run a second 'safety' car, for the RAF.

* * *

Andrew Cowan had grown up on an adjoining farm in the Scottish border country to twice Formula One world champion and Indy 500 winner Jim Clark. They were close friends. They tested themselves on the twisting roads around Chirnside and

Duns, and on weekends they chased girls in Jim's Triumph TR 2. They rallied together, but when Jim went motor racing, Andrew, strapped for cash, stayed on the farm and kept rallying. After Jim had won his world titles and Indy, he tried to get Andrew to translate his immense talent to the track. Jim arranged for Lotus boss Colin Chapman to have Andrew test a Formula Three car, but the madness of his first race, in the wet at Goodwood with cars interlocking wheels, convinced Andrew to remain a rallyist.

On the afternoon of 7 April 1968, with the marathon firmly under preparation, Andrew was heading home from the Granite City Rally in Aberdeen when his service crew flagged him to the side of the road. They'd heard on their car radio that Jim had been involved in a massive crash in a Formula Two race at Hockenheim. 'I drove straight on to his home, but when I got there a friend was standing in the window and he just shook his head,' Andrew said.

Jim had been killed.

Had Jim ever been in the frame for Rootes' 'marathon seat'? 'I never asked him,' Andrew said, intrigued with the idea. 'He was busy at the time. It just never entered my head.' Instead, Andrew and brother-in-law Brian Coyle got the wild man of British rallying—wilder than Roger Clark—Colin Malkin as their third team member, setting up a dynamic in the car that was never quite comfortable and which demanded that Andrew asserted his leadership from the start.

* * *

In Australia, Ford simply called up its rally team, including its in-house engineers. Holden decided its entry through *The Daily Telegraph* was outside company policy and did not allow its engineers, among them competent race and rally drivers such as Tony Roberts and Bob Watson, to participate.

'It was a big mistake,' said Ian Vaughan, a Ford engineer who was to claim a marathon podium and be the highest-placed Ford in the event. Ford Australia's team was all over the preparation, and it showed. Vaughan was a good example. He'd joined Ford out of university and was an up-and-coming engineer (much later to become a director of the company and the 'father' of the Ford Territory SUV). Vaughan's marathon, along with co-drivers Bob Forsyth and Jack Ellis, was both professional and personal. His young wife, Suzie, travelled with him to the UK, intending to be part of a follow-the-marathon tour all the way back to Australia. The tour was cancelled, so Suzie organised her own, turning up across Europe and Asia to cheer her man through. It was an incredibly risky and brave decision on her part. When they arrived in Europe, Ian hired a car in Paris and drove to Istanbul. It was his only opportunity to refamiliarise himself with European driving.

The team's Number One driver, Harry Firth, took long-time co-driver Graham Hoinville. The two had won everything there was to win in Victorian rallying and had claimed the inaugural Australian Rally Championship that year. They chose a South Australian competitor, Gary Chapman, to accompany them. Firth was a huge star. He'd won the Bathurst 500 and its predecessor at the wild and windy Phillip Island four times. He'd been instrumental in staging a 112,000-kilometre Ford Falcon endurance test at Ford Australia's proving ground in the You Yangs. He was so instrumental in Ford's success that he was one of the select group of Ford heroes invited to Walter Hayes's Cortina d'Ampezzo bobsled extravaganza, match-racing drivers such as Jim Clark.

Bruce Hodgson, bush mechanic, went with Doug Rutherford, who would become the 1969 Australian co-driver champion. When Frank Kilfoyle, another national titleholder, declared himself unavailable, they elected to remain a two-person crew.

Ford Australia assigned a young executive, John Gowland, to manage its marathon assault. The appointment created immense friction with Firth. He'd survived the North African desert campaign of World War II on his own initiative, and he had an ingrained distrust of authority. Sometimes, even in the face of sound logic, it could be his undoing.

* * *

David McKay's choice of crews in the Holden team had not been his own—but with fast footwork he resurrected it as best he could. When his man on the ground in London, David Lewin, became unavailable, McKay was able to move Armstrong 500 winner George Reynolds into his car with his trusted motor-racing mechanic, David Liddle. Doug Whiteford and Round Australia Trial winner Eddie Perkins took the second car with the quietly spoken and near-invisible Jim Hawker. The 'rogue' team was car 76—New South Wales rally champion Barry Ferguson, David Johnson and Doug Chivas. None was McKay's choice. While he was away on his recce, *The Daily Telegraph* had come to a commercial arrangement with Castrol. McKay had hoped to secure Stirling Moss and Jack Brabham—a vain hope, as both declared themselves unavailable. Team dynamics were on edge. It was fifty years on that David Johnson discovered a McKay-produced detailed route chart for Europe and Asia that he claimed he was never given by the team leader.

Ford dynamics—country to country—were not that much better. When the Ford Australia cars were flown into the UK, they were garaged separately, not at Ford's Boreham HQ. At least Ken Harper, Ford Australia's sole mechanic on the Europe and Asia legs, was allowed on the Ford aircraft.

Ford Germany went with two-person crews. It was a carbon copy of the Ford UK program. The lead car was Gilbert Staepelaere and Flying Finn Simo Lampinen. Racing driver Dieter Glemser, who'd prove himself in touring-car racing in the coming decade, was teamed with Martin Braungart.

The 'safety' car was Ford Motorsport's Herbert Kleint with Günther Klapproth. The two would go on to become highly credentialled long-distance competitors. Lampinen was the star of the team. He would win the RAC Rally just two days before the start of the marathon, co-driven in a SAAB by John Davenport, who would contest the marathon in one of the Porsches.

Lampinen was as close as you got to motor-sport royalty in Finland. His grandfather had founded the sport in the country, and his father was a multiple motorcycle champion, the best Finland has produced. It was a close-knit society. Rauno Aaltonen's father was Lampinen's godfather. When Lampinen caught polio at age thirteen, Aaltonen, five years older, was his constant companion and mentor. When Lampinen, in a supporting boot he wears to this day, had his first rally in his mother's Jaguar, Aaltonen led the cheer squad. Three years later, Lampinen was national champion, qualifying for inclusion with Aaltonen in the exclusive club known as the Flying Finns.

Gilbert Staepelaere was nominally lead driver in the car. Staepelaere had racked up more than 50 rally victories in partnership with his father, Jules. But as soon as Lampinen and Staepelaere tested, the order of driving preference became clear. 'He said to me,' said Lampinen, "'You do the special stages, and I will drive the transports".'

* * *

Simca went with two-person crews. Simca motor-sport manager Pierre Boucher would be captain-coach, driving with wealthy enthusiast Georges Houel, once owner of a works Mercedes-Benz 300 SL Gullwing, in which he co-won the Tour de France Automobile with Stirling Moss. Roger Masson, in the second Simca, carried a different and unusual distinction—that of pushing his car further around the Le Mans course than any other driver. When he had run out of fuel, he pushed the vehicle 7 kilometres to the pits rather than running for a can of gas. He still finished sixteenth outright.

DAF also elected to run two-person crews. Rob Slotemaker, skid school owner at the old Dutch Zandvoort circuit, was in one car. The other was driven by David van Lennep, who was genuinely Dutch royalty, carrying the title of Jonkheer. It was ironic that, for all his skill, Rob would die a decade later at Zandvoort when he lost control of his Chevrolet Camaro and spun into a parked course car.

Moskvitch went with a pair of twos and a pair of threes—all travelling in convoy. The best Estonian rally driver of the twentieth century, Uno Aava, led the four-car team. He'd twice won the USSR Rally Championship, in 1959 and 1963, and he was chairman of the Estonian Automobile Federation's motor-racing committee. Aava drew second-last starting position in the marathon. The Moskvitchs had always planned to travel as a team, and they fell back to gather around their hero to guide him to Australia.

* * *

Servicing arrangements were the real challenge. A marathon moves in one direction, all together. Service crews need to leapfrog the field to clear customs with equipment that needs special permission, be available within precise time spans and also be flexible to chase down a missing car—and stay awake.

The marathon simply could not have occurred without the dedicated service of suppliers to the industry. Castrol had an association with better than 65 per cent of the field, and its fuel dumps with petrol of what was hoped to be guaranteed octane would keep the marathon moving. Dunlop was the largest of the tyre suppliers, but Goodyear and Michelin were there, too, servicing their teams. As much as possible, decisions taken in conjunction with the works teams were capable of being supported. But there would be errors of shipping and customs clearance and of local supply that would create massive heartache.

The factory teams had people working full-time on visas, carnets and air travel. Advance parties came to arrangements with local suppliers to lay down parts and tools and to use their facilities.

Ford and DAF both had aircraft but at different ends of the spectrum. It helps when your company is rich beyond measure. Ford simply commandeered one of their corporate Gulfstreams. Even now, that sounds excessive. Back then it was awe-inspiring. Management and mechanical teams from the UK, Germany and Australia would travel on it.

DAF's chartered Douglas DC3, even then, was past its use-by date. Volvo had put a plane on to service its private entrants, and AMOCO, the fuel company, had its Piper Navajo that had flown all the way from Australia just to go back again.

The media plane, a Vickers Viscount with four turbo-props and configured for 28 passengers, would carry journalists, marathon organisers and event partners such as Castrol on sixteen flight legs to Bombay.

Beaverbrook Newspapers assigned a journalist for each of its two titles—the *Daily Express* and the *Evening Standard*. I was to go for *The Daily Telegraph*, along with the paper's UK-based foreign correspondent. Our editor-in-chief, David McNicoll, would represent both newspaper groups on the first leg to Bombay. For a young reporter, it was an experience beyond measure. To call David Benson from the *Express* a reporter was a vast understatement. Urbane, worldly, well connected, a social climber covered by the press almost as many times as he wrote for it, he was the most sophisticated human being I'd met. He was a confidant of Stirling Moss and, with a touch of scandal, was known to be close to Shell Oil heiress Olga Deterding.

Ian Morton, from the *Standard*, was more my speed but only just. He and his wife, Jennifer, lived on a houseboat on the Thames and kept their Aston Martin DB2, not expensive then but so stylish, in a lockup on the dock.

Harold 'Dev' Dvoretsky, born in Perth and the *Telegraph*'s man in London, was part journalist, part diplomat and part messenger for Sir Frank Packer and McNicoll. Want it fixed? Get Dev. London was his patch, and he let me know it. I was chosen out of the Sydney newsroom almost a year before, seconded to write and organise. I had some experience in motor sport and had been a small part of David McKay's team, but this was another world.

There were others, too—Paul Savelieff, John Hart and Lloyd Coulson from Sir Frank's radio and television stations.

I was to drive with David Benson in the just-released Jaguar XJ6 all the way to Le Bourget outside Paris, crossing the Channel on the *Maid of Kent* ferry with the marathon teams. Then we'd pick up the aircraft. Ian, Dev and the others would leave from Gatwick and be waiting for us.

A hierarchy developed on the charter. David McNicoll and his travelling companion, Snow Swift, variously known as the *Telegraph*'s pilot and Sydney's best-connected man about town, were up front. Then there was an unseemly rush of moths trying to get close to the flame. Vic Blackman, *Express* photographer, and I avoided the crush. Back of the bus was our natural position.

The commercial airlines were winners, too. Travel agents devised complex means of moving vital service crew between locations. Sometimes, because of the marathon schedule, the commercial flights would be better than our charter. *The Times* of London, a rival newspaper to the *Daily Express*, scooped us by getting to Kabul before the media aircraft.

Most teams relied on ground service. Service crews were covering huge distances and putting in punishing hours, full of fatigue. Bill Price for British Leyland left London nine days before the marathon started. He was driving a comparatively massive 4-litre Vanden Plas, and he took it all the way to Bombay. 'They were hard to sell in Great Britain, so the company thought why not turn two of them into service cars?' Bill said. 'They were heavy, and they broke up on the drive.'

As well as servicing marathon cars, crews were working hard to keep themselves going. Initially, Price's car was in the lead, forging a way down the marathon roads so he could warn the upcoming team cars. For the last part of the journey—once the second critical special stage was completed—Price dropped back to chase, ready to pick up any works or customer car in trouble. In the absence of any chase vehicles from marathon organisers, it was an invaluable service.

9

Wheels and Water

ON 31 AUGUST 1968, with the start of the London–Sydney Marathon less than three months away, Tommy Sopwith won the first *Daily Express* Cowes–Torquay–Cowes powerboat race in a tactical tour de force that, for anyone who was watching, was a guide on how to win a marathon. In so many ways it was a frivolous thing to do, but for Sopwith it was life itself. To put this adventure on hold for another was unthinkable.

His win provided a masterclass in marathon strategy.

Sopwith was not driving the most powerful boat in the UK's premier offshore race, nor was it the largest, fastest or the most comfortable. But it was purpose-built for the task.

A combination of stealth and tactics along with bulletproof reliability in tumultuous seas delivered a victory so crushing that the race favourite only became aware of Sopwith's challenge when he crossed the finish line to discover Sopwith had arrived 11 minutes earlier.

The marathon influenced Sopwith's victory and vice versa. He'd learned a lot about long-distance endurance in the past six months, and he'd applied it to his all-out attempt to win his second Cowes race—this one the first to travel not only to Torquay but back to Cowes, double the distance at a boat-breaking 196 nautical miles.

Race-boat architect Don Shead had designed Sopwith's diminutive 25-foot (7.6-metre) *Telstar* to a strict power-to-weight ratio formula with an accent on hull rigidity to withstand the worst chop of the Channel while delivering maximum power at all times through a unique futuristic prop and rudder system. *Telstar* was light, just 2.5 tonnes; narrow, just over 2 metres beam; and, in a race until then won by twin engines putting out 1000+ horsepower, Shead allowed for just one 7.9-litre 600-horsepower Daytona Scarab engine, admittedly the absolute epitome of race engineering, to save weight and fuel use. *Telstar* was so narrow that Sopwith and his navigator, Charles De Selincourt, would stand one behind the other for the entire six hours of the race, braced against bulkheads.

When the 58-strong field fanned out across Cowes in the spectacular mass start, it was the elegant 40-foot (12-metre) pencil-shaped monsters such as defending champion the Gardner brothers' new boat *Magnum Tornado* and Italy's *White Tornado* that leapt to the lead.

Sir Max Aitken not only owned the race, but also raced in it, never quite reaching the top step of the podium, and for 1968 he'd had a new racer built, a 40-footer he christened *Gypsie Girl*. He was to finish fifth. It was a family affair. The adventurous Lady Violet Aitken was there in *Ultra Violet* but failed to finish, an unusual disappointment for the regular class contender.

The Channel was a killer. It wasn't delivering 'waves which became mountains', as the commentator claimed, but a huge and unpredictable swell combined with turbulent chop presented an uneven surface and a challenge few competitors were able to fathom.

People die in powerboat racing. Misjudge your angle of attack or your speed, and the wave wins. French Formula One driver Didier Pironi and his two crew died off the Isle of Wight twenty years later when they hit a wash far too hard at a crazy angle.

In 1968, Italy's Vincenzo Balestrieri escaped death but sunk *White Tornado* without a trace when he, too, adopted the crash-or-crash-through approach. *White Tornado* and the Gardener brothers in *Magnum Tornado* had plotted the shortest route on the new extended course, regardless of sea conditions. Balestrieri paid the price, and the Gardners eased back to avoid the same fate.

But Sopwith knew there was more than one route. On his charts, a longer course delivered a smoother ride, and he took it. He powered through the sea mist back into Cowes to victory while the Gardners were still looking back over their shoulders for the boat coming second.

It was a salutary lesson for marathon competitors. Sopwith knew things the top teams were only just starting to discover. There were mountain passes that provided a short-distance high-risk solution and bypasses that presented comparative safety but at the price of time. There were roads so rough that they could dictate exactly what sort of car should be built for the task—and roads so long and straight that they would favour exactly the sort of car that wasn't built to handle the rough stuff.

And yet Tommy Sopwith was the first to tell anyone he wasn't the expert on how to compete in a marathon. 'Not my job, old boy.' His task had been to blaze a pioneering route through the bureaucracies of eleven countries, to gain permission for borders to be opened if only momentarily and to achieve the permission of governments, juntas and dictators to let the marathon pass, all the time under the eye of the distrusting superpowers, Russia and America, which had 'beneficial' interests in the regions.

He'd learned about management technique from his father. Stick with the big picture, and let others sweat the details.

PART 2

The Race

Calais to Paris

Distance: 283 kilometres

Time allowed: 4 hours 32 minutes

Approximate average speed: 64 kilometres per hour

10

The Start

MISS WORLD, PENNY PLUMMER, was thrilled to be asked to flag away the greatest motoring adventure of modern times. Penny was the first Australian to wear the Miss World crown, awarded in 1968. Penny's personal contribution was a great deal of natural poise, which was perhaps beyond the brief.

Starting the marathon on Sunday 24 November, alongside Desmond Plummer (no relation), chairman of the Greater London Council, was one of her first assignments.

The Crystal Palace race track was already an anachronism. Close to the city of London and now surrounded by urban sprawl, it had opened in the same year that Francis Birtles left London for Australia. It had hosted the London Grand Prix in 1937, won by Prince Bira in the renowned ERA R2 B known as *Romulus*.

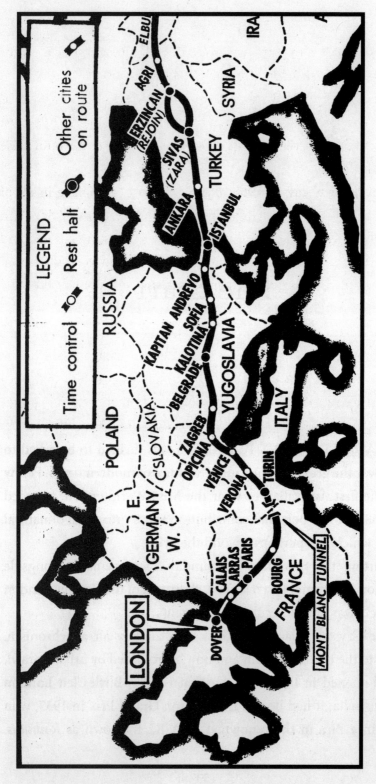

Map 1: Map showing the race route from London to Erzincan, Turkey.

The BBC had staged the first-ever outside broadcast of a motor race from the 2.2-kilometre track in the same year.

Now it was under threat. Like many race tracks that had escaped the long-term thinking of town planners, it was restricted to just five active days a year and its days were numbered. It would close six years later.

But on that day in 1968, there was no better place in all of London to start the London–Sydney Marathon. After two weeks of UK drizzle, the skies cleared, a weak sun emerged and rally jackets—the gun ones were the black-and-yellow Dunlop versions that signified a member of the in-crowd—were cast tentatively aside.

In the early morning, chief steward John Gott called teams together for a final briefing. It was mandatory to be there, and some were running late, victims of a crush of spectators that had grid-locked access to the circuit. Some were held up by the very police force that had been brought in en masse to control the crowds. Gott went straight to the heart of that lesson.

'The marathon has attracted the attention of every police force through which it passes,' he said. 'Take it easy, and you won't have any accidents. If you do have one in a foreign country, you will find yourself behind bars. Pronto.'

The tension was explosive. It took Gelignite Jack Murray to relieve it—with an explosive. Murray threw a double bunger into the midst of the meeting. He was going to do it sometime, and it seemed prudent even then to do it 'in club' rather than unleash it among the spectator crowd outside. Gott was unperturbed. 'Thank you for that additional report, Jack,' he said. And he continued the briefing.

Organisers were overwhelmed with the public response. The *Daily Express* had made preferential car parking available at

10 shillings per car with no maximum limit on the number of people who could be carried in each vehicle. More than 10,000 cars crammed the official car parks alone, and many more lined streets in surrounding suburbs. Many spectators avoided Crystal Palace entirely and headed for the CBD. The marathon route was intended to show off the landmarks of London: Big Ben, the Houses of Parliament, Westminster Bridge. Many members of the world's press had stationed themselves there to get the iconic shot, rather than simply a starting ramp.

Crystal Palace was memorable for a number of reasons. There was no real crowd control. Spectator access was not limited, and so crews who had spent months preparing their cars for their grand adventure now needed to defend them from close contact with well-wishers. Organisers had also turned on entertainment.

The most British of British racing drivers, Graham Hill, had won his second Formula One World Championship only three weeks before in Mexico, and he'd brought his Cosworth DFV Lotus 49 to do hot laps. For Hill to be undertaking parade laps in his Gold Leaf Lotus in front of such a huge and enthusiastic crowd was a fitting tribute to the man and his machine. Betty Hill, Graham's wife, was there, too. The two of them drove the circuit in *Chitty Chitty Bang Bang*—the automotive invention of James Bond author Ian Fleming, whose book that year had been translated into a major musical comedy movie of the same name. Betty also drove the female support vehicle: *Truly Scrumptious*. As a piece of product placement, it was way before its time, and the crowds, eight to ten deep behind the wicker safety fences of Crystal Palace, enjoyed the spectacle.

The starting ramp was tall, perhaps 2 metres above the ground, and the entrance and exit were both steep. At the top was a reinforced platform large enough for one car at a time and a crowd of besuited officials, among them Sir Max Aitken and David McNicoll representing Sir Frank Packer. A grid girl would lead each car up the ramp, carrying the flag of the competing nation, and Raymond Baxter—a voice of great authority—would introduce each team to the crowd.

Starting was at 1-minute intervals, and the starting order had been preordained, apparently by a fair and equitable lottery draw. It was an episode of conjecture. No consideration had been given to the relative speed of the competing cars or the skills of the crews. It was quite possible that the faster cars would want to move up through the field to keep pace with schedules they'd set for themselves. Rest at control points was considered to be one of the great opportunities for teams to retain freshness, and so there was pressure to move quickly, not stupidly, between controls, even in sections where plentiful time was allowed. On stages that appeared impossible to clean—and there were two between Turkey and Afghanistan—it was imperative that the quick competitors were able to use their speed to maximum advantage.

In Australia, there would be a new starting structure, based on finishing order in India. For the major teams in outright contention, there was an incentive to lose minimum points across Europe and Asia to gain an advantageous restart position out of Fremantle. But on the run down to Bombay, the guns knew they had a problem. They hoped they could rely on those ahead to move politely out of the way, but there was always the risk of low visibility caused by night, fog or dust—or a combination of all three—and there were rocks. Every time you got close to a car on an unmade surface, there was the risk of a rock being thrown up by the car being passed. Windscreens were at risk, and so were radiators. Puncture a radiator, and an engine can overheat and blow up. It would not be the way to end a marathon.

Bill Bengry in the Cortina GT was first over the ramp. He asked for and received a 'good luck' kiss from Miss World, resplendent in her fur hat, and with air horns blasting—a cause of some distress to London police, who cautioned several drivers in the run through the city—he and his team undertook one lap of the Crystal Palace circuit and headed off on the highway. Harry Firth had drawn number 2, Tony Fall was four. But it was time to give consideration to those in major contention: Bengt Söderström would start 38th, his Ford teammates Roger Clark and Ove Andersson almost mid-field in 48th. Paddy Hopkirk was 51st; Simo Lampinen, 57th; Andrew Cowan, 75th; and towards the tail of the field in 87th came Bianchi and Ogier. The last car away, as the first was nearing Dover, was the tiny works Simca of Pierre Boucher and Georges Houel.

There'd been some confusion about the starting rules. The works teams had a handle on them, but the privateers were less informed. Some had believed they were not allowed to start with a full tank of fuel; in fact, they believed they were to start on minimal fuel load and fill up outside the circuit. Where that came from no one knew, but Innes Ireland left Crystal Palace with less than a litre in reserve.

It was hair-raising. Just 10 kilometres from the start, the first of the works Fords was in trouble. Eric Jackson and Ken Chambers, surely the most experienced long-distance competitors of all, misjudged a traffic island in Parliament Square and knocked down a traffic signal. Their car was undamaged. Their reputation not so.

Twenty minutes out from Crystal Palace, the Blick Racing Team—Fritz Reust, P. Gratzer and Axel Béguin—made a chilling discovery: their road book was missing. The road book was essential. It had to be presented and stamped at each control. Without it, there was no proceeding. They were lucky—they were early on the road, number 11. While two dismantled the car's interior, another hopped a motorcycle back to Crystal Palace, through the immense crowds, in the hope he'd find it. There were no mobile phones, no communication. Desperately he searched, and returned downhearted and empty handed to discover his teammates had found it under the front seat. In the week ahead, they would join a queue of people with similar stories, some not so fortunate. Cabin management was the first rule of marathon competition.

It's a long way from Crystal Palace to the Eastern Docks at Dover. David McKay used the A20 to clear the spark plugs on his Monaro. Spark plugs would foul on competition cars, especially if the engine was not run in the intended revolution band, and McKay was convinced his had fouled.

'It felt fine on light throttle opening, but the moment I gave her full throttle she missed and banged,' McKay said. 'There was little chance of running hard for more than a few seconds at a time because of the traffic and England's 70-mile-per-hour [110-kilometre-per-hour] limit, but we stretched her out whenever we could and after about 20 miles [32 kilometres] she suddenly came into full song. It was as though someone had pulled the loud pedal down under my foot, and the speed increased immediately.'

He was lucky to get away with it.

In the cavalcade to Dover, there was an equal mixture of police and spectator activity. Nick Brittan counted three road accidents as a direct result of non-marathon drivers losing attention as the competing cars went by. In David Benson's media XJ6, we had our own excitement. In front of us, Terry Hunter and John Davenport were running somewhat above the speed limit in their Porsche and we were keeping pace. Suddenly, a white Humber police car interjected itself between us and brought the Porsche to a halt. We thought, 'Too good an opportunity to miss' and pulled over, too. Faced with the full glare of media attention, the police issued a warning and quickly departed.

There was no need to speed. The first time control lay on the other side of the English Channel at Calais. The run down to Dover was the only stage of the entire marathon that was truly transport alone. The only requirement was to reach the dock in time to board the *Maid of Kent*, the 10-year-old cross-Channel ferry that had been chartered to take the entire marathon to France in one transfer.

Most teams made it with hours to spare. Some squandered the time. One put their entire marathon effort at risk. At an auto-repair shop in Dover, according to Berwyn Williams (Austin 1800), another crew had taken a pair of windscreen wipers and failed to pay. Williams covered the cost. It was probably accidental, but in a marathon where rules were remarkably few, one that stood out was the penalty for failing to pay any bill en route: immediate disqualification.

Perhaps of greater concern to the rally was a warning given as an aside by Tommy Sopwith. He had heard—but not been officially informed—that French authorities had that day requested the marathon not run down the autoroute from Calais to Le Bourget. In order to keep use of the two-lane super highway clear for other traffic at midnight on a Sunday night, they'd suggested the marathon use alternative B-roads. That rumour, for that is all it was, spread through *Maid of Kent* like a tsunami. Crews who had planned their first day on the road to the last minute, including rest and service stops, were now wondering what additional time they should allow—and worse, what additional maps they would need to acquire. Not easy in Dover on Sunday evening.

The works crews were somewhat immune. They had people to do that. At Dover, most were met by the first of their service teams. Even Mercedes-Benz, clearly not a works team, had service available. One team, Rootes, had thought through every eventuality, no matter how trivial or embarrassing. Colin Malkin, brilliant behind the wheel, was a little vague when out of the car. He liked to wander, loved a chat. Rootes assigned one mechanic to him at Crystal Palace and Dover, to ensure he made the start and the ship.

The Channel crossing is merely 90 minutes—port to port. Loading, disembarking and clearing customs take the time. Most of the crews had not given thought to the best use of the time. Ford had. Arriving early into Dover, their teams were fed while they waited for embarkation clearance, and then, as soon as they'd boarded—first, of course—they went to a pre-purchased cabin. By the time everyone else had come on board, they were already into the first hour of a near-three-hour sleep.

Some teams bribed stewards for cabin use, but it was pyrrhic at best. By the time they had undertaken the negotiation, all they had achieved was the satisfaction of knowing they'd got one up on their competitors.

* * *

At Calais, the main point of entry into France from England, it was still Sunday night. Compared to the mild conditions with which the marathon had left Britain, competitors were met with a blast of chilly air and a warmth of unexpected and perhaps unwanted hospitality.

Calais was the first true time control of the marathon. Crews needed to check into and out of the control desk, which had been set up in the customs hall, prior to starting the 283-kilometre drive to Le Bourget, France's principal airport (Charles de Galle had not then been built).

There would be a passage control midway at the town of Arras, when the route would split either to the autoroute or to B-grade side roads. But in the midst of this orderly procedure was an invitation to proceed to the first floor for an official welcome. The French— whether it was tourism authorities, the government or the FIA (world governing body of motor sport), no one knew—had turned on champagne. It was a Brut, vintage 1961. There was a crush in the reception room, but it appeared not too many marathon crews attended. It was one of those occasions when it was best to risk offence.

The issue of using the autoroute or secondary road was not being resolved. Here was the quandary. The marathon made very few prescriptions as to what roads could be used. As long as crews checked into control on time and from the right direction—a point that would on several occasions become critical—then they were okay. If the French police had asked that the autoroute not be used, then that was between the individual competitor and the gendarme (or similar) who pulled them over. Thinking it through, the issue was not whether crews would be breaking marathon rules but what the penalty would be for having a prolonged negotiation with a policeman.

What had John Gott said? 'You will find yourself behind bars. Pronto.'

There was the strong possibility, the conservatives reasoned, that they could spend considerable time talking their way out of a confrontation, maybe so long that it would eat up marathon points—so why risk it in the first place?

Andrew Cowan thought otherwise and made his call: 'I thought it was all a complete waste of time, and saw no reason why we shouldn't go down the autoroute.' Ford felt the same: 'The Ford crews got together and decided to use the motorway route. We agreed to stop before we reached toll booths and cover up our marathon numbers.'

No one who went down the autoroute ran into any police intervention.

Everyone who elected to play it safe and take the B-roads spent a night in anxiety, and some even lost points.

At 10 p.m. on a moonless night, Bill Bengry checked out of Calais control bound for Arras 1 hour 15 minutes later and then Le Bourget at 2.32 a.m. Every reasonable estimate said he'd be early at both, probably by up to 90 minutes into Paris. It was a horrible night. Light drizzle turned to rain. The further crews strayed from the intended route, seeking the B-grade road alternative, the less illumination there was from streetlights, and the fewer sign posts.

For Cowan, the decision to stay with the main road was dramatically vindicated as his Hunter manoeuvred through a small town on the way to Arras. 'I was following a Citroën not entered in the marathon when suddenly a cyclist just appeared from under his wheels,' Cowan said. 'The Citroën stopped, and I was forced to swerve to miss both him and the bike rider.'

Everyone made Arras, and then the separation started: the brave ones heading for the autoroute; the conservatives, not game to take a risk but not quite realising the risk they were taking, heading for the B-roads. A normal rally moves in an orderly direction. This was not normal. Across a broad area, there was a confusion of headlights—and, for that matter, tail-lights, adding to the dysfunction.

And then there was the curse of early breakdown. Why does it happen? You've built a car to go 17,000 kilometres, and it breaks down in the first few hundred. Barry Ferguson at the wheel of the Holden Monaro was on the B-road, desperately seeking Paris, when a red light lit up on the dashboard and a squealing sound announced that the fanbelt had come loose. You cannot continue like that. But at midnight, with rain pouring down and the outside temperature nudging zero, there were precious few service stations open to fix the problem. If only they'd stayed with the autoroute. But then Doug Chivas, older and a bit more experienced than his two teammates, effected a fix they'd never seen before. 'He got under the bonnet with spanners, in the pitch dark, and tightened the belt with the engine still going,' David Johnson said. 'The battery had lost all its power. We knew if we stopped and tried to disassemble and fix it in the normal fashion, we were gone. The battery would never restart us. So Chivo did what he'd done on rallies in Australia—a temporary fix that worked perfectly.'

Innes Ireland in the Mercedes had no mechanical expertise on board. His red light indicated an alternator failure. The battery was discharging rather than charging. With patches of fog quickly becoming a white-out as the clock passed midnight, Ireland turned off the headlights and fog lamps and continued to drive towards Paris on sidelights alone. The pressure was immense. In a service station, he found a private motorist and explained the problem. The local enthusiast—who was out looking for marathon cars—willingly agreed to become tour leader. At high speed, he led Ireland towards Le Bourget and increasingly, as they sped through towns and even explored smaller C- and D-grade roads, known to the locals, they picked up marathon strays. Cars that had been irrevocably, irretrievably lost hooked on to the caravan. By the time they saw the bright runway lights of the airfield, there were twelve cars in the convoy.

Eileen Westley was not one of them. The *Tortoise* had made it off the boat just fine, but for some reason the tap that switched from the main fuel tank to the auxiliary tank had stopped working. The all-women crew were on the B-grade road, searching for petrol stations to top up the only small fuel tank that was working. And that would make them late into control. They took a massive 12-point hit and lost a lot of confidence.

Elsie Gadd's crew did not have the same excuse, but still took a 6-point penalty. There are things you don't think about when you start out on a grand adventure, but maybe you should. Crew compatibility is one. Driving expertise is another. When they came off the boat in Calais, Jennifer Tudor-Owen took the wheel because she was the only one of the quartet who had driven on the French (right-hand) side of the road. That's daunting enough in itself, as a lot of the amateur crews quickly found. But it is compounded when you're driving a right-hand-drive car. Suddenly, the driver's position of control, closest to the crown of the road, is lost. As a driver, you are at the mercy of your co-driver to call conditions ahead. If you're not a well-drilled team, full of trust for each other's judgement, tension is the logical outcome. Add to that your determination to take the long way to Paris, on the side roads, and it's pretty certain you're either going to be lost or lucky. They weren't lucky.

Neither was Robert Eaves in the privately entered Austin 1800—down 3 points, despite a desperate dive at the airport control point.

The control was a story in itself—too small to accommodate both in and out traffic, it became a flashpoint of confusion. One gate was too tight to allow two cars to pass, so traffic management attempted to exercise its limited wisdom according to perceived priority.

One car claimed its place in the queue with air horns blaring. David McKay made it to control in the Monaro with just six minutes to spare. He was tense, flummoxed and anything but a model of the unflappable racing driver. His team had become boxed in among increasingly smaller villages and tighter roads as it made its cross-country way. McKay had taken back the wheel and was driving as if it were a Mille Miglia. His speed increased with the decrease in remaining time. They thundered through French towns. 'We should have been here more than an hour ago,' he breathed. McKay had a speech impediment, a stutter. It tended to go away with tension. He was speaking very clearly.

Ken Tubman made it on time, but he, too, was harassed. 'You could drive up to any intersection and see lights coming at you from all directions,' he said. 'We saw one competitor several times, and each time it was from a different direction.'

Lieutenant Jack Dill in the Royal Green Jackets' Porsche 911 T started tenth in Calais and arrived first into Le Bourget by a considerable margin. He covered the distance in a little less than two hours at an average speed of 150 kilometres per hour. Tony Fall (Austin 1800), who had started fourth, followed the Porsche into control, and Alfredo 'Freddy' Bombelli, who'd got away eleventh, a minute behind the Porsche, was third in his privately entered Lotus Cortina. Comparatively high speed was neither foolhardy nor dangerous, but perhaps slightly unnecessary.

Le Bourget would be the first opportunity for vehicle service before the long haul of almost 800 kilometres to Turin in Italy, with a longer distance immediately afterwards to Belgrade. Some teams had service at all three locations. Others had split their service crews across the two waypoints, bypassing Turin. Rootes and Simca had shared resources. They'd each service in Le Bourget and then Simca would do Turin as a stand-by, should the Hunter run into difficulty.

Le Bourget, in the middle of the night, was not a particularly happy place. It was all klieg lights and confusion. There was no accommodation, although a couple of teams had caravans. Others simply bunked down in their cars in the pre-dawn chill, waiting for their turn to check out and get back on the road.

The adrenalin of the previous day's start at Crystal Palace—had it only been twelve hours ago?—was fast wearing off. Already there were tired faces and frayed attitudes. Perhaps the dawn would bring new vigour.

Andre Welinski was the story, and the envy, of the privateer teams. Parked alongside his Volvo was a Rolls-Royce. It had been driven in by the chauffeur of his ageing aunt, who had turned up to wish her nephew *bon chance*. She brought out champagne and canapés from a wicker basket in the trunk, and they toasted each other, discreetly, before Andre went off to bed in his rally car. They'd both been refugees from war-torn Poland. And they'd both done very well in their lives. There was cause for quiet celebration.

Paris to Turin

Distance: 782 kilometres
Time allowed: 13 hours 20 minutes
Approximate average speed: 61 kilometres per hour

Turin to Belgrade

Distance: 1161 kilometres
Time allowed: 21 hours 12 minutes
Approximate average speed: 56 kilometres per hour

Belgrade to Istanbul

Distance: 969 kilometres
Time allowed: 15 hours 31 minutes
Approximate average speed: 64 kilometres per hour

11

Paris to Istanbul

BENGT SÖDERSTRÖM AND GUNNAR PALM were in dire trouble. Exiting the Mont Blanc tunnel on the way to Milan, their works Ford Cortina Lotus had ground to a halt. It was something internal in the engine. There'd been no warning, just a sudden stop. Only 24 hours into the marathon, and it seemed likely the Ford backup car—the second hare, in the wake of Roger Clark and Ove Andersson—was the harbinger of potential problems. Was this—whatever it was—a one-off or was it a warning that needed to be heeded by the entire team? Söderström and Palm, starting 38th on the road out of Paris, were barely out of their car and under the bonnet when Clark, starting 48th, arrived behind them.

What happened next was strictly against the rules—but who was going to see, and on the 'do unto others' principle, who was going to report them? The Number One team took a pillow from their car, inserted it between their roo bar and the rear bumper of the stricken Ford and then they began to push. For 100 kilometres, two Cortinas forged towards Turin on the power of one engine. Clark kept a close watch on his engine temperature and was prepared to pull out of the shunt at the hint of trouble.

They coasted into Turin, straight to Ford service, hours before they had to go to the official control point. The rescue, officially, never happened. Nick and Jenny Brittan, travelling close behind the train, were prepared to take responsibility if news ever got out. Better that they faced official sanction than Clark and Andersson. But nothing ever happened. 'They just struggled in under their own power,' Nick told me. It wasn't the only time it would happen.

* * *

There is a monument at Le Bourget Airport to Charles Lindbergh, commemorating his landing there in 1927 from America in the *Spirit of St. Louis*. It was a true feat of daring and determination and, for the 98 marathon competitors, it was humbling.

Nerves were on edge. It was hard to keep them in check, even if you were one of the top teams. The true test of car and driver was edging closer, now less than two days away, when the field would face the first 'impossible' stage on the Asian continent in Turkey. Driving from Paris to Milan, it was not possible to win the marathon, but one error, mechanical or human, could lose it. Ask Söderström and Palm.

Take the Boulevard Périphérique, the maze-like ring road still under construction in 1968. It remains a puzzle for tourists in

Paris, opening through a series of *portes* to the pleasures within. But which one to take and how to get to it? Authorities promised a solution. A battalion of police motorcyclists would be available to guide the marathon. The offer caused more confusion. Were the French saying the marathon would pass through all of France under police guard, or were they offering a sensible solution to the immediate problem of how to clear Paris?

After the run down into Le Bourget, not too many competitors were willing to risk another B-road debacle. But the need to obey, or disobey, never eventuated. The police were nowhere to be seen, and the marathon navigators were on their own.

Eileen Westley's *Tortoise* took more than an hour of precious time to find the autoroute south of Paris. She finally relied on the kindness of strangers, four young men in a Mercedes, who led her car to the right road.

Crews were looking forward to the high-speed run across France and the roof of Italy. The road book called for them to cover 782 kilometres in 13 hours 20 minutes. They'd leave Le Bourget before dawn and be in Turin in the late afternoon—most of them a lot earlier. It was a time to settle down and, in many instances, to learn about their cars. It seems strange, but many had not had seat time. Some did not even know where the switches and controls were and what they did—at least not intuitively, which is what is needed in an emergency. Lighting was a particular challenge. The marathon cars were festooned with lights for every occasion: headlights, using the newly released quartz halogen bulbs, which appreciably increased the sweep of night vision; driving lights, which could look far into the distance with pinpoint precision; and fog lamps, which spread a puddle of orange light capable of cutting through a white-out without bouncing back into a driver's eyes. Most of the marathon cars had a complex wiring system that allowed lights to be mixed and matched in a multitude of ways. The sequence needed to be learned.

On the Autoroute du Sud, it was possible to go ton-up without trouble. ('Ton-up' is a mixture of imperial and metric measure. It means 100 miles per hour, and cars were averaging well above the metric equivalent of 160 kilometres per hour, eating up the distance as they passed and repassed each other.) There was time, if you were willing, to call into roadside cafes for quick refreshment and then rejoin the marathon, catching up to the cars that had just sailed past. Quickly, the atmosphere was becoming festive.

The Mont Blanc tunnel had been opened only three years before—16 July 1965—in a joint ceremony presided over by presidents Charles de Gaulle from France and Guiseppe Saragat from Italy. The tunnel was a masterpiece of engineering: 11.6 kilometres of dual carriageway, 2.5 kilometres beneath the surface of the Aiguille du Midi, it cut more than 30 minutes off the cross-country journey and, despite being claustrophobic in its dampness and darkness, it was a safer bet than the mountain roads, especially as snow and some ice still covered the higher sections. The marathon crews were happy to pay their 40 francs for a one-way journey.

France had been full of fog. Italy was in sunshine. It could have been a state of mind but, as crews cleared customs, the realisation was that the marathon was running substantially ahead of schedule. They'd be able to bank more sleep.

But not all of them.

Uno Aava, the most favoured of the Russian Moskvitch competitors, found himself stuck in gear. The Moskvitches had been travelling as a quartet. They shepherded the stricken Aava to Turin and assisted with a major pull down and rewelding of the gear linkages. Three of the four Russian cars checked into control on time. Aava lost 24 points and fell to the tail of the field. It was a crushing blow. No one knew, exactly, what lay ahead, but to lose points—any points—on a transport stage was not good.

Jean Denton and Tom Boyce were struggling in the MGB. Their wiring loom was all wrong. It linked the wiper motor, the starter motor and their electric overdrive. Turn on one, and the others failed to function. Boyce created a makeshift system, keeping wipers and starter in play but disabling overdrive. It meant they'd rev harder and use more fuel.

Ian Vaughan's Falcon GT was screaming: a high-pitched howl from the gearbox signalled what he thought would be the end of his marathon. Bruce Hodgson arrived from behind.

'Settle down', he said. 'Bloody Harry [Firth] hasn't run in the bushes on the shaft. Stick it in third gear for 20 minutes, and you'll be all right.'

It worked. 'I thought we were out on day one,' Vaughan said.

At the Mont Blanc tunnel exit, a curious ceremony had taken place—with totally official sanction. Free of the threat posed by French requests, the marathon ran into an offer of leniency presented by the Italians. The law in Italy prohibited any rally to travel on a public road at an average of more than 50 kilometres per hour. The solution proposed by the Italians was that these brightly coloured, purpose-built vehicles with lights, air horns and roo bars simply cover their numbers and, for the purpose of crossing Italy, become normal tourists. That way, they could legally travel at 180 kilometres per hour or more, waved happily through by the police.

Dieter Glemser and Martin Braungart (Ford 20 MRS) took full advantage of the offer. They were first into Turin control, from fourteenth restart position, covering the distance in less than eight hours at an average speed of 140 kilometres per hour. They were more than five hours ahead of the allowed schedule. Terry Hunter and John Davenport were next, in the car best built for high-speed Continental touring: the Porsche 911 S. And then came one that wasn't: Harry Firth's Falcon GT, drinking fuel at a great rate on the autostrada but happy to do so while supplies were plentiful.

Ahead of them all was the media contingent. When the last car left Le Bourget, we'd travelled across Paris to its secondary airport, Orly, where our charter was waiting. The marathon had had more sleep than us. We'd been interviewing and filing copy for better than 24 hours, so an hour or so's sleep on board was welcome as we winged across the Alps to Turin. We were waiting at the Agip Motel, north of Turin on the main Milan–Ivrea autostrada, when Glemser rolled in.

The Italians were not prepared. As more and more marathon cars arrived in the car park, so did more and more spectators. Everyone wanted to be fed at the same time, and the queues and frustration were growing in intensity. Then Giancarlo Baghetti pulled into control. He was the one the locals had been waiting to see. His tiny Lancia disappeared beneath a tide of Italians, and both he and co-driver Giorgio Bassi, each with three days of designer stubble making them ruggedly handsome (long before it became the fashion), were hoisted shoulder high and chaired to the control desk. For the two former Formula One drivers, this moment was as good as it was going to get.

There was full British Leyland and Ford service in Turin, but nothing specific for Rootes except access to the Simca team in an emergency. The next major service for the Hillman Hunter was scheduled for Belgrade, behind the Iron Curtain.

Both the Ford and British Leyland teams were distracted by things that shouldn't have captured their attention. BL spent too much time on the Eileen Westley *Tortoise*, attending to a faulty speedometer cable that was making it difficult for the crew to accurately compare in-car odometer readings with the marathon's route instructions. At some stage the works service crews would have to establish priorities, but not yet.

Ford was mightily embarrassed. They had thought of everything. They had spares for their spares. Everything—except a timing chain tensioner spring, which is what had broken on Söderström's Lotus Cortina. Works mechanics—and several journalists pressed into action—began telephoning local garages. They discovered three Lotus Cortinas in Turin, one for sale on a nearby second-hand lot. The solution became known as 'The Great £100 Scandal'. The part was worth £2 in a parts bin. The car-yard owner demanded £100. When he got it, he thought he had achieved the sale of the century. In reality, Ford would have bought the car. The organ transplant occurred clinically, and Söderström checked in without points loss. But, as with most transplants, it takes time to assess rejection. Söderström was on borrowed time.

Second of the works Citroën drivers, Bob Neyret had used his initiative in Turin. Like everyone else, he was early into control, so he'd breasted the reception desk while others were joining the food queues. To his amazement, he secured a room and room service—two for one action. All he had to do was lodge his passport with the desk, returnable when he checked out. Except—it wasn't there when he went to get it. Bob is Gallic; the Italians, Italian. The argument was never going to end with a peaceful resolution. As it escalated, time was slipping away. Neyret was 74th on the road. He checked out from control, on the clock, then returned to the reception desk. Belgrade was 1161 kilometres away. Time allowed was 21 hours 12 minutes, an average of only 56 kilometres per hour. Neyret knew that if he took off without his passport, it was unlikely he'd be allowed to cross the border. For ten hours, the search continued—half the allowable time to Belgrade—and then, good fortune. The passport had been taken by another competitor, who'd sensibly left it at the border customs post. Neyret took off at a rush. He would need to average 140 kilometres per hour to get to Belgrade in time—and he did it.

* * *

Cecil Woodley liked a smoke. It relaxed him in times of stress. Getting from Turin to Belgrade had been just that. Although the autostrada was wide and fast, fog and an enfolding night had made the going tough for drivers not used to this high-paced, long-distance discipline. Keeping concentration is stressful, especially when the road you're on is a mass of marathon cars, passing and repassing at varying speeds, as well as trucks and general road traffic. The trucks. They were getting bigger, faster and more aggressive the longer the night wore on. It's one thing to be passed by a marathon car, but to have a 28-tonne behemoth bear down on you and sweep past with what seems like millimetres to spare is daunting. Woodley wasn't a professional.

After the Yugoslav border, the autostrada had turned to a series of sweeping corners and tunnels—built for the enjoyment of the professional, who could sweep through them in fluid motion, taking delight in the transition from left to right to left. For an amateur, at now well after midnight, it was all hands to the wheel. When the esses turned to motorway, or at least straight road, it was time for a cigarette. Steven Green and Dick Cullingford were asleep when Woodley lit up. It took maybe two minutes to drag it down to the last puff, and then he flicked the butt out the window.

But the breeze blew it back. It flew past his head and onto the back seat, where his co-driver was sleeping. Instinctively, Woodley reached behind him to pick it up—and that's when the Vauxhall Ventora ploughed straight off the road.

Andre Welinski and Gerry Lister were the first to arrive at the crash scene. They were only 146 kilometres out of Belgrade, just one-tenth of the distance to control to go. 'The car was upside down in a sea of mud more than 50 metres from the road,' Welinski told me in Belgrade. 'The three drivers were out of the car and wandering around, obviously in shock. The lights were still burning, the heater was on and fuel from the fractured tank was spilling everywhere. Gerry reached inside and turned off the ignition and then [incredibly] we pushed the car back on its wheels. It was a write-off.'

Woodley had broken his collarbone. That was confirmed by Australian doctor Alec Gorshenin, who was flagged down by Welinski. Doctors at the Traumatoloska Hospital in Belgrade administered painkilling drugs, and British embassy officials arranged to have Woodley flown to London for an operation. Green and Cullingford stayed behind. There was the matter of getting the battered wreck onto a truck and exporting it from the country, otherwise import duty would be payable.

By the time Woodley had had his accident, Roger Clark was already asleep in the Metropole Hotel in Belgrade. He had arrived eleven hours early, and the control area was not open. Officials were not travelling as fast as the marathon. As there was no advantage to arriving early in control, there was no real reason to open the control early to receive first arrivals. So if you were half a day early, like Clark, then it was up to you to park, go away and rest and be back on time to clock in, lest you receive a late-arrival penalty.

Some would not make it to Belgrade.

Peter Harper, a seasoned rally professional in the Tecalemit Lotus Cortina, had his water pump fail—ironically as he passed Venice—and he'd called back to Turin in the hope of getting a replacement. It was to be delivered by taxi. But he never booked in to Belgrade control, incurring an automatic penalty of 1440 points. Same at Istanbul. Officials knew he was out there somewhere, but now out of all contention. By the time of the first special stage at Sivas, he was an official retirement. It was a huge disappointment. Of all the privateers, Harper had been one of the best prepared, and in the private entrant stakes he had been one of the favourites.

David Corbett achieved the distinction of being the first to pull out. His Austin 1800 threw a rod through the engine block within sight of Belgrade and, although he was towed in, there was no hope of repairing it. Tom Fisk, an Australian working in England, had got the call to join the crew of the Corbett car only two days before the marathon started. Now he was stranded in Belgrade, 'a lifetime away from home'.

Belgrade was a grey ghost of a city. The Metropole Hotel was its own haunted castle, overlooking a city square with green trees and colourless people. Perhaps it's because I was expecting my first look behind the Iron Curtain to be something like this that my expectations were met. The Metropole had once been grand. The plumbing, huge chromed pipes exposed and standing proud from the walls, gleamed in an otherwise drab interior. Throw open the high French windows, and the street below, with tramcars clattering past, was all the better for the splash of colour the marathon cars brought to the streetscape. The Belgrade Autoklub, where the control was situated, was only half a kilometre away down a side street.

Bill Bengry strode into the foyer, his story of near disaster still fresh in his memory. The Number One Cortina GT had still been in Italy when it had approached an autostrada toll booth way too fast. Driver John Preddy locked up all four wheels, but it was still obvious he was going to hit the queue of cars in front.

The entries to autostrada booths are wide. They funnel you down from a soccer pitch–sized entrance to a final cattle race where you pay your money. In the scant time available, Preddy steered from one booth to another, looking for the greatest possible stopping distance. Finally, all this in a fraction of a second, there was one with only two cars, and one was moving out. He slammed the Cortina into the gap, cutting off the second car, and paid his toll as if it was the normal thing to do.

Perhaps it had been drowsiness that had led him to his mistake. Already the marathon competitors were learning a lot on the run. If it got cold, as it had the previous two nights, they turned on the heater, but that had the effect of making them tired. Eyelids started to droop; not good, especially in a two-person crew.

The solution crews were finding was to run cold. They used their own clothing to layer up against the cold, but ran without heaters. David McKay's decision to insist on air conditioning was looking more sensible by the moment.

The 'buddy system' was also working—especially intra-team. Concentrating over a long distance is tiring. Rather like a cyclist taking his or her turn on the front of a peloton, it was possible for small groups of marathon cars to travel in a pack. If you trusted the car in front well enough, you could drive off its cues, including its navigation, significantly reducing the onus on the following crews. Then after a while you'd change position.

But no amount of buddying up was going to solve the very real challenge as competitors struggled to check into, then out of, Belgrade. The early-morning calm had turned into a late-morning crush. The half-kilometre drive to the Autoklub, surely no more than a five-minute amble, had become a half-hour traffic jam. And people were running late. Marathon cars were charging down tramlines, with trams coming in the opposite direction. They mounted footpaths and went the wrong way up one-way streets. The police looked on and took no action, positive or negative. Lieutenant Jack Dill in the Royal Green Jackets' Porsche took a 21-point loss; Terry-Thomas–sponsored Peter Capelin in the Ford Cortina 1600 E went down 3 points; and Australian Geoffrey Franklin (Cortina GT) dropped 1 point, despite a determined last-ditch sprint.

* * *

Bandits roamed the Yugoslav–Bulgarian border. They'd lay a thick coating of oil on the roads over the mountain pass in order to cause tourists to crash. Then they'd swoop on them and rob them of their valuables. There had been reports of deaths. Tourists' cars had gone off the side of cliffs and plunged into the ravines below. If the crash didn't get them, it was rumoured the bandits would. It was rough country. Several recce teams had noted the bandit action as fact, and the marathon was on high alert.

The Yugoslav military had reacted before the marathon passed through, sending troops into the region to issue stern warnings.

When Peter Capelin spun on the mountain pass, wiping out a row of guide posts, the crew feared the worst. They were over the lip of the road, with their roo bar wedged on a ledge. When they peered beyond, they saw they were precariously balanced on the precipice of a much larger drop. They abandoned ship, called for assistance and were towed out. Incredibly, they reached Istanbul without penalty.

Max Winkless and John Keran were only 150 kilometres past Belgrade when the special high-performance Repco cylinder head in their Volvo 144 S bent a valve. Gerry Lister, arriving shortly afterwards, lent them tools but sped on. Winkless and Keran dismantled the engine by the roadside, then hitchhiked back into Belgrade to buy new parts. The Volvo dealer offered professional courtesy to his Australian counterpart. He initially volunteered a complete car, but that was forbidden under the rules, so he arranged entry to a nearby workshop, an Iron Curtain Atomic Energy headquarters. It took Winkless and Keran a full day to rebuild their car, destroying their marathon chances, but they sped off in pursuit of the field, and caught it when it was well into Afghanistan.

The face of Europe was changing. It was still only Tuesday. The marathon was less than 48 hours old and, as if through a time warp, the familiar scenery of the Western world had disappeared. Broad autostradas had become rocky roads; Vespa motor scooters and motorcycles had been replaced by herds of goats and horse-drawn carts.

Cheering crowds remained, but they were dressed differently and some, not all, were more aggressive, perhaps even threatening, in their attitude. Wherever a marathon car stopped, a crowd appeared. Passing through villages drew tight bunches of people—most of them cheering. 'It was like the Mille Miglia,' Innes Ireland said. 'There was definitely a feeling that they were cheering a race.'

Crew compatibility is everything in a rally or a marathon: the ability to get along, complement each other's thinking, work on in-car discipline and hygiene and to contribute to mutual success is all important.

In some cars it was already being sorely tested.

No one doubted that clear favouritism to win the Ladies' Prize rested with Rosemary Smith and Lucette Pointet. As professionals, they were streets ahead of their amateur opposition. But Ford had a lot of work to do on its star pairing. They hated each other—and, 50 years on, they still do not have a good word to say about one another.

The atmosphere inside the Lotus Cortina was frosty, bordering on toxic.

'Rosemary said, "This is my car." I didn't drive it once, not once, except to park it,' Pointet told me.

'She critiqued me the whole way,' Smith retorted in a separate interview. 'Every time I'd go into a corner, there'd be a *tutt, tutt, tutt* from the co-driver's seat.' The language of the route chart was

English, but Smith did not believe Pointet's French-accented call was up to the task. Try spending a week in a car without speaking to your companion.

'And then there was the smell,' Smith said. 'In Europe, someone, her mother I think, shoved a garlic sausage through the window, complete with a knife. She would carve off small pieces of this foul-smelling meat and eat it, all the way to Bombay. The smell was horrific.'

'There was no *bonhomie*,' Pointet countered. 'I think she did not like French people.'

Perhaps the fault was Ford's. The two women had met in PR activities before the marathon, but the first time they sat together in the car was at the start. There'd not been a lot of work done on team building.

Evan Green was having a hard time keeping a lid on antagonism far more aggressive in his Austin 1800. You'd think travelling the world with Gelignite Jack Murray would be a laugh a minute. George Shepheard was doing his best to keep the placid Green focused (sensational on the big picture, not too flash on detail), let alone deal with what he saw as the harping and carping of Murray.

'Jack was always clowning around,' Shepheard said. 'You try to keep an even keel in the car, but I had to tell him to settle down. The only time I dared to sleep was when Evan was driving. When Jack was at the wheel, I couldn't trust where he'd go.' One of Murray's stunts was to drive for ten minutes, then wake his co-driver and tell him he'd done a full two-hour stint. It worked in PR runs with Green, but it didn't wash in the marathon with Shepheard.

Murray didn't take Shepheard's criticism lying down. There was soon to be a huge argument in their shared room in Istanbul. Barry Ferguson and David Johnson walked in on it and then quickly walked out again. 'Jack had been tearing into George, who was in the bathroom behind a locked door. It was more than just raised voices; Evan was in the bedroom with Jack, trying to restore calm,' David Johnson recalled. 'And you don't want to get Jack angry.' The former wrestling champion had a formidable temper matched by a formidable physique.

Innes Ireland, Michael Taylor and Andrew Hedges found a ready way to relieve in-car tension. Each driver, each day, was allowed one rant. Whatever the topic, whether it was about the car, teammates or life in general, it became a much-anticipated event. A negative became a positive.

The Ford team was big on hygiene. Roger Clark and Ove Andersson were always clean-shaven, neatly and newly dressed, and spotless in appearance. 'It's amazing the difference a razor will make to your general demeanour,' Nick Brittan told me after the marathon, when we got together for several days to compare notes. 'If you brush your teeth and shave your face, it's almost as good as a shower, which may not always be available. After just a couple of days, it was obvious which teams were in trouble just by the look of their general demeanour. If they were unshaven, dirty and dishevelled, you knew they were less likely to go the distance.'

The Australian Ford team were the only ones to install toilets in their cars. The specially designed potty sat unused in the rear of all three cars. They were, perhaps, a step too far. In India, they tried to give them away but could find no one to accept such an unusual but thoughtful gift.

Crossing from Yugoslavia into Bulgaria had been identified by recce crews as one of the struggle points of the long run to Bombay. No one had passed between the two countries without extreme difficulty. That's why crews sped towards the border from Belgrade, to allow themselves more time for clearance. But the Bulgarians had cleaned up their act. In an extreme act of good PR for their country, they'd streamlined entry, slowing it down only to allow gifts from the local auto club to be showered upon crews as they passed through.

Bulgaria, though, was a different country. It was as if a light had been switched off. The good roads disappeared, and the bad ones became the norm. The Dragoman Pass near the border was difficult, and there were stories of several cars spinning out—but not crashing—on the suddenly changed surface. The marathon was moving at high speed.

Giancarlo Baghetti's Lancia punctured a tyre, and the Italian crew did not have a jack. The two Formula One drivers built a plinth of stones, raising the car high enough so that they could manoeuvre the wheel off. Then the plinth collapsed. They tried again and again before they succeeded. In Istanbul, they laughed about it.

Sofia, the capital of Bulgaria, a magical but frustratingly difficult city to navigate, had been bypassed. But if the marathon wouldn't come to Sofia, then the city would come to it. In the early morning hours long before dawn, the increasingly cut-up road was lined with cheering well-wishers. Intersections were patrolled by police, and marathon cars were waved enthusiastically through.

The border into Turkey was 180 kilometres before Istanbul. It was almost like a homecoming. Turkey had extended a fine welcome. All the way along the road into Istanbul, soldiers stood as sentinels, marking the way. But they were still soldiers, heavily armed. It was a taste of things to come. The road had not been officially closed, but it was still remarkably free of traffic. A high average speed into Istanbul was made possible, but rain spoiled that. From nowhere a storm of increasing ferocity grew, blowing almost horizontally across the road. For some of the smaller vehicles, control became a challenge.

For Keith Schellenberg in the Bentley, it was like an Antarctic expedition. Unprotected, the crew were chilled to the bone.

Bengt Söderström and Gunnar Palm made the most of it. They covered the distance from Belgrade in less than eight hours to lead into Turkey. Ford was 1–2–3 on the road into Istanbul, with Roger Clark and Eric Jackson closely behind the Swedish-crewed car.

Marathon organisers had made a last-minute change to the route. The control was to have been at the Sports Arena in the middle of Istanbul, but it had changed to the giant Cinar Hotel complex near the airport at Yesilkoy, way outside the city. There'd be no iconic views of the Blue Mosque, no side visits to the Hagia Sophia. Worse, the hotel was overbooked. Several crews, even the works teams, found themselves under-accommodated. For the first time in nearly three days, tired marathon drivers were sleeping in stairwells. There was a feeling of disgruntlement. The marathon was getting unnecessarily hard. At least the military division was happy. They'd passed through the Iron Curtain without difficulties—in fact, they'd been made welcome.

If you counted the marathon in continents, stage one was now officially over. Ninety-five cars remained in contention; eight had incurred penalty. The mighty Bosphorus Strait waited to be crossed, and the first elimination section from Sivas to Erzincan was just up the road. At 9 a.m., Jack Sears, who had travelled with us in the media plane, left in a car to drive almost 900 kilometres to Erzincan to confirm for himself that the road remained suitable for sorting out the serious operators from the dreamers.

Istanbul to Sivas

Distance: 934 kilometres

Time allowed: 12 hours 25 minutes

Approximate average speed: 75 kilometres per hour

Sivas to Erzincan

Distance: 299 kilometres

Time allowed: 2 hours 45 minutes

Approximate average speed: 109 kilometres per hour

12

The First Special Stage

IN THE MIDDLE OF A DESPERATELY DARK, clingingly cold night, on a road so daunting it made the amateurs gasp, Roger Clark and Ove Andersson seized the lead in the London–Sydney Marathon by such a convincing margin that they left astonishment and disbelief in their wake.

With Clark at the wheel and Andersson calling the corners on the longest special stage ever run on pace notes, the pair danced the Lotus Cortina across 298 kilometres of mountainous goat track, holding the law of gravity to account as the underbody of their car set the flintstones alight.

The only witnesses to their awesome skill were local goatherders and the competitors they thrust their way past and who tried in vain to cling to them as their tail-lights receded in the distance.

If there was any doubt that there were two divisions in the marathon, this first special stage, from Sivas to Erzincan, had set the record straight.

The first fourteen cars were all professional. The first privateers, Bob Holden—arguably, under marathon interpretation, a private entry in his works-assisted Volvo—and Stewart McLeod in his definitely self-built Alfa Romeo 1750, had done an amazing job to fling their cars down the mountainside to claim fifteenth and sixteenth ahead of the Porsche of Sobieslaw Zasada.

The marathon, after an exploratory feint and jab, a first tentative 3200-kilometre joust across Europe, had suddenly exploded into full-on competition.

It all started on the morning of day three in the race to the ferry to cross the Bosphorus, the daunting expanse of water separating Europe and Asia. There was no bridge then, only the slow-moving, flat-bottomed boats that plied between the two shores of Istanbul crammed with local people and produce, without rationale or order. Organisers had made no arrangements for crossing. Instead, they piled on the pressure.

The distance from Istanbul control to check-in at the tiny town of Sivas, the start of the first super special stage, was 934 kilometres. The time allowed was 12 hours 25 minutes. That translated to an average speed of 75 kilometres per hour, by far the highest point-to-point average yet demanded. It was achievable, but there were obstacles. For a start, the marathon would be running for the first time on substantially dirt roads. Secondly, the dreaded Turkish traffic that had not materialised on the run into Istanbul was a real and ever-present danger. And thirdly, there was the ferry crossing.

As crews checked out of Istanbul, 25 kilometres from the ferry terminal, an atmosphere of urgency overcame the control area. For the first time, people were pushing and shoving at the desk when their route card was stamped. Cars were pulled up close by, their engines revving and the passenger's door opened ready for the co-driver to scramble in. Cars left with a squeal of tyres, with the co-driver sometimes not fully on board.

Those who missed the first ferry would be able to get the next, but the delay could be measured in multiples of minutes—and it was all on the clock. For the professionals, it was a case of slow breathing, keeping their head as all around were losing theirs. For the amateurs, 'the dreamers', this was what in one respect they'd signed up for—the adrenalin rush of keeping pace, of involvement in a race. Innes Ireland, with a foot in both camps, noted 'from the minute the gangway went down, there was a great jostling match to get ashore. Hyde Park corner in the rush hour had nothing on this.'

Nick Brittan told me: 'It was just like a race track. Everybody was weaving and chopping each other off. Even the little DAF was doing around 150 kilometres per hour.'

The first crash happened less than 10 kilometres from the ferry exit.

Peter Lumsden, Peter Sargent, Redge Lewis and John Fenton in the Australian-made Chrysler Valiant station wagon they'd borrowed from Rootes in Adelaide were fifth away from control, but they'd dropped back in the pack in the race into Asia and more and more people were coming up behind. Lumsden and Sargent were experienced racing drivers. They'd both competed in the pressure cooker that is Le Mans. And yet, with cars coming up behind them and with a slow-moving non-marathon vehicle in front, they pulled out to pass, despite the presence of an oncoming truck. They'd been warned about Turkish truck drivers. They think they own the road. 'He only had to move over a foot, and I would have gotten through,' Sargent said. 'But he didn't budge.' The crash ripped the front and side out of the Valiant. The crew were uninjured, but their marathon was over. Bert Madden, travelling behind in the Holden HK, saw it all. He claimed the truck had pulled out from behind another, putting four vehicles across a two-lane road.

There was indignation, but the message was clear. The marathon was travelling through another culture. Apart from in exceptional circumstances, such as they'd experienced driving into Istanbul the night before, no one was going to move out of the way.

Nick Brittan hit a horse.

It came from nowhere—except they always come from somewhere—and Brittan was left with no alternative except to lose as much speed as possible. He was doing 150 kilometres per hour. The horse catapulted off the roo bar, into the windscreen and then up onto the roof and back onto the road. Co-driver Jenny Brittan had been asleep when she awoke to be confronted by darkness, glass, immense noise, blood and excrement. There was, amazingly, no one in sight. They laid out their sleeping bag so they could kick the windscreen clear of the car's A-pillar. It was then that three young men arrived, each, Nick felt, claiming to be the owner of the horse. 'I had heard of situations like this and felt it was best to be out of there as soon as I could,' he said. Resourcefully, he took the shattered windscreen from the bonnet and passed it to his confronters, giving them something to do with their hands. Then he and Jenny leapt back in their car and sped away. It was, in hindsight, not in the spirit of the marathon, but the Brittans were genuinely in shock and in fear for their lives. They drove the rest of the way into Sivas wearing the goggles Ford had thoughtfully provided.

Rock-throwing children were a major hazard. In the myriad small villages through which the marathon passed, up to 200 by some counts, they would appear from nowhere, hurl their weapons and disappear with the wraith-like stealth of guerrillas. It was anything but youthful enthusiasm and nowhere near funny. It was an epidemic. Colin Forsyth's BMW 2000 was struck side and rear, shattering glass and narrowly missing crew members. Nobuo Koga's Vauxhall windscreen was shattered. The *Telegraph's* Holden team suffered dents on both sides.

Reliability was becoming a factor.

Barry Ferguson stopped several times in an unsuccessful attempt to clear an engine miss every time he kicked down to full power. At the back of the field, private entrant Dennis Cresdee had found a telex machine with which he contacted organisers to say he was out. His tiny Austin 1300 Estate had cried enough.

In the chill—no, the cold—of a dark early evening in Sivas, Ford was nonplussed. Bengt Söderström and Gunnar Palm were out—the first major works withdrawal. The organ transplant in Turin had not taken. Or, to be more precise, the damage done when it dropped its valve had apparently been terminal to the bottom end of the engine, and they had limped into Sivas with no hope of repair in time under the rules. At least Palm was able to offer up his car as replacement parts to the Brittan team, and they removed his windscreen and worked a way to fit it to the severely damaged bodywork of the other Cortina.

Without Söderström and Palm in contention, Ford was reviewing its strategy. It had started with two sprint teams and one slower saver—the Jackson–Chambers car. Surely now they'd have to instruct their one remaining 'hare' to back off a bit as he faced the first true test.

If you ignore the jokes about Nick Brittan, Sivas was a one-horse town. The start control for this all-important special stage lay in a darkened, muddy car park at the edge of a sports field.

The professionals and the near professionals busied themselves preparing. Tyre choice would be critical. Dunlop, Goodyear and Michelin were all supporting works teams, and each had brought special gravel tyres to the start.

British Leyland, the Hillman Hunters, Holden and many of the privateers were on Dunlop, and a specialist tyre technician and manager, Jeremy Ferguson, had become the go-to man of the marathon with his knowledge of the road ahead. The Fords were running Goodyear; the Citroëns were exclusively on Michelin. A works team had the choice of high-speed road tyres, capable of covering great distance without overheating, and off-road tyres ranging from those that were lightly grooved to serious mud pluggers. There were even studs available, should snow and ice become a problem. The icepick-like devices embedded in the tyre were capable of digging into the surface to gain traction.

Fuel was another issue. For maximum performance and reliability, competition cars needed to run on 100 octane. The trick of mixing on the run from reserve tanks was a good stand-by, but when the teams started a special stage like Sivas–Erzincan, there could be no doubt. Rootes had found even better—120 octane Avgas (aviation fuel) at an airstrip in Erzincan, and they'd sent it back to Sivas for themselves and to share with the British Leyland team. Helping an opponent may seem strange, but it was still early in the event; a favour offered early on might be reciprocated in a critical moment later.

Weight was a major consideration. Every kilogram removed from a car is a small percentage of power gained. In Sivas, the works teams stripped their cars and sent onboard baggage forward. Even privateer Innes Ireland hired a Sivas taxi and had most of his onboard equipment taken around the long way to Erzincan, hoping it would be there when he arrived.

The biggest issue of all was the route. There were two roads to Erzincan, both legal under marathon rules. The northern road went over the mountains, climbing to 2500 metres. It was marginally longer and marginally slower. The southern route seemed to be the logical way, except it was prone to becoming so muddy as to be impassable.

No one was sharing information. Ford and British Leyland had current intelligence. They knew which way was passable and fastest, but they weren't telling. Citroën had knowledge that was not quite as current; they'd communicated with team manager René Cotton, who'd made a call. Andrew Cowan had flown out specially before the event to survey the southern route, but he had no immediate feedback on its condition.

Cowan and Colin Malkin argued. 'We had arranged for someone in the forestry commission to telegraph us in Sivas, but the telegram never arrived,' Cowan said. 'We'd heard the others were heading north, but sometimes this is disinformation and we were suspicious. Colin wanted to bet it all on the southern route. I was undecided. If everyone went south, and we'd never know until it was over, and if we went north we'd be way back in the field. If everyone went north and we did, too, we'd at least be in contention. But if we went south, they went north and we got bogged, our event would be over at the first hurdle.

'Colin made it worse by telling me mid-argument that "it was my decision". No one needs pressure like that.'

As they sat in the queue, waiting for their turn to go, Cowan made his call. He'd take the northern route.

To describe the conditions in control as basic is an understatement. Every rally competitor needs a comfort stop before the start of a stage. Even if they don't really want to go, it's a tradition. Graham White's Austin 1800 was 65th in the queue. He wandered away from control in search of relief. Out of the klieg lights he was suddenly in pitch darkness, and he stumbled into a 2.5-metre-deep inspection pit. David Benson heard his cries for help and pulled him out. White was complaining of chest pains, and a local medico strapped his chest tightly. Any hope of driving was gone, but he took the back seat, holding on gamely as John Jeffcoat and David Dunnell flung the Austin towards Erzincan. They wouldn't be fast—mid-pack among the privateers—but by the time they reached Erzincan, White was unconscious. Rushed to the small general hospital, he was diagnosed with a ruptured kidney. It was removed on the spot.

At the head of the pack in Sivas, Harry Firth, the wily fox of Australian motor racing but also one of the most aggressive and, truthfully, selfish of competitors, made his own decision. He was number two on the road in his big V8 behind Bill Bengry in his four-cylinder Cortina. Harry walked the town and found a short cut from the control to the trail head where the road narrowed down to one lane. It was only a few kilometres. Bengry would be starting one minute ahead of him and not going slowly. When Graham Hoinville sprinted back to the Falcon with his route book stamped, Firth took off, showering mud and stones behind him. Down back lanes he reached speeds bordering on dangerous, and when he converged back onto the rally road he was able—just—to squeeze by Bengry. He was the leader on the road, and it was a lead he'd not lose to the end of the stage, almost 300 kilometres away. He wouldn't be fastest, but he wouldn't be held up, either. Holding that lead would come with great controversy.

Ove Andersson, the tough, implacable Swede, swore to me years later that he and Roger Clark never came under team orders in that opening stage, regardless of the loss of Söderström and Palm. The team existed for its fastest car. Andersson's job was to hold Clark back on the transport stages. On the special stages, where time could only be lost and loss had to be held to a minimum, his job was to lift Clark onto maximum attack.

Across that amazing night-time stage, Clark and Andersson lost an average of 1.2 seconds a kilometre. The average loss for the entire field was 15.48 seconds. The average loss for the top ten was 3.4 seconds.

Starting 48th on the road, Clark and Andersson were passing cars on both sides of the road at will. They were, compared to everyone else in the field, on another plane. They dodged accidents and debris and avoided route calls that were wrong.

Sixty kilometres into the stage, they caught the car that had started twelve minutes ahead of them. David McKay had already run into problems, but nothing could have staved off Clark's attack. 'We were privileged to see Roger Clark at work as his lights glared behind us and announced his arrival,' David said on the onboard tape he handed me at control in Tehran the next day. 'I pulled over on a mountain descent as soon as George Reynolds told me Clark was within passing distance, and in a flash the Briton had taken the opening and was past. We had a chance to watch him for only a few moments. Sparks were flying off his undertray and exhaust as he flung the works Lotus Cortina this way and that, keeping the car in a continually checked slide.'

Clark and Andersson reached Erzincan with a late time of just 6 minutes. The nearest to them was the German-entered Ford Taunus of Gilbert Staepelaere and Simo Lampinen. The German car's crew made an extraordinary decision to start with a light fuel load and refuel midway. At roughly 1 kilogram per litre, they'd jettisoned up to 75 kilograms of weight in the hope that they'd make up more time than the two to four minutes they'd spend at their fuel dump. It was a calculated gamble, and perhaps it paid off. They sprinted home with a loss of 14 minutes—two minutes clear of the field, but still more than double the time lost by Clark.

Lucien Bianchi was the stealth fighter of the field. Running on Michelin's super off-road tyres, he tore through the stage with a 16-point deficit, enough to be third quickest. No one saw that coming. His teammate, Bob Neyret, dropped 36 points in a supposedly identical car. Bianchi, simply, was on the very top of his game.

British Leyland drivers Paddy Hopkirk and Rauno Aaltonen, and Lampinen's Ford teammate Dieter Glemser, all sacrificed 17 points. Australia's Bruce Hodgson was the fastest of the V8 Fords, down 18 points. Firth lost 20, as did Tony Fall.

Fall was ropeable. He'd started from position four and had caught Firth on the road. But the Falcon would not let him past. Worse, the big Falcon had thrown up rocks, shattering the Austin's driving lights. It was not the only complaint made against the Australians.

Way back in the field, Andrew Cowan had started in 75th position, but he'd soon been passed on a long straight stretch by Barry Ferguson, whose Monaro had found its missing full-throttle power. Into the next corners, Cowan was all over the back of the Monaro, looking for a way through. 'I kept on his tail all the way, with him chopping me off on the corners. The stones from his car broke our windscreen and those lights which were not protected by our roo bar.' Cowan backed off for a full 100 kilometres, one third distance, before he had another—this time successful—go at passing. 'It was annoying because we dropped 21 minutes, and if we hadn't been baulked we could have been closer to the 1800s.'

Ferguson tells it differently. 'The Monaro loved that stage,' he said. 'Sure we passed and repassed Andrew, but our power was the advantage. It was only when our brakes started to fall to pieces that we backed off.' Ferguson lost 26 minutes. When they went to service the brakes, they fell apart in their hands.

For Cowan, all the predictions he'd made at the outset were proved correct. He knew he didn't have the fastest car in the event, and now he knew by how much. Cowan calculated that he passed 31 cars in the stage, but it was a struggle. 'We would catch them through the corners, but as soon as we hit a straight they would accelerate away.' Cowan caught a Cortina 1600 E in a corner, lost a drag race on the straight and finally begged for permission to take the lead.

Cowan had been too polite. In-control Lucien Bianchi, the racing driver, gave Andrew Cowan, the confirmed rally driver and reluctant racing driver, some tough-love advice: 'Be forceful. I'd let that happen for two corners, then *bang*, I'd be through, no questions or apologies.'

Cowan's lost 21 points still had him ahead of Evan Green and Eric Jackson, both 22 points down, and Ian Vaughan, whose deficit was 25 points. Vaughan thought he was going okay: 'Then I saw the lights of Bruce Hodgson's Falcon blazing behind me. He'd started five minutes back. It was a huge wake-up call, so I got stuck into it. Bruce never passed me but it was a close call, and he finished ahead on points.'

Just eighteen crews made it with a loss of less than 30 minutes. Only three of them qualified, with some dispute, as privateers—Bob

Holden on his magnificent 25, McLeod on 26 and veteran Ken Tubman in another factory-built Volvo on 29 points. They split the fastest Porsche, Sobieslaw Zasada in the works car, who was seventeenth on 28 points. His brakes failed at half distance, and Marek Wachowski became the brake man, working the handbrake as best he could. Edgar Hermann, in another of the Porsches, had the same problem, dropping to mid-field with a loss of 58 points. The two Porsche teams discovered a similar crack in their brake master cylinder and repaired it on the spot.

Sivas to Erzincan had been a crew and car breaker and a massive wake-up call for the inexperienced. At least fifteen cars ploughed off the road. One muddy field in particular caught out the unwary who were driving on trust on the Castrol notes, which had neglected a right-hand corner off a narrow bridge. Those going too fast went straight ahead into the field.

It was a big lesson—unless teams had written the notes themselves, they were never to be absolutely trusted. Fifty years on, the issue of using 'bought' notes is still a pressing safety concern.

David van Lennep's tiny DAF flew off the corner and landed on its sump. The car was stranded all night until it could be towed back to Sivas for repairs. Although the support aircraft left parts, they turned out to be the wrong ones, and van Lennep spent a day with a Sivas blacksmith fabricating a new timing chain.

Peter Capelin's Ford Cortina 1600 E went off into the quagmire. The entire Moskvitch team, travelling in convoy, saw him bogged, stopped and lifted him back onto the road.

David McKay was another visitor to the field, but he kept the power on and his off-road tyres let him spin and skid his way back to the road.

But that's as good as it got for the lead Holden driver.

It's possible McKay had had the red mist descend. He'd been passed by Clark, then by McLeod. Co-driver David Liddle was working the Halda Speedpilot and, although they had no real marker against the opposition, they knew their own target time was slipping away. When they came to one of the narrow bridges that dotted the course, the Berwyn Williams Austin 1800 had spun across it. The crew were doing their best to push it out of the way, but McKay made his call to squeeze past. The side of the Holden was gashed in the process and, perhaps, its rear wheel was dislodged. Within kilometres, McKay stopped for what he thought was a flat tyre to discover the wheel studs had stretched and the wheel was hanging loose, broken. The crew replaced it, leaving the cracked wheel at the side of the road. By the time McKay arrived at control, he'd dropped 66 points. Any hope he'd had of winning the London–Sydney Marathon had evaporated on the first serious stage. The mood in the car was dark.

The Australian soon-to-be Formula One driver David Walker thought he'd killed his co-driver, Doug Morris. Their rear suspension broke mid-stage and, at the side of the road, Morris had gone under it to effect repairs. The jack slipped in the mud, and the car crashed down on Morris's head. The next car along was the Holden of Bert Madden, Jack 'Milko' Murray and John Bryson. The trio leapt to the stricken Vauxhall. With Walker and his third driver, Brian Jones, they lifted the car off the unconscious Morris. 'The only problem was that we were all holding the car up, and no one was able to reach him to pull him out,' Murray said. Four of them took the weight while the fifth grabbed Morris. The bodywork cut deeply into their hands.

With his hands hurting and bleeding, Murray was to leave the road only kilometres later. Despite both incidents, the team still lost only 34 minutes. Morris, incredibly, would continue in the marathon, not as a driver or as a navigator but as essential cargo so the team would not be disqualified for losing a crew member.

Keith Schellenberg's marathon ended on the Erzincan stage. The mighty 1930 Bentley pulled to the side of the road, and Schellenberg and Norman Barclay stepped out of it, leaving the Hon. Patrick Lindsay in the back. At that moment, the road collapsed under the Bentley's weight. Some said it was 3.5 tonnes. It rolled down the culvert, fracturing Lindsay's collarbone. The 'Spirit' of the event had been extinguished.

Bobby Buchanan-Michaelson bent the gear linkages of his Mercedes-Benz on a rock, requiring a lengthy stop to fix them. Then he hit another rock, forcing the radiator back onto the fan. Innes Ireland escaped vehicle damage, but a hard landing triggered immediate neck pain for co-driver Michael Taylor, who'd broken his neck in the Spa Formula One crash eight years before. Taylor would continue, but in a brace.

At 11 a.m. the next morning, Max Winkless and John Keran made it to Sivas, now only twelve hours behind the field. They didn't stop but sped on to Erzincan. With no one to tell them otherwise, they took the southern route, believing it to be faster, and they got bogged past their axles. It took the tired, despondent but still-determined crew an hour to dig themselves out. Andrew Cowan's decision to use the northern road had been vindicated.

Erzincan to Tehran

Distance: 1465 kilometres
Time allowed: 22 hours 1 minute
Approximate average speed: 67 kilometres per hour

Tehran to Kabul

Distance: 2495 kilometres
Time allowed: 23 hours 33 minutes
Approximate average speed: 107 kilometres per hour

Kabul to Sarobi

Distance: 76 kilometres
Time allowed: 1 hour
Approximate average speed: 76 kilometres per hour

13

The Road to Afghanistan

THE ARMED MEN CAME ON BOARD the media plane at Sivas as we were about to take off. Three of them, young soldiers, soft faces and frightened eyes. It could have been the extreme cold, but two had shaking hands as they clutched their semi-automatic weapons to their chests. The third walked through the plane, demanding our documents. We felt obliged to comply.

They left with our passports, retreating to the only hut on the airstrip, icicles hanging from its eaves.

We had created confusion and suspicion.

The marathon had left Sivas the night before, and our plane had flown off, too, taking some of us to Erzincan to cover the finish of the special stage.

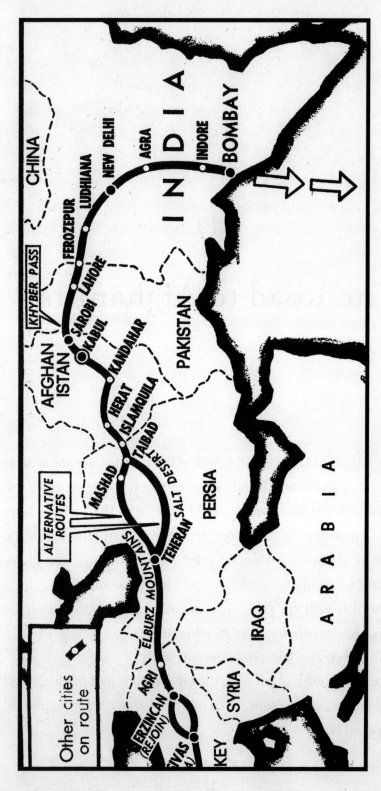

Map 2: Map showing the race route from Erzincan, Turkey, to Bombay.

Now it had returned, via a seemingly unscheduled stop at Ezurum, a renowned US spy base, the closest NATO facility to the USSR border. The explanation was simple. We were being collected, and Ezurum had provided a refuelling opportunity for the plane.

But they didn't want to listen.

We sat there for more than 90 minutes—frozen in time—the open door of our aircraft allowing blasts of sub-zero air through the cabin. We were due in Tehran in the afternoon, not only to cover the marathon but also to deliver vital parts to the *Telegraph* team. Back in London, we'd agreed to act as their courier.

David McNicoll snapped. 'Smailes,' he said to me, his face ruddy with cold and anger, white moustache bristling, 'come with me. I shall command their attention whilst you retrieve our passports.' He spoke like that.

We marched across the tarmac, noting that ours was the only plane on the strip—not much assistance available. When we entered the hut, McNicoll let loose bombastically, pushing past the front desk to the obvious commander at the rear of the building, dragging the others in his wake. Our passports sat neatly stacked on the counter. McNicoll was magnificent, a command performance. How good would it have been, I thought, if he'd chosen Benson and not me—the two of them born thespians. But what he needed was a sneak thief. He kept glancing at me and at the passports, his instructions quite obvious. At that moment I decided I feared my editor-in-chief far more than the Turkish military, swept the entire stack under my rally jacket and headed for the door. There was no small arms fire. Five minutes later, McNicoll arrived at the plane's steps with the military commander.

They shook hands convivially. 'We can depart now,' McNicoll said, and we did.

* * *

Sid Dickson demolished a house just out of Ankara. It's hard to know why. There was no hurry. Officials had allowed 22 hours 1 minute to cover the 1465 kilometres from the end of the special stage in Erzincan to the massive service facility at the Philips electrical factory in Tehran. There was only one border to cross, one mountain to pass—Mount Ararat, the fabled resting place of Noah's Ark—and a battalion of out-of-control trucks and buses to miss. Most people had covered the distance in half the time on their recces.

To be fair to Sid and the crew of the red-white-and-blue Rambler, there was a snow storm blowing and visibility was minimal. 'We came to an intersection and couldn't decide which way to go,' his co-driver, John Saladin, said. 'By the time we did, it was too late and the house was right in front of us. Our car wasn't badly damaged—and nobody was screaming about the house, so we reversed out and kept right on going.'

That was the official version. Later I learned that people had come running and that the third man in the Rambler, Jerry Sims, had pulled a gun on them. Onboard weapons were not widely discussed on the marathon, but it was known that several teams were packing. The risks across the Asian continent especially, but also in Eastern Europe, had encouraged some to seek the reassurance of at least a handgun. Paddy Hopkirk's co-driver, Alec Poole, had one, given to him by a friend in the Irish police force. It had had its serial numbers removed, what the cops call a throwdown. He had received no

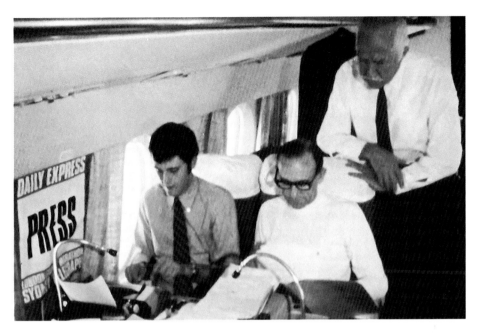

On the press plane: author John Smailes and *The Daily Telegraph* senior representative Harold 'Dev' Dvoretsky work under the supervision of *Telegraph* editor-in-chief David McNicoll. Covering the marathon in a collar and tie.

Pakistan and India threw out a huge welcome to the marathon, but the crowds were overwhelming and dangerous. From his co-driver's seat in the works Porsche (through the 'roo cage'), Marek Wachowski took this picture of Barry Ferguson's wide-body Monaro clearing onlookers.

On the docks in Bombay: the cars were under Parc Ferme rules, and no one was going to get near them.

Steam cleaning cars and removing fuel from tanks were necessary steps in preparation for travel on the SS *Chusan* to Australia. The Innes Ireland, Michael Taylor and Andrew Hedges Mercedes-Benz 280 SE gets the treatment.

The SS *Chusan* came with its own set of challenges. Nine days of enforced confinement on board eased the stress of getting the cars in the hold, but disembarking the precious cargo was fraught with concern.

Lucien Bianchi and Jean-Claude Ogier cross the restart line at Perth's Gloucester Park. The Citroën team was to stay on the pace of the Fords and outlast them for a time.

Compared to the crowding during the first leg to Bombay, service points in Australia were expansive. But at key points, service crews still jostled for prime position for their teams.

Australia's outback presented a unique opportunity to race hard. The Simca team, down on power, took full advantage of the wide, open spaces.

Paddy Hopkirk landed too hard just once in Western Australia, and it cost him enough points to lose the marathon. But he didn't learn that until later, so never stopped trying.

The only 4x4 in the marathon—modified to 4x2 to comply with the race rules—was driven by a team of four from the 17/21st Lancers. The cumbersome Land Rover finished 49th.

Miss Elsie Gadd's Volvo 145 S Estate won the Ladies' Prize. Much of her team's success was due to Max Winkless and John Keran, who blew up their own Volvo early and spent the remainder of the marathon guiding the women's team home.

The smallest car in the marathon, John Sprinzel and Roy Fidler's MG Midget, came close to winning the privateers' trophy but broke on the penultimate day of competition.

Everyone was worried about kangaroos. No one had considered the emus.

Roger Clark and Ove Andersson speed through Brachina Gorge, after breaking down on approach to Port Augusta. It was a sensational comeback drive, but ultimately not enough.

Andre Welinski and Gerry Lister (Volvo 144 S) finished thirteenth, two places behind the best-placed Volvo of Ken Tubman and Jack Forrest. The two Australian-driven Swedish cars split the *Telegraph* Holden team, which came twelfth and fourteenth.

Simo Lampinen and Gilbert Staepelaere were in winning contention right up until the last stage, when their Ford Taunus 20 MRS hit a post beside a cattle grid. Teammates Herbert Kleint and Günther Klapproth came home seventh to Lampinen and Staepelaere's sixteenth.

Ian Vaughan came into his own in Australia. The quiet achiever was eleventh in Bombay and a podium placegetter by Sydney.

The magnificent Moskvitches. Four cars started, and four finished. They didn't win the teams' prize—that was taken by the Australian Ford team—but it was a superhuman effort from the Russian cars.

Telegraph Holden team leader David McKay drove the most troubled of the Monaros. He finally retired in Broken Hill—so close to home—after co-driver George Reynolds rolled the big V8 in soft sand.

After the last sensational night of competition, Lucien Bianchi and Jean-Claude Ogier were clearly in the lead—eleven points ahead of their nearest rivals. They only needed to cruise to victory.

Australia's Alec Gorshenin and Ian Bryson drove the only Mercedes-Benz sports car in the event. They were going well but retired in Moralana Creek, on the 'special' rally road through the Flinders Ranges.

On the last night, Sobieslaw Zasada and Marek Wachowski blazed through the Australian Alps in their Porsche, but their glorious challenge came too late in a field of fast-finishing professionals. They came fourth. Photograph by Bruce Thomas.

On the last truly competitive stage of the marathon, Hindmarsh Station, Simo Lampinen crashed, so he used an embankment as an inspection pit. Harry Firth, seen passing him here, would also break down during this stage when his differential finally gave up.

The only US-built car in the marathon, Sid Dickson's Rambler American, finished 46th. It had a gun-turret hole cut in the roof for news cameraman Jerry Sims. Photograph by Bruce Thomas.

Lucien Bianchi and Jean-Claude Ogier are out, due to a head-on crash during the transport stage up to Nowra. The Mini Cooper S that collided with their Citroën has been pulled to one side, clearing a narrow path through which the marathon field could pass. Both cars were extensively damaged.

The defining moment of the marathon: Andrew Cowan's Hillman Hunter squeezes through the gap to claim first prize.

Lucien Bianchi is still trapped in the wreck. Jean-Claude Ogier is talking to reporters, including Walkley Award-winner Bob Bottom (right).

The Hillman Hunter drives triumphantly into the Warwick Farm finish, with cameraman Rob McAuley perched on the boot. More than 10,000 people flooded the race track, and a live broadcast all afternoon on Frank Packer's TCN9 beamed pictures all over Australia.

NSW Premier Bob (later Sir Robert) Askin congratulates, from left to right, Andrew Cowan, Brian Coyle and Colin Malkin.

Not the last car to finish, but the one to finish with the fewest original parts left on it. Brothers Pat and Tony Downs nursed their VW 1200 the entire distance and got most of it to the finish line in 51st place.

The marathon paraded through downtown Sydney. Along George Street, Andrew Cowan leads Paddy Hopkirk and Ian Vaughan: first-, second- and third-place winners, respectively. Photograph by Roger Parsons.

Shortly afterwards, a recovered Jean-Claude Ogier and Lucette Pointet went on to win the New Caledonian Safari in another Citroën and then returned to France to marry in their native Grenoble. They became one of the most successful husband-and-wife teams in the sport.

Andrew Cowan (standing) has bought back his winning Hillman Hunter from the Scottish Museum. On occasions, he allows it to be shown—this time to author John Smailes.

instructions in its use. Tony Fall's Austin 1800 carried a .22 Beretta. Innes Ireland had a sawn-off shotgun.

Sid Dickson persuaded his co-driver to put the gun away just as the locals arrived. Instead of being hostile, they wanted to be helpful, and it was they who pushed the Rambler out of the front room of the house.

It was a long and arduous climb over the mountains to Tehran. Tired crews found it difficult to maintain concentration; visibility in the freezing conditions was stretched. Australian Geoffrey Franklin (Cortina GT) left the road and retired. It was reported that his engine had blown.

There seems to be a rule in motor sport that when good fortune abandons you, the errors only compound. Two of the most organised people in the marathon, those whose preparation would have appeared to make them immune from mistake, were suffering.

Nick Brittan left the road—again—and was towed back on. The windscreen popped out, and he and Jenny endured another long-distance drive with goggles and cold air tearing at their faces.

David McKay, downcast and embarrassed, came close to risking disqualification when he reached tyre service in Erzincan. Import rules stipulated that Dunlop account for every wheel and tyre assembly, and he'd left his broken rim at the roadside. He was about to depart with a brand-new spare he'd commandeered from the Dunlop lockup when he realised that he wouldn't have the paperwork to get through the border into Iran. Reluctantly he took off without a backup. Then he hit and killed a dog, speeding on when the owner approached him with his gun drawn.

For both Nick Brittan and McKay, the situation would only get worse.

Reg Lunn in the Falcon GT paid the price for not listening. His gearbox broke near the Turkish border, a direct result of not having made the fix recommended to him by Ford. John Gowland, Ford's Australian competitions manager, shipped another box back to him from Tehran, but it was fitted with the wrong ratios and allowed him a maximum speed of just 110 kilometres per hour. By the time he crawled into Tehran, he'd lost time, engine performance and enthusiasm—and was out.

Crossing the border from Turkey into Iran was illuminating. The road immediately improved. It was suggested that the last 100 kilometres into Tehran had been built as a freeway so the Shah and his family could enjoy their Ferraris.

Tehran had caught marathon fever. The streets were like a Grand Prix race but unstructured.

The difference between works teams and privateers was never more evident. The Philips factory had made itself available as the marathon control point, and outside was a tent city of service facilities into which the works cars could be pushed to undergo major service while their crews were taken to hotels to sleep.

Privateers instead were intimidated by the large and unruly crowds that drove dangerously and crushed perilously in on the cars when they came to a halt. The early evening Tehran experience was daunting for a crew without support.

Rootes went best of all for Andrew Cowan's team. Iran National, a local company, was assembling and selling Hillman Hunters under the name Peykan. So the arrival of the Hunter was something special. The Cowan car was met at the outskirts of the sprawling city and guided to the factory through the manic traffic. There the crew was debriefed, and mechanics set to work on their car. In the meantime, the crew was taken one floor up to a pop-up complex of showers and bedrooms, as well as a dining room where they were served a full baked meal. When it came time to leave, they were also guided out of the city. For many crews, departure was fraught with high anxiety. A wrong turn in the Tehran maze of streets could cost immense time.

The factory teams had been working overtime to resolve a growing spare-parts issue. Marathon organisation had been strong in some areas, weak in others. Customs clearance and freight transportation times had been the weaknesses. Advance crews had spent several days sorting out the mess. Rootes got its parts just two hours before Cowan arrived. It was a close run.

The *Telegraph* team almost missed out. The media charter from Sivas, due in the mid-afternoon, arrived at 7 p.m. and was shuttled to a lonely parking bay a long way from the terminal. David Lewin, McKay's recce partner, was there and borrowed a BOAC car to illegally go airside. He'd gotten to us and mounted an aluminium ladder we'd lowered just as the pilot fired up the engines to taxi elsewhere. With the spinning propeller close to his head, Lewin leapt for his life. The chase across the tarmac was farcical; the recovery of the Holden parts from the hold in packages that were sodden and collapsing equally so; and the cross-city dash in a taxi, going the wrong way through roundabouts, was dangerous. For one night I had become not a reporter but a team member.

Lewin and I got to the Holdens, especially Barry Ferguson who needed new rear brakes, just as they were preparing to leave. Those in front of the Holdens never got to tell their story to the media before they hit the road for the longest stage of all—across almost 2500 kilometres out of Iran and into Afghanistan.

No automotive event had ever attempted anything of this magnitude. Crews had 23 hours 33 minutes to cover the distance,

an average speed of 107 kilometres per hour. It wasn't an elimination stage in the manner of Sivas to Erzincan or the upcoming
super special across the feared Lataband Pass, but it was equally
daunting. This section was a reliability trial that could break cars
and crews. In a short, sharp, percussive stage, a million things
can go wrong, but they are almost predictable. On this run, crews
didn't know what they didn't know.

* * *

'You can tell they've got something to hide when they approach
you, not the other way around,' Andrew Cowan grinned. Henry
Liddon and Paul Easter, Rauno Aaltonen's two co-drivers, had
just walked up to Cowan and Coyle and inquired, nonchalantly,
which route they were taking to Kabul. It was a game of bluff.
There were two known roads across Iran—an undulating northern
route across the Alborz Mountains, so rough it could shake a car to
pieces, and a rock-hard southern route through the desert, so corrugated that it threatened to pitch a car off at every turn. Both joined
up just before the Afghan border and, depending on prevailing
conditions, one would be more secure than the other.

Des O'Dell, the Rootes manager, had heard that the southern
route was blocked, but he didn't trust the information. The day
before Cowan arrived in Tehran, O'Dell hired a local Mercedes
and went out to see for himself. He drove more than 150 kilometres into the desert to where the giant wash-out was alleged to
have occurred. It was dangerous stuff, spurred by the desperation
of the moment. He went without backup, spares, food or water.
A breakdown would have left him stranded, perhaps at great
personal risk. But the wash-out didn't exist. He drove on to make

sure, then sped back to Tehran with the news. Rootes would take the southern route.

'We told them we were going north,' Cowan said. Liddon and Easter nodded in agreement. It seemed the sensible way, they concurred. But neither team was telling the truth. British Leyland had found a third way—shorter and straighter through the centre of the other two routes. It was their secret, and they weren't letting on. It would also be, for the Aaltonen car and for Tony Fall as well, their downfall.

* * *

David McKay was hailed as first into Kabul, claiming, controversially, a special prize from the Shah. After the rocky northern route out of Iran, the big V8 had sat effortlessly at an average of more than 160 kilometres per hour on the concrete super highway across Afghanistan. The Afghan road had been built in a remarkable, totally unwilling joint venture between the Americans and the Russians. Both superpowers were courting the Afghans, and this magnificent ribbon of road seemed symbolic. The Shah had ordered his road shut for the marathon, increasing the opportunity for speed. All along the road, soldiers stood like telegraph poles one in sight of the other, a human chain of communication. They were all armed.

As McKay wound up the big Monaro, he gobbled up the competition. He caught and passed Innes Ireland, finally outdistancing the Mercedes. It was quite a race between the two open-wheeler drivers. Ego took over from common sense, and McKay had to open the Monaro right up to inch ahead. But he didn't catch Firth, and he didn't see Evan Green. Then on the outskirts of the ancient city, there they both were, at service. Firth had simply outpaced them. Green had used British Leyland's secret central route, proving it to be shorter. McKay thundered straight past. His team had no service point scheduled in Kabul. He would perform his service at the control point.

The crowds were massive. McKay had to use his air horns, lights and gentle nudges from his roo bar to get through. The Kurds, mountain people, had come down from the hills to see the marathon. It was rough country. The control in the car park of the Hotel Spinzar was surrounded by high wire with barbed wire on top. Militia, armed with clubs and whips, were struggling to hold the crowd in check. It was crowd control at its most brutal. McKay pulled into the compound, and Stuart Turner told him to go away—he was too early. McKay argued that he had nowhere to go and, besides, until the control officially opened in several hours, it was now not governed by marathon rules. He was allowed to stay.

And that's how he came to be awarded the Shah's prize of four magnificent Afghan woollen coats for being the first into Kabul. The prize was a surprise to all—determined on the spot as a PR exercise by the local administration. Harry Firth was incensed. He'd rightly been first in, but he'd parked out of sight at service. Roger Clark was equally aggrieved. He was the leader of the marathon, and surely the prize should go to the leader.

It was a valid point.

Quickly, a make-up was put in place. Clark also was awarded the Shah's coats, but because he'd reached the control first, McKay got to keep his. The papers in Sydney the next day made conflicting claims: the *Telegraph* and its associates claimed victory; the opposition Fairfax media went with Firth.

* * *

Rauno Aaltonen and Tony Fall both broke their Austin 1800s across the middle route. Since the British Leyland recce, the surface had become a washboard, so corrugated that it attacked their cars' suspension. Bound and rebound, the opposing forces that determine ride comfort fell seriously out of synchronisation. The Austins' hydrolastic suspension could not cope and neither could the struts and suspension towers that held it in place. Tony Fall's car was the first to snap. Its front suspension simply separated, giving Mike Wood and Brian Culcheth a huge moment as the car, out of control, came down from speed to lie broken on a desert sand dune. Aaltonen, speeding past, promised to send back help. As it turned out, Wood and Fall found their way into a nearby town and brought back assistance, but with the late time of more than five hours (304 points) into Kabul, they were out of contention.

Aaltonen was the next to go. The Austin landed badly, bending the suspension towers. The resourceful crew worked on a makeshift repair. The Austin 1800s carried a small hand winch, and they used it and their roo bar to rig a sling to hold the suspension in place. 'It was so tight that it was tuned to the key of C,' Liddon quipped. They made it out of the horror stretch without penalty. Evan Green loved the short cut. He'd spent years driving the corrugated roads of outback Australia, and he instinctively knew how to balance a car on the plane. There's a moment where car speed, suspension movement and road surface meet in perfect harmony. Get it right, and it's like trimming out a big powerboat. The waves become your friend, and you simply skim over the top. Paddy Hopkirk wasn't getting the technique quite as right but he, too, popped out the other end without discernible damage. At a roadside service near the Afghan border, he sent a British Leyland crew back to help the fallen.

* * *

On both the northern and southern routes, cars were breaking and struggling to get through. Thirty-two cars—effectively one-third of the field—would lose points on what had become a horror stretch. The entire Simca team lost points. Three of the four Moskvitches sacrificed time as they urged each other home. To reach Kabul without loss of points was a real achievement. Some would not make it at all.

Nick Brittan hit a truck. He was just 80 kilometres north of Tehran. The Brittans had been through hell. Their nerves were shot, they had reached the point of physical and mental exhaustion, their vision was impaired by a succession of makeshift windscreens and their judgement was awry. Brittan arrived at a corner too fast, simple as that. In the freezing cold conditions, there was ice on the road, unseen to him but perhaps obvious to a crew who were more alert. The Cortina skated forward, straight into the path of an oncoming truck. The impact was immense, frightening. It tore the front off their car, and this time there was no coming back. Nick fell over as he leapt from the car, a double victim of the ice. But their nightmare was not over. 'It took us 36 hours of negotiation with seven different government departments to clear ourselves of immediate blame,' Nick told me much later in Sydney. 'They'd confiscated our passports at the accident site, and in the small township where we'd been taken there was no sympathy for the marathon. Ford was not able to help. They'd moved on—2000 kilometres away.'

Further up the road, Peter Wilson's Ford Corsair hit a rock and flipped over. It was mountainous country, and driver Keith Dwyer reported that the car had ended up on its roof on the edge of a 20-metre drop. The crew were in a taxi, heading back to Tehran, when they came across the Brittans. Keith stayed with Nick while Jenny was taken back, shaken, into the city. Without the Wilson intervention, the Brittans' fate could have been much worse. They were not thinking clearly.

Dieter Glemser and Martin Braungart were in a strong position. Their Ford Germany Taunus 20 MRS had breezed across the Sivas–Erzincan stage with a loss of just 17 minutes, only three behind teammates Lampinen and Staepelaere. They were lying equal fourth, tied with the fastest of the Austin 1800s and only 1 point behind the fastest Citroën. They were having a dream run. And then—the engine stopped. They'd come through the roughest of the route and had enjoyed a roadside Ford service at Herat before joining the super highway. Now they were isolated, a long way from assistance. The problem was later diagnosed as a broken camshaft causing the engine to detonate. It didn't matter. They were out, and the professional division was left with one less major contender.

Leadership in the privateers changed as well. Stewart McLeod, Jack Lock and Tony Theiler were motoring happily well within themselves, when the differential of the Alfa Romeo began making noises. Finally, it locked up. A British Leyland sweep vehicle driven by Bill Price, who'd come all the way from England in a personally heroic effort in a Vanden Plas 4-litre R, found two straight black lines leading up to the back of the car where the wheels had locked solid. Bill tried to help them, but there was no solution. The Alfa went on the back of a pick-up truck and travelled to Delhi, where it was retired.

Price also picked up the *Telegraph* women. Their hydrolastic suspension line had chafed through. He was able to fix that, but his biggest contribution was in lifting not their car but their spirits. 'I came across them again at the side of the road. They were lost— even though the road was easy to follow.' Fatigue was taking its toll. He led them to Kabul.

Bobby Buchanan-Michaelson ploughed into a metre-deep ditch. The Mercedes' radiator was already vulnerable after two repairs. This time, with the water temperature gauge on red and then dropping to cold, indicating there was no water left to measure, they staggered into the town of Farah Rod to confirm they'd blown a head gasket. They were halfway between Tehran and Kabul, and they caught a taxi all the way to control to announce their retirement.

Terry Hunter and John Davenport went on three cylinders in their air-cooled Porsche. They kept feeding the hungry beast with oil, but it was only so it would deliver them to civilisation. They retired in Kabul.

Ford's flying service unit had landed on an airstrip alongside the road near Herat. Each Ford simply pulled in for a very meaningful spanner check after the long, rough blast over the mountains while the crews went inside the plane for food, a freshen up and a change of clothes. There were haves and there were have-nots.

But Ford was in trouble. Rosemary Smith popped and banged into service. Her Lotus Cortina had gone onto three cylinders. It was beyond repair at the roadside, and the service crew simply blanked off the cylinder. They'd lost the Brittans, they'd lost Söderström and Palm, and now Smith and Pointet were likely terminal. The British Army Motoring Association Lotus Cortina of David Harrison and Martin Proudlock was their get-out-of-jail card. They called on it for the all-female team. Harrison and Proudlock would stay with Smith and Pointet all the way into Kabul.

'We'd stopped at the roadside, and suddenly we were surrounded by local tribesmen,' Smith recalled much later. 'They started touching us, pulling at my hair, taking things from the car. They took two little cans of oil. They thought it was Coca Cola.' Smith and Pointet were in fear. 'Then we heard a car coming. It was Martin and David. There was a *bang, bang, bang,* and the tribesmen disappeared. Martin and David stayed with us all the way to Kabul.'

Towards the end, the Ford team attached a tow rope between the two cars to give them enough mobility. It was against the rules, but there was no way the women were going to be left alone in the desert. 'We swapped cars, too. Martin drove mine for a while in the hope he could coax more out of it,' Smith said. North of Kabul, the military men let the ladies' team loose to coast into control. 'Stuart Turner was waiting for us. He stamped the book at whatever time we were supposed to be there. A darling.'

Smith found that the only bed available was in a room with six men. 'I slept in the foyer.'

* * *

Des O'Dell was determined that if he was to support Andrew Cowan in his desire to take the southern route, he'd give him every possible backup. He sent a fuel truck into the stage well ahead of the Hunter, so that they'd have 100 octane available to them the whole way. Then, at the last minute, he commanded local mechanics to load a road car with suspension spares, so heavy that the car was bottoming, and sent them off to chase Cowan.

O'Dell was operating on a 'need to know' basis. His words were commands, not requests. As they were preparing to leave, he found one of the locals in a corner of the Tehran garage, writing a letter instead of loading the car, and exploded. The local explained that he was writing a letter to his wife. He'd come in to work on the marathon for one overnight stop. Now he was being sent on a journey of at least three days, maybe longer. She deserved to know. O'Dell was suitably humbled.

In the second Hunter, the RAF crew of David Carrington, Tony King and John Jones were in many respects forerunners for the Cowan car. Running at 45th on the road, they were starting 30 minutes ahead of the works car. On a stage of this length, they expected to be overtaken, so they'd also act as backup.

Cowan was shepherded out of Tehran, his enthusiastic local guide setting a cracking pace that left him unsettled in the chaotic traffic but saved substantial time. Cowan was even more disturbed when he saw the RAF car coming back into the city. Could the southern route be blocked after all? Had he lost time? But the reality was different. The flyers had hit a wash-out and bent their front suspension, narrowly avoiding a rollover. The backup car O'Dell had arranged to follow Cowan now sprang into action on the RAF machine and had it back in action in two hours.

Cowan drove on. In the village where they'd agreed to refuel, there was no sign of their tanker. Increasingly desperate, the crew drove back and forth through the town, but there was no tanker. Malkin and Cowan again clashed. Malkin was shouting from the back seat for them to find petrol somewhere—even to siphon it from a parked car. But that wasn't a solution. A dose of bad fuel would cripple them. They needed fuel they could trust. Cowan remembered another village 80 kilometres away and determined to chance it all on a fuel station there being open in the middle of the night. It was a huge risk, one that could have ended their marathon chances, but they took it—an economy run in the middle of a speed event. They got their fuel and later learned that the tanker had been where it said it would be—it was just not the vehicle they'd expected.

It was a small, unmarked van with a fuel drum inside, and the driver was asleep.

* * *

At Kabul control, it was getting dangerous. Police were unable to hold back crowds, and people were storming the compound. Stuart Turner was unable to set up his control desk. Instead, he used the bonnet of David McKay's parked Monaro as a temporary control table, signing in cars as best he could. Police were becoming more aggressive. On the steps of the relatively modern Spinzar Hotel— fascist architecture with huge columns, an imposing staircase and an atmosphere totally devoid of hospitality—police had set up a human barricade and were beating people back. Cameraman Rob McAuley and I were standing behind them, and Rob was filming. A boy, maybe fourteen, rushed forward, and the policeman beside us raised his whip, a cat-o'-nine-tails with ugly talons, to slash it down on the boy. Rob and I both reacted, perhaps a bit too spontaneously. I grabbed the policeman's arm and, as he turned on me, Rob used his battery-powered portable light, a high-intensity sun gun, and turned it on right in the policeman's eyes. He was blinded, and Rob and I retreated inside the hotel.

There were fewer rooms than there was demand. In the large reception hall, marathon competitors who were supposed to take major advantage of this first scheduled break in four days were grabbing what comfort they could in armchairs. There were no phones. David Benson, Ian Morton and I decided that to clear copy we had to go elsewhere. We hired a taxi and headed across town to the British embassy. In the madness of the moment, a police VW gave chase. Our driver, wisely we thought, was disinclined to stop. Instead, we kept going faster. My companions swore shots were fired. I wasn't so sure, but the relief when we reached the British compound and the gates slammed shut behind us was immense. Later that night, we snuck back to the Spinzar.

* * *

Gunnar Palm snuck out of Kabul at the same time. He'd rented an old Morris Minor 1000, and he was off to do a last-minute recce. The Lataband Pass was only a little less than 80 kilometres long. Time allowed was exactly 1 hour. And yet every one of the lead competitors knew that right there their future in the marathon could be decided. The stage would be run in the pre-dawn with the early morning light threatening clear vision. Either dark or light is good. Half-light is deceptive.

Palm came back with good news. The goat track with its huge, tyre-eating rocks was rough but not as much as some earlier recces had indicated. The Afghan authorities had pulled out all stops to make their country's experience the best of all. The first hint had been at the border with Iran. There were two customs controls. The Iranian side was basic, clinically efficient, certainly determined not to waste precious time. The Afghans had laid out the red carpet. It was on top of the sand, and all competitors had to do was walk along it, getting their passports stamped and, if they needed to, change money. They were also handed a single sheet of welcome. 'Dear competitor,' it read, 'the people of Afghanistan welcome you to our country, which you are just crossing now.' Among the guidance it gave was: 'From Kabul you leave the asphalt road to go via the Lataband Pass, a treacherous rough road, till you join the highway again at Sarobi. The road would be good but the Rishman Tangi—Silk Route—has treacherous bends, which you have to traverse with caution.'

'Would be good'—what did they mean? The explanation came further down: 'The Lataband Pass, described as "enough to shatter the illusions of the toughest competitor" by your organisers, has been attended to which is not as bad as described [sic]. We apologise to have done it because your organisers had chosen it for its ruggedness. We hope they would not sue us for our playing foul.'

There it was—in black and white. The Afghanis had put a blade over the Lataband Pass, taking the edge off its treachery. But could what they said be trusted? That night, Gunnar Palm saw several other cars on the mountain pass, among them taxis, their drivers cowering in fear as the marathon entrants tested their mettle.

There was a long way round to the town of Sarobi. Service crews and media took it to join Stuart Turner at the control desk set at the roadside, just over a blind brow. Modern rallies insist on a flying finish so that cars can flash through at high speed. Their time on stage is electronically recorded as they pass through light beams, then there are 200 to 300 metres to slow down before arriving at a control desk to have their time ratified and their road book notated. Not so in the marathon. You were on the clock until your book was stamped so, in a super-stage where time could be lost, the co-driver needed to be a sprinter, door open, belts off and ready to run to the control desk to hit the official clock.

At 4.42 a.m., with darkness all around him, Bill Bengry sped out of the Kabul control. Harry Firth would be only a minute behind him, and this time Bengry was determined to be in the lead when they hit the single lane. More so than Sivas–Erzincan, the Lataband Pass was a technical stage, more suited to the nimble Cortina than the lumbering Falcon. Firth would only hold Bengry up.

They were virtually side by side as they hit the trail, but Bengry held his nerve and his line. With rocks flailing from the tyres of the Cortina, Firth was forced to drop back, looking for a passing place. He couldn't find one. Bengry arrived at control in 69 minutes—a loss of 9 points. Firth also lost 9 points and was crying foul. Bengry wouldn't let him pass. He could have been faster.

Bengry's time was truly sensational. But so was that of Bob Holden, starting from position 63 in the Volvo. He, too, lost only 9 minutes. With McLeod out of the marathon, Holden's inspired run across the Lataband had confirmed him, cumulatively, as the fastest of the privateers. But he would hold the lead for only another section before a crash put him out.

After Sivas, all eyes were on Roger Clark. He was expected to be fastest, and he was—but only equally so. Paddy Hopkirk and Lucien Bianchi both lifted to the task, carving past cars in front to lose just 5 minutes each, the same as Clark; Lampinen in the Taunus, perhaps a little put off by Glemser's retirement, was another minute behind. Bob Neyret, this time right on form, equalled Lampinen, only 1 minute behind teammate Bianchi. Andrew Cowan, carrying minimum weight—including a light fuel load sufficient only for the stage—was on a 6-point deficit as well.

The Lataband Pass stage was one of those motor-sport moments that remain forever etched in your memory. Standing up stage from control, you'd hear them before you saw them, exhaust notes on and off again as drivers fought the switchback bends. Then you'd see their lights, flashing through the passes, even in the early morning as the pre-dawn light began to fill the sky. And then a noise, unheard before, like you'd imagine rapid-fire gunshots to sound, and you realised it was the rocks being flung from the tyres, cannoning off the cliff faces. As the light came up, you'd see you were not alone. All around you were grey figures, the inhabitants of this remote land, some standing, many squatting, silently watching. They'd taken positions on rocky promontories, looking down on the cars passing them by. Anyone male, no matter his age, seemed to be armed.

At the control desk, officials and spectators, including David McNicoll, suddenly fled. Rob Slotemaker had arrived over the brow 50 metres away without brakes. The king of drift threw the tiny DAF into a semi-controlled slide and skidded to a halt just past the control desk. 'That's the way I always come into control when I'm in a hurry,' he joked.

* * *

Back in Kabul, David McKay had struck another problem. His car had been parked in the freezing overnight cold within the Parc Ferme—the secure area for entrants' cars in which no mechanical work can be performed. In London, the crew had disconnected the automatic choke to give the Monaro better breathing. To fire up the V8 meant that the crew had to lift the bonnet and manually activate the choke. But Parc Ferme rules prevented them touching the car. They checked out and pushed the car away from control before beginning their starting procedure. McKay wanted to make up the lost time in the first kilometre. Around a corner he hit a kerb, putting his wheels out of alignment, making driving across the Lataband even more hazardous, especially on left-handers.

His 'handbrake' came in the form of Alec Gorshenin in the Mercedes coupe. Gorshenin steadfastly refused to give way to McKay. 'We lost 20 minutes,' McKay said at control. 'It should only have been ten.' He was quite right in his assessment. Eddie Perkins, multiple winner of the Round Australia Trial, and Barry Ferguson, New South Wales rally champion, in the two Monaro team cars each lost 11 minutes. Ian Vaughan lost 12 in the Falcon GT; his teammate Bruce Hodgson, 18, having stopped to replace wheel nuts that had popped off one wheel. His solution was to take one nut from each of the other wheels.

The harder you went, the more you risked punctures. The rocks were jagged, and a slide across them could rip a tyre. Sobieslaw Zasada dropped 12 minutes and arrived in control with his left-hand rear tyre torn to pieces on the rim. Gerry Lister in the Volvo reached control with news that Clark could have been faster. Lister's tyre tore off the rim as Clark came up to pass him: 'I had no option but to press on for another 6 kilometres until I could find a place to stop,' he said. It's not as if there was much passing room. The choice in many places was a cliff wall or a sheer drop. Gelignite Jack Murray, 8 minutes down with Evan Green brilliant at the wheel, delivered his well-worn cliché: 'The drop was so great, my clothes would have been out of fashion by the time I hit the bottom.'

Just 7 minutes separated the top fourteen finishers. All were professionals except Bengry and Bob Holden.

With two elimination stages complete, and not another one scheduled before Bombay, Roger Clark and Ove Andersson extended their lead to 9 points with a total 11 lost, from Lampinen–Staepelaere on 20 points; Bianchi–Ogier, 21; Hopkirk–Nash–Poole, 22; Aaltonen–Liddon–Easter, 24; Cowan–Coyle–Malkin, 27; and Firth–Hoinville–Chapman, 29.

Two cars had come around the long way. The *Telegraph*'s *Tortoise* and Rosemary Smith's ailing Lotus Cortina had been persuaded that the Lataband Pass was no place to be slow. The risk, with cars pushing to pass, was too great.

They arrived the wrong way at control, and Stuart Turner rushed at them, stopping them before they entered the control zone. Entering control the wrong way carries immediate exclusion. Failing to report to control carries a 'fine' of 1440 points. Turner could have played by the rules and checked them in, but he wanted to be fair. He persuaded both to cop the fine and remain in the event.

One car, parked in Kabul when we left, didn't make it at all. The Italians Baghetti and Bassi had lost their marathon documents. Instead of heading east they went west, back into Iran in search of their papers. They were seen again in Bombay, still without their road book, and they were refused passage on the *Chusan*.

* * *

Kabul without the marathon was a cold and lonely place.

Ian Morton and I drove back around from Sarobi to file copy before joining our aircraft.

There were no crowds, no police: life had resumed in the dusty streets, and horses and camels mixed freely. Covering a marathon is no way to see the world, but for a moment we were tourists in a strange land.

We walked into the vast Spinzar lobby, and it was empty—a hundred seats or more spread around the gigantic high-ceilinged space. It was then we saw him, sitting alone in the centre of the room. His eyes were red rimmed and his face aghast, way beyond tiredness.

Robbie Uniacke, co-driver in the most upbeat car of all, the Pan Australian Unit Trust BMW 2000, the entry of money managers and optimists, had just received word from England. His wife, Sally, had been driving home from the start at Crystal Palace on Sunday. There'd been a car crash, and she had been killed.

We were moving at such a pace that the news had only just caught up.

We sat with him for a while. There wasn't much we could say. His teammates, Colin Forsyth and James Rich, had driven on in the hope of being allowed to continue with only two in the car.

We had a marathon to cover so we, too, left him there, to find his own way home.

Sarobi to Delhi

Distance: 1158 kilometres

Time allowed: 17 hours 55 minutes

Approximate average speed: 66 kilometres per hour

Delhi to Bombay

Distance: 1405 kilometres

Time allowed: 22 hours 51 minutes

Approximate average speed: 62 kilometres per hour

14

The Way to Bombay

THERE WAS A LOT OF OPTIMISM in the air. In Sarobi at the end of the Lataband Pass, locals were throwing flowers at the cars, not rocks. The route chart said bitumen all the way to Bombay, 2563 kilometres away and, with just under 41 hours to make it, the average speed required was only 63 kilometres per hour. It was Saturday morning, the sun had risen on the brightest of days and the Khyber Pass, the most evocative of all of the landmarks on this ancient Silk Road—the trade route for centuries—could be driven at tourist speed.

But by the time the marathon reached the Bombay docks, two crews were in hospital after serious, life-threatening crashes, another four cars had been eliminated, and nerves, already raw and on edge as a result of extreme fatigue, had reached the point of no return. Wars were breaking out within cars over things as trivial as when to use air horns, and between cars—over serious things such as following distances—on roads that were the most dangerous the marathon had presented. It was no exaggeration: lives were at risk.

Rosemary Smith reversed over the steepest point of the Khyber Pass, the 50-kilometre ravine that links Afghanistan to Pakistan in the north-east corner of the Afghan kingdom (it would become a republic eleven years later). Down to three cylinders, she found her Lotus Cortina was labouring, and to avoid putting more, perhaps fatal, pressure on it she remembered her father's advice that reverse gear is always the lowest. So she turned the car around and backed it up the steepest slopes.

She was surprised to find Australia's Channel Nine news crew at the summit. John Hart and cameraman Lloyd Coulson had forgone the race across the Lataband Pass in order to capture magic vision of the marathon crossing the Khyber. They'd gained special permission to go in before dawn, carrying two armed guards, one perched on the bonnet of their car, to warn off bandits who still roamed the area. Crews were happy to stop and do interviews. They thought the last elimination phase on the Asian continent had finished, and now they had only to prepare for Australia.

Driving under the Khyber Pass gates, in the path of Genghis Khan, every competitor received a gift, a bulbous horn of the type used by local herdsmen. Crossing the Khyber was far more ceremonial than competitive. Bill Bengry's lead car, number one on the road, was regarded with reverence. Bengry was asked—and could not refuse—to carry a major dignitary from the area with him through the Pass. It was a great honour for both.

Even the border crossing presented a spirit of goodwill. Marathon organisers had experienced great difficulty, taking up to six hours to cross. Now the Pakistanis set out to beat the Afghanis. Every competitor passed straight through. But it proved to be a highway to hell. There were riots in Pakistan—nothing to do with the marathon, but political unrest. The marathon added fuel to the fire of discontent. Crowds that had terrified drivers on the way into Kabul magnified tenfold through the densely populated areas of Pakistan. Suddenly, there were reports passing from car to car of collisions with spectators as crowds got out of hand.

Innes Ireland passed by a bus, surrounded by an ugly crowd of young men. 'They were stoning the bus, with people still inside it,' he said. The arrival of the marathon Mercedes took them by surprise, and it was only at the last moment they turned their attention to it. The car's windscreen was shattered, and driver Michael Taylor suffered several cuts to his face, requiring treatment. They sped on, wisely not wanting to stop. A short while down the road, they came across another stoning—this time a truck. Taylor put his foot down and charged past.

In fairness, there was perhaps no threat intended to the marathon. There were occasional banners welcoming 'The Magnificent Men in their Machines', but to the marathon crews, intent on their competition, the mass of people was threat personified. 'I rounded a corner at 110 kilometres per hour to find an army truck stalled in our path and the roadside completely covered with spectators,' Laurie Graham said from his hospital bed (he'd taken over the driving duties in the Bob Holden AMOCO Volvo 142 S). 'My choice was the truck or the people, so I took the truck. The local police told me later I should have aimed for the crowd. Apparently, a truck is worth more to them than a few human lives.'

Graham and Holden were severely injured. Holden needed major plastic surgery and was in the Delhi Hospital for more than two weeks after having his facial structure and particularly his nose rebuilt by a surgeon who had only that week returned from residency in a leading British hospital. He was 'fortunate' the crash happened in India and close to New Delhi. His medical expenses and his welfare were both seen to by a maharajah who befriended the two drivers.

Only 500 kilometres before, Holden and Graham had been greeted with genuine enthusiasm at the Pakistan–India border. The marathon had brought a seemingly willing easing to the tensions between the two nations. When the Pakistanis were short of power to light their control desk, the Indians had run a lead across the no-man's-land between the two borders. But it was a tenuous truce. Swarthy and goatee-bearded Andre Welinski had been given a woollen fez hat in Pakistan and wore it proudly even after he crossed the border. 'The crowd was getting very ugly, and we couldn't understand why,' Gerry Lister said. 'Then we realised they thought he was Pakistani.' Lister had been struck on the chest with a thrown rock aimed at Welinski.

It was important not to stop for fear of being swamped. When slower, more tentative cars eased to a near halt, genuinely concerned for the welfare of the crush of people, competitors behind would blast their air horns. Bruce Hodgson had found the best way through was to open and shut his front doors 'like a giant bird flapping its wings'.

Andrew Cowan came close to being involved. Near New Delhi, the Mercedes-Benz 280 SL of Alec Gorshenin hit a cyclist. Ian Bryson was driving, and Gorshenin filmed the rider going over his roof. Cowan was close behind in an unintended convoy with the

SAAB of privateer Alister Percy and Major John Hemsley's Rover 2000 TC. All four cars came to a screeching halt, but police waved them on. Gorshenin was distressed, because with his medical training he may have been able to assist.

The control check at Delhi was necessarily short. Although a service area had been established, it was deluged with people. Stopping, even for a tyre change, was regarded as hazardous. 'Because we were travelling so slowly, our spark plugs had fouled,' David Johnson, in the Holden Monaro, said. 'We were forced to stop to change them, and we chose a place where miraculously there did not appear to be a soul. But even as Doug Chivas pulled out the first plug, red hot, it disappeared into the hands of an Indian who had suddenly materialised. All eight plugs went the same way to a huge crowd which just appeared.'

Max Winkless and John Keran caught up with the marathon at New Delhi, presenting organisers with a problem. They'd checked 74 cars through control bound for Bombay, where the SS *Chusan* had room for just 70. All the forecasts of 50 or fewer reaching the halfway point had exploded in a bliss bomb of determination. The organisers, pleased on the one hand, were embarrassed on the other. Competitors, like homing pigeons, were finding their way to Bombay. If they couldn't arrive by marathon car, then they'd get there by other means. Embarking on the *Chusan* had become a quest. Gunnar Palm and Bengt Söderström had jumped on the press plane because their own Ford plane was full. Max Stahl and David Seigle-Morris, Nick and Jenny Brittan, Stewart McLeod, Jack Lock and Tony Theiler had used a combination of taxis and aeroplanes. Giancarlo Baghetti was still using his own Lancia, but of all of them he'd be turned away.

Roger Masson and his co-driver, Jean Py, in the Simca 1100 were the first to offer a solution: they crashed. They'd approached a bridge far too fast, and at 140 kilometres per hour they'd become airborne, wrapping their Simca around an immovable post. It was a silly accident. There were no spectators involved and no time to be made up. Incredibly for 1968, a helicopter airlifted them to hospital, where they were cleared of serious injury. They were no longer looking for passage on the *Chusan*. At least Ronald Rogers and Alec Sheppard, British amateur back markers who started in position 96, could claim to have made crowd avoidance a priority. Just outside Agra, they chose a truck over people and, after the initial collision, rolled their Ford Cortina 1600 E down a two-metre embankment. Rogers broke his collarbone. There were now 72 green bottles hanging on the marathon organisers' wall, and the marathon still had to pass through the tightest crush of all.

'Indore turned on the worst street-scenes of the whole route,' David McKay told me on his tape. 'The law was completely ineffective against the thousands who jammed the road ahead of us. David Liddle was driving, and where he had been cautious and slow yesterday, today he was fired with the desire to get to Bombay at all costs. Liddle hooked the lever into second and kept the car at around 50 kilometres per hour, headed directly into the mob. You would have to experience it yourself to believe the sight and to feel some of the resentment of these people, who beat the car with sticks, threw stones at it, broke off the aerial and spat at us. Only once did we have a moment and that was when we got tangled up with a pushbike that was a little slow getting out of the way. We had to back off it, and Liddle made a mental note that pushbikes were better avoided.'

The London–Sydney Marathon had been wonderfully bold. It had already gone further than any speed trial before it. It had conquered roads and climatic conditions that were beyond the experience of all who had entered. It had tested cars and their drivers past known limits of endurance. There was a lot of which to be proud. Yet in its last 40 hours, it had entered another world— that of humanity.

The marathon had imposed itself on an entire population. It had assumed the right to pass through at speed and with impunity. That no one was known to have been killed was, in the circumstances, a major miracle. There were rumours, but they were never proved. There were reports from crews of 'hitchhikers' riding on the marathon cars like train surfers do now—putting their lives at risk for the thrill. Ford's Ken Chambers said he looked in the rear-vision mirror to see an uninvited passenger on the boot lid. He accelerated hard then braked violently. When he looked again, the person was gone. Roger Clark reported an old shoe wedged under the grab handle of his boot lid. Had he had a joy-rider? Harry Firth was certain he'd run over feet. 'There was nothing you could do to avoid them,' he said. 'If you stopped, you could bank on sitting there for hours while your car was literally pulled to pieces around you.'

Innes Ireland, Michael Taylor and Andrew Hedges were the first car into Bombay. They claimed to set a record. They had left New Delhi at 1 a.m., and they arrived at Ballard Dock on the Bombay wharves at 3 p.m., covering 1405 kilometres at an average speed of 100.4 kilometres per hour. The previous record, unofficial, and a full two hours slower, had been set many years before by a maharajah in a Bugatti, complete with motorcycle outriders. Ireland's claim would remain unofficial as well for obvious reasons.

They were sent away to service their car; control would not open until late that night. There was a flurry of servicing. Once the cars moved into the dockyard, they were regarded as being in Parc Ferme, untouchable, and that lockout would continue all the way to Fremantle in Western Australia. Although the cars would travel on the same ship as the crews, there would be no sneaking below to service in the hold. The only relaxation of the no-work rule was an hour allowed to drain the cars of fuel and to steam clean them so they would comply with Australian import regulations.

It was prudent to get as much of the serious work out of the way in Bombay as possible. Decisions depended on the availability of spare parts, the fitness of service crews—in the case of many of the privateers, their own state of preparedness to work—and, to a degree, the mental alertness of the team managers. A decision taken in haste now could have dire consequences in Australia. John Gowland, Ford's team manager, argued with his lead driver, Harry Firth. The Falcons were scheduled to have rear axle and drive-train assembly changes in Bombay. It was preventative maintenance. Lying seventh, tenth and eleventh, the Ford team were in good spirits. Even Roger Clark had praised the drivers of the big Fords for their pace over the technical super special stages that so much favoured cars like his. The Ford team were confident of their performance in Australia. But Firth declined the axle change. 'There's nothing wrong. Don't touch it,' he told Gowland.

'You can't argue with Harry, especially when he thinks he's in charge,' Gowland said. He should have pulled rank; the fact that he didn't rankles him even half a century later.

The *Telegraph*'s Holden team elected to leave major work on their cars until they hit the safe shores of Australia. They'd been operating with minimal external assistance, and they did not want to risk a major change now that could not easily be reversed in Australia. British Leyland were, uncharacteristically, in some trouble. The cars had beaten the service crews into Bombay, and the drivers undertook their own service. They needed nothing more than a good wash and a spanner check, but a local mechanic cross-threaded Evan Green's sump plug and broke it. With no time or ability to repair it, the sump plug was glued in place and the car was pushed on board the *Chusan*.

Ford serviced in Bombay. They were down to four cars to fettle. Rosemary Smith received a new cylinder head. The Fords had been fast but fragile. All four cars received new suspension struts, weakened from the hard pounding across Asia. Citroën did virtually nothing, and the Porsche drivers undertook their own service. Both knew they would be joined in Australia by works teams. Huschke von Hanstein would come to Australia for Porsche. René Cotton had already elected to fly ahead to meet with Citroën's east-coast agent, Ken Murden, to arrange support vehicles and to recce the course. He'd pick up as a valued assistant Jim Reddiex, Citroën's concessionaire in Queensland, who would go on to become one of the company's most successful international rally competitors.

The most important service undertaken in Bombay was that on Andrew Cowan's Hillman Hunter. Car speed was unlikely to win the marathon for Rootes. Iron-clad management would be the team's point of difference. The plan they'd laid down at the start was holding up well. Cowan, Coyle and Malkin were sitting in sixth position, 16 points behind Roger Clark, which was a little disappointing, but they viewed Clark as a firecracker. He could go off at any second. Their equal focus was on the Austin 1800s and the Citroëns—with a big saver on Jackson and Chambers in the second Ford.

Rootes had placed its service at Ballard Dock to maximise the time its service crew of four had with the car. They'd brought with them the second Hunter, which had been left in Bombay from the recce. It was like a motor-racing pit stop. Within ten minutes, the axle was out and the front and rear shock absorbers and suspension struts had been removed for replacement. Most importantly, a new cylinder head was placed on the car. Cowan had been running a low-compression cylinder head across Europe and Asia to deal with the variation in fuel quality. Rootes suspected that the failure to do exactly what they had done was the reason Ford had been having their problems. They had tried too early to be too fast. Fuel consistency in Australia was going to be much better, so the new cylinder head, developed by specialist tuner Holbay to provide greater horsepower, was going on. The old head was examined closely for hot spots of wear. There were none. The plan had worked. There was a small crack in the Hillman's windscreen that could grow on a rough, corrugated Australian road, so they replaced that, too. Then they went through the car methodically with a spanner, and properly—unlike Evan Green's hapless service crew—torque-tightened every nut. Cowan took the car for a run up and down the dock, looking for problems, before he checked it in on time.

Roger Clark and Ove Andersson were presented with the Carreras Guards Trophy and a cheque for £2000 for leading the marathon to Bombay—and then they were very nearly excluded from the event. Inexplicably, the Lotus Cortina's registration papers had gone missing. They had their licences and their marathon road books but, without proof of ownership and registration, the car was not welcome on the ship. Team manager Henry Taylor arranged for it to be flown out from the UK. It was presented just 45 minutes before loading time.

Officials had intended to give a Private Entrants Award, sponsored by P&O. They elected it would go to John Tallis and Paul Coltelloni. Their Volvo 123 GT had arrived in Bombay down 57 points, with losses of 38 and 19 points in the two super special stages. Michael Taylor, Innes Ireland and Andrew Hedges were incensed. They'd lost only 50 points, accumulated from 32 and 18 in the two special stages. The impasse was presenting itself as a major embarrassment. Taylor had entered privately, but organisers fully recognised the car had come from Mercedes in Stuttgart and had received Mercedes service across the route. For the sake of peace and propriety, Tommy Sopwith tried to get Taylor, the owner of the car, to back down. He wouldn't and reluctantly—because a gentleman is always unwilling to make a fuss—entered a protest that could not, according to marathon rules, be heard until the end of the event in Sydney. To save some face, the single trophy was presented to both teams in a ceremony at the Bombay Motor Club.

The argument again raised a serious issue—the definition of a private entrant and the distinction between a true privateer and a works entry. Thirty-three entries had been placed in the marathon in the name of an individual who was listed as the entrant. Another 32 non-works crews had entered under company names. Some of those companies were owned by the entrant or were small sponsors. Because they were sponsored, did that make these entrants any less 'private'? It was a totally perplexing situation, and everyone ran a mile from it. Did Bill Bengry, a former British Rally Champion and garage owner, sponsored by a retreading firm, have any more or less right to private status than John Tallis? If he was deemed a private entrant, he would have claimed equal rights to the trophy along with Ken Tubman and Jack Forrest, who were driving a Volvo 144 S on behalf of a Perth television station. Both had arrived in Bombay with a loss of 47 points. On the other hand, Sobieslaw Zasada and Bob Neyret had entered under their own names. Zasada's Porsche had lost 40 points; Neyret's Citroën, 42. Obviously, both cars had been works prepared, and organisers had excluded them from private-entrant status on that basis. But it wasn't clear and it wasn't right. In Bombay, the general consensus was that the best thing to do was ignore it. Australia would most likely sort out the situation organically, on the road.

It was worth at least looking at the relative performance of the various divisions, no matter how you defined them. In the private-entrant category, fourteen of the 33 entries had retired by the time the marathon reached Bombay. Of the sponsored non-works entries, there had been eight retirements from 32 starters, and four of the 25 teams that were entered by manufacturers had retired. There were eight military teams entered under either regimental or armed services motoring-club banners, and all had soldiered on to Bombay.

The restart in Perth would be according to the order of points lost. For the first time, the quick teams, which had been faced at every regroup with a struggle to get through the field, would now be able to start in their approximate order of performance capability. Roger Clark and Ove Andersson in the Lotus Cortina would be first away, instead of 48th. They would be followed by Gilbert Staepelaere and Simo Lampinen in the Ford Taunus and then the Citroën of Lucien Bianchi and Jean-Claude Ogier.

The Austin 1800s of Paddy Hopkirk, Tony Nash and Alec Poole, and of Rauno Aaltonen, Henry Liddon and Paul Easter would be next away in front of Andrew Cowan, Brian Coyle and Colin Malkin in the Hillman Hunter. All of them Europeans.

The Australians would be led by Harry Firth, Graham Hoinville and Gary Chapman (Ford Falcon GT) in seventh and Evan Green, George Shepheard and Gelignite Jack Murray (Austin 1800) in eighth. Eric Jackson and Ken Chambers were right where they needed to be, backing up Roger Clark from ninth, ahead of the other works Ford Falcons of Bruce Hodgson with Doug Rutherford, and Ian Vaughan with Bob Forsyth and Jack Ellis. The first Holden was that of Barry Ferguson, David Johnson and Doug Chivas, tied on points with Vaughan. In the top eleven there were four big Aussie V8s, and there was a lot of conjecture about how quick they'd be once they were on home soil. If you discounted the mercurial Clark, just 17 points separated the top ten behind him. He had a buffer to play with, albeit slight, but most people thought that was not Clark's way. He'd go for broke from the off.

You had to look back to position 17, Bill Bengry, to find a car not prepared by a factory, and to position 22 to discover the organiser's nomination for the first private entrant, John Tallis and Paul Coltelloni in the Volvo. John Sprinzel and Roy Fidler in the tiny MG Midget were in position 24, exactly one-third into the field, with a loss of 66 points. There was so much talent and expectation bristling in that top 33 per cent that Australia was shaping up as a sprint beyond compare. As for Clark, there wouldn't be a lot of percentage in holding back.

Marathon organisers let 73 cars on the SS *Chusan*. The rules allowed for passage for the first 70. The final two to arrive,

David van Lennep's DAF and Duncan Bray's Lotus Cortina, had both lost more than 10,000 points and were totally out of contention. But they were standing on the dock, bruised and battle weary. Sopwith could not in conscience turn them away. 'We'll get them on board if we have to hang them from the yardarms,' he said. He made no such concession for Baghetti and Bassi. They'd failed to locate their road book, had missed the controls across Asia, and were excluded from passage.

Privately, Colin Forsyth and James Rich arranged for their BMW 2000 to travel on the *Chusan*. They were no longer in the event and would not face the restart in Perth, but they were determined to get to Sydney. As a mark of compassion, Tommy Sopwith did not oppose their plan.

Keith Schellenberg arrived in Bombay in his Bentley but did not seek passage for the car. He'd driven on with Norman Barclay after the injured Patrick Lindsay had returned to England. John Jeffcoat and David Dunnell in the Hy-Mac-sponsored Austin 1800 were in a similar predicament without their third driver, Graham White. The unlikely pairing had motored all the way to Bombay. While Schellenberg shipped the Bentley home, Dunnell called his sponsor who agreed that he should attempt to beat the record for driving solo from Bombay to London. He did it in ten days—much slower than marathon pace, taking two days off the record—and arrived home on Christmas Eve.

* * *

We boarded the SS *Chusan* at the turn of the tide. It was a metaphor. The marathon would bring great change to the *Chusan*. People took long sea voyages because they wanted to, not because they lacked an alternative. They dressed for dinner, promenaded on the open decks, took deck chairs with rugs and were treated with polite civility by their stewards. Their clothing and the essentials for an extended voyage were sent ahead in trunks and laid out in their staterooms, awaiting their arrival. There were 200 such first-class passengers on the *Chusan* when the London–Sydney Marathon invaded mid-voyage. We were all booked in first and, unlike our more genteel travelling companions, we were all operating on high levels of adrenalin.

To be fair, some of the marathoners had joined in the spirit of their grand adventure. Bobby Buchanan-Michaelson, Michael Taylor and Keith Schellenberg had had their essential accoutrements taken on board in London and had dined on the ship there to ensure all was in place. Their wives had flown from the UK to join them on the nine-day voyage to Australia. It would be such fun. But for most others of the marathon crew, the *Chusan* was some form of seaborne purgatory, an enforced respite to be endured. Most had never travelled so slowly. Still, as it was mandatory, best to endure it as well as possible. 'Rosemary, don't go in the pool, you'll lose your bikini.'

'Well, what will be, will be,' the bright-eyed Irish driver replied.

It was generally agreed that what happened on the *Chusan* stayed on the *Chusan*. That covenant couldn't last. There were too many media on board and their newspapers were hungry for daily bulletins from the ship's meagre and costly communications. A special rate had been negotiated between P&O and the *Express* and *Telegraph* to make the transmissions affordable. P&O even put a PR person on board to maximise their opportunity for positive coverage. It was a challenging assignment.

The *Chusan* was a two-class ship—first and steerage, split roughly half and half: 500 up front and 500 down the back, with the same number of crew to serve and separate. Much was made of sorties by marathoners into the less-refined and perhaps more liberated tourist sector. A small steering committee was set up, comprising marathon organisers, the ship's captain and, of all people, David Benson, to manage a situation that in its own little microcosm was threatening to tear down the very fabric of polite society. It missed the point entirely. The marathoners and those in steerage were quite happy for the ship to live by the rules of the swinging sixties. It was the entrenched first-class passengers, entrapped in their fantasy world of titanic sea voyages, who were aggrieved. And even then only some of them. I dined one evening, by gilt-edged invitation, at the captain's table with the proprietor of an Australian newspaper chain and his vivacious wife; he in his dinner suit, she in something silk, the captain in his dress whites, me in my only string tie. The tone of the conversation led me to believe that but for propriety she would have most preferred to join the fun.

Gelignite Jack Murray and, in a more subtle way, Graham Hoinville did their best to destabilise the European opposition. Murray piled on stories of yowies, a nocturnal Australian cousin of the yeti, so large and so terrifying that it had caused whole communities of Aboriginal people to disappear without trace. Its footprints could create massive holes in the road into which a speeding marathon car could fall. Hoinville told stories of the hairy-nosed wombat, a renowned ditch-digger. Somehow their tall tales became intermingled and were largely dismissed. A pity, because Hoinville's were true—as several competitors would discover.

Kangaroos commanded universal attention. Whether they were Gelignite Jack size: 'Honestly, I hit one on the first REDeX Trial. I thought it was dead, so I dressed it in my jacket and stood it up at the front of the car for a photograph and that's when it woke up and took off with my jacket and my wallet.' Or whether they were the rock wallabies that dance and skip their way around the Australian Alps, there wasn't a European driver on board not filled with dread.

Dev Dvoretsky worked his magic on the European media. A Perth native with a Chips Rafferty drawl and a laconic look on life, he convinced them and himself that they were all facing certain death if precautions were not taken. When the ship docked, he led a land party straight to an army disposals store, a phenomenon of the 1960s, to buy slouch hats, webbing belts, tin canteens, army knives, blowfly nets and, most importantly, supplies of corks and string to hang from their hats to ward off things that sting. The international media corps was instantly recognisable at the restart in the Perth CBD.

Stewart McLeod had come onboard minus his car but carrying a route chart that he guaranteed provided a faster way through the Flinders Ranges and was, he said, the key to marathon victory. His asking price started high and diminished as we approached Fremantle. Ultimately, he gave it away—only to later learn that his route had been discovered anyway. But McLeod's spruiking kept the urgency alive. It was all too easy to be brought off the boil by this imposed interlude. As we approached the edge of the Roaring Forties, a rough sea passage made far more tolerable by the *Chusan's* state-of-the-art stabilisers, there were gatherings of marathoners. Self-help groups were setting up. The Moskvitch team had formed an alliance with the Polish Porsche drivers, Zasada and Wachowski.

And the Ford teams, which had been distant with each other, were holding strategy meetings. Ian Vaughan, lying equal eleventh, was aware that there was a gap in Ford's knowledge of the upcoming Lake King section out of Perth. He borrowed some of the media's radio-telephone time to call ahead to Fremantle to speak to team manager John Gowland. When he got there, Gowland had a light aircraft waiting to fly him to Southern Cross so he could drive the section. With some degree of irony, he used a Holden borrowed from the local dealer. He flew back to Perth just in time to make the restart.

All across Australia, service crews and tyre and oil companies were setting up depots. There were more than 30 points identified as critical to replenishment. Even then, they missed the flashpoints where a crew could be stranded for hours waiting for help to arrive. In broad terms, the competitors were adopting the attitude of 'no more Mr Nice Guy'. A Dunlop crew in Southern Cross came to blows with a Goodyear crew who tried to set up on top of them.

There were 5664 kilometres to cover across Australia in 67 essentially nonstop hours. That's an average speed of 84 kilometres per hour. There would be fourteen special stages, and four of them would definitely be elimination super specials, impossible to be cleaned. From the time the flag dropped, the next three days would be flat out, a time of maximum attack and dirty tricks, of intended baulking and misdirection.

Tension was rising on the *Chusan*. On Friday, 13 December, as it came alongside the Fremantle docks, certain lead drivers were surprised to see that their works teams had flown out their wives. There they were, waving from shore, almost face to face as the ship approached the wharf. There was a hasty reshuffling of deckchairs onboard.

'What did you think of the nine days at sea, Paddy?' a television reporter asked.

'It's a great advertisement for air travel.'

Not exactly what P&O wanted to hear.

Perth to Youanmi

Distance: 547 kilometres
Time allowed: 7 hours
Approximate average speed: 78 kilometres per hour

Youanmi to Marvel Loch

Distance: 393 kilometres
Time allowed: 4 hours 3 minutes
Approximate average speed: 98 kilometres per hour

Marvel Loch to Lake King

Distance: 192 kilometres
Time allowed: 1 hour 59 minutes
Approximate average speed: 97 kilometres per hour

Lake King to Ceduna

Distance: 1442 kilometres
Time allowed: 14 hours 52 minutes
Approximate average speed: 97 kilometres per hour

15

Australia

MISS AUSTRALIA, SUZANNE McLELLAND, was thrilled to be asked to flag away the restart of the greatest motoring adventure of modern times just a day after they'd arrived, battle scarred, in Fremantle. In the crowd at Perth's Gloucester Park, on the country's far west coast, almost unnoticed stood Australia's 1962 Miss Universe, Tania Verstak. The statuesque Ms Verstak was Australia's beauty queen of queens. She popularised and could well, if she wished, have patented the genre. But the limelight was being taken by the Western Australian premier, David Brandt, and the towering presence of the federal leader of the opposition, soon to be prime minister, Gough Whitlam.

Wharf labourers at Fremantle docks had received an 18-gallon (81-litre) keg of beer in anticipation of a trouble-free unloading

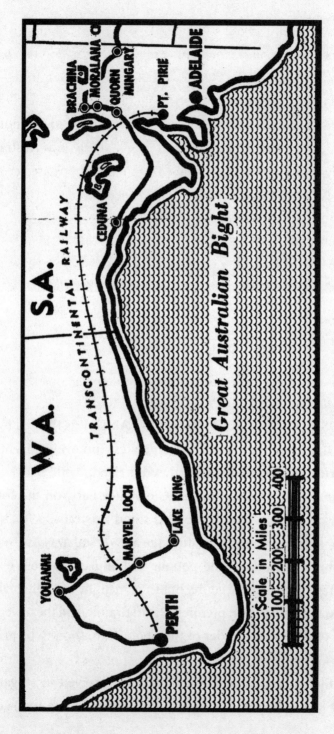

Map 3: Map showing the race route from Perth to Mingary, South Australia.

of the cars, but some were still dented. Marathon organisers had worked in close cooperation with police and customs officials, but 27 marathon cars still received defect notices—most for safety items such as air horns and driving lights, banned under local licensing laws. A marathon bulletin warned private entrants not to raise the issue of importing their cars permanently into Australia and selling them at marathon's end. 'Any negotiations are certain to delay customs clearance, with the consequent risk that the competitor may miss the start in Perth.'

Competitors were continually warned of Australian speed limits—60 kilometres per hour in town, and 110 kilometres per hour outside city limits—yet police led the escorted 20-kilometre drive from Fremantle to the start at the trotting track at Gloucester Park in Perth at 120-plus. Officials were sending mixed messages.

Competitors were given the option of taking their cars out of Parc Ferme at the penalty of a point a minute or to wait until the rally restarted to effect repairs in their own rally time. In Europe it would have been an easy decision, but in Australia the police attitude to speeding was a consideration. Crews had 7 hours to make the 547-kilometre drive up to the first control at Youanmi, a former mining town and now a collection of shanties. After service, most would only have a tight six hours in which to arrive. From the start, they needed to speed straight to garages around Perth for the service they needed. Their required average would be more than 90 kilometres per hour and, depending on the police, that might not be so easy.

Some crews, who were now committed to simply getting to Sydney, took the first option. The Downs brothers, Pat and Tony, had already rebuilt their VW once, and it was becoming a grandfather's axe, barely within the rules, as they again strengthened it for the run home. The *Telegraph*'s *Tortoise* team, the Winkless–Keran Volvo and the Jack 'Milko' Murray Holden would forgo the first special stages, incurring maximum penalties in order to make Sydney.

The other Murray, Gelignite Jack, fired off a bunger to signify the 2 p.m. restart. The crowd appreciated its local larrikin. Roger Clark was first away. The *Telegraph* Holdens each went to separate dealerships to cut down the waiting time to have the rear axles of their cars replaced; John Sprinzel, in contention for the Private Entrants Award, had a new windscreen fitted by a local crew that had practised the job for two days on a car in their showroom.

Sobieslaw Zasada was the first to be pulled over by police. His multi-roo-barred, low-slung Porsche was a cop magnet. Thirty kilometres out of Perth, a police way station—you wouldn't call it a roadblock—was road-worthy checking the 27 defected marathon cars. All passed, but at some cost to nerves. The first kangaroo struck just out of the city limits. David Harrison and Martin Proudlock hit one, damaging their spotlights. But theirs was the only sighting. Between Perth and Youanmi, neither police nor kangaroos posed a threat.

Next morning at dawn, three dust-stained cars stormed into the tent town of Lake King, fighting for the lead after clean-sheeting the first three stages. Roger Clark was frustrated. 'We should have been faster,' he said.

Clark had discovered a phenomenon unique to Western Australia—the ball-bearing surface. In Perth, being first on the road is a two-edged sword. On the one hand, the blinding dust that can make visibility near impossible and slow your car is behind you. But Western Australia has a low-grip surface strewn with small granite-like pebbles. In later rounds of the World Rally

Championship (Perth was the venue for the Australian round for almost twenty years from the late 1980s), the 'ball-bearing' gravel would become notorious. Teams would do anything to avoid being first on the road, where they would be nothing more than road sweepers, clearing a racing line for others who would have far more traction and better car speed.

But in 1968, Clark and Andersson had no knowledge of the ball-bearing problem. What they did know and were somewhat upset about was that organisers had agreed to a three-minute dust gap between cars across Australia. It had been one minute across Europe and Asia. The longer gap allows dust to clear and provides visibility, good for the cars behind, but was an equaliser that gave Clark and Andersson no advantage.

Through that long first night, Clark and Andersson slid around, clearing the rocks and carving a path. Simo Lampinen and Lucien Bianchi, travelling behind, became the beneficiaries, getting more traction and their ability to stay with Clark was relatively easy. But the dust—even at three minutes, it still hung in the air, creating false shadows and making visibility treacherous.

Behind the leaders lay a melee of wrecks, accusations of unfair play and the start of a snakes-and-ladders board of changing positions. Rauno Aaltonen was up to fourth from fifth. Paddy Hopkirk was down to eighth from fourth. Andrew Cowan dropped points but still advanced from sixth to equal fifth with the first Australian, Evan Green, who had been eighth. Harry Firth was 2 points behind Green, clinging to the seventh place with which he arrived from Bombay. Firth's two teammates, Vaughan and Hodgson, with the benefit of their impromptu recce, moved up, while Jackson and Chambers in the Lotus Cortina dropped to eleventh from ninth.

Clyde Hodgins in the Australian Safety Car was making serious accusations. All the way down from Youanmi to Marvel Loch, the next control, he'd been baulked, he claimed, by a British Leyland service car that had no business being on the marathon track. 'When I did get through, after 50 kilometres, I had to drive at speeds of up to 160 to make up time—and that's when I ran off the road.' Hodgins was out, although he, Wait and Lawler would drive cross-country to the finish in Sydney.

His complaint was the start of several claiming interference from vehicles associated with the marathon.

John Tallis and Paul Coltelloni were also in a ditch and gone. A British Leyland service vehicle—surely not the same one—arrived in the tiny township of Southern Cross to report them stuck on course with a broken axle. They had been fighting with John Sprinzel for the lead in the Private Entrants division, and now they were out. Another Volvo, the William Chesson–driven Lydden Hill Race Circuit–sponsored 122 S, lying 38th, blew up as a result of extreme over-revving in the soft soil. It was a mistake many crews were making.

With some poetic justice, Gelignite Jack had collected a roo, although Evan Green was at the wheel and driving the marathon of his life. Amateur Captain Fred Barker's Mercedes took one, and it slid underneath the car instead of up into the windscreen. Barker lost 20 points in the service park. The Southern Cross service lay just before the Marvel Loch control. It was there for a quick refuel and for emergencies. 'We'll pull up over there next to that person who looks like von Hanstein,' I said to David Benson.

'That is von Hanstein,' he replied. It was a surreal moment. The core media team had split into two small aircraft, leapfrogging each other to the stages as we struggled to keep up with the speed of the marathon. The last place you'd expect to see the imperious Porsche competitions boss, Huschke von Hanstein, was in the abandoned goldmining town of Southern Cross.

*   *   *

Youanmi to Marvel Loch had been an eye opener. If there were any thoughts that the marathon would move at European pace, they were now dispelled. Thick dust, even with the three-minute gap, made vision difficult, and in the middle of the night dead reckoning was essential. A Tripmaster that was not properly adjusted to log accurate distances could lead crews to miss a turn—little more than a hint of a sidetrack in the bush—and they'd be off in the wrong direction. Tony Fall, already way back after the Kabul disaster, lost another 25 points.

The set average for the 393 kilometres was high, even taking into account the last 70 were on bitumen. Crews were finding it hard, although not impossible, to maintain the required 98 kilometres per hour. But while they'd been ahead of schedule in Europe and Asia, with time to rest before checking out on the next stage, they now had time only for a splash and dash.

Lake King had turned into a tent city. More than 3000 people had come from the district and cross-country from Perth to cheer the cars into control. The 192-kilometre stage south from Marvel Loch required the same 96 kilometres per hour average. It was best to make up that time early. The last 20 kilometres were along unmade tracks, around tree stumps and across fence lines. Ken Tubman and Jack Forrest in the Perth television Volvo 144 S were lying 18th in the marathon on 47 points. 'Tubby', a genius in territory like this, reckoned a top-ten position was on the cards, better if others started to falter. He and Jack Forrest had found a quick way to control. It was far longer than the set route, but it was far faster, too. It ran along a dog fence, a high-wire mesh that also extends well below the ground to prevent dingoes, the scourge of livestock, from digging under it. The pair sped into Lake King, going hard and on time. It appeared only the top three cars in the entire field were going to clean the stage, and now they would be the fourth. Except . . . they were on the other side of the fence, trapped behind the tent city. Control officials could see them, and they could see control. But they could not bridge the gap, and event rules insisted that cars be within 50 metres of control when the route card was stamped. With time running out, they began bush bashing through the scrub, seeking a way across. And all they were doing was getting more bushed. Forrest leapt from the Volvo and directed Tubby backwards.

'But I didn't see him and ran right into him. I trapped him against a tree, grazed both his arms and bruised his chest. By the time we were back in the car and had driven onto the right road, we had lost 16 minutes.'

* * *

Paddy Hopkirk was determined to clean the stage. He was lying only 1 point behind Lucien Bianchi, and he was aware that now, in the stages that were supposed to be unable to be cleaned, was when the cars in front would give it everything. He had to do the same. Fifty years on, we are sitting in the office of his sixteenth-century home at High Wycombe—Paddy, Alec Poole and I—and I asked them to describe the stage. Both of them clouded over; they were about to describe, and admit to themselves for the first time, that this is where they lost the marathon.

'We didn't think we were going to win it in an Austin 1800,' Paddy said. 'It was too heavy and too slow. I think if I did it again I would do it with two people, to save weight. We had carried a lot of spares across Asia, fewer in Australia to keep the weight down. The Marvel Loch to Lake King track was nothing more than a path between high bushes.' Even most of the Australians had never seen anything like it—although Evan Green had. 'Drive to the tree tops,' was his advice. 'You'll get it right most of time.' Like Paddy said— they were playing the long game.

'I came up to a bush. Tony Nash was calling the shots. Was it to be left or right, surely not through,' Paddy recalled. 'There were wheel marks to the right but left seemed straighter, and I made a decision on instinct.

'The Austin 1800 hit hard rock, perhaps even a concrete slab— that's what it felt like. The wheel marks had been the giveaway. There were enough to indicate that the leading three had gone right, and also that "the locals go that way".' Paddy's crew stopped immediately to change a damaged front wheel, but there was a terrible noise from underneath. Then a rear tyre blew, and they stopped to change that as well. They arrived at control 14 points down. That's all it took— one moment in time, and they felt the pain fifty years on.

'When you look at the final results—6 points between me and Andrew Cowan, that's where we lost the marathon.'

The Scotsman lost five minutes on the stage and could have been faster; he caught the crippled Hopkirk, passed him and then was trapped in Rauno Aaltonen's dust.

Evan Green came through the stage with a loss of only 2 points. It was his best drive of the marathon. It elevated him from eighth to equal fifth with Cowan. There was a major service at Lake King before the second-longest stage in the race—all the way across the

Nullarbor Plain—and there was plentiful time to rebuild Hopkirk's front end. They'd broken the steering rack in the impact.

* * *

At Marvel Loch, John Sprinzel in the MG Midget came rushing back up the track the wrong way. He'd noticed that his route card had not been stamped and feared what would happen if he arrived at stage end. He argued with officials, didn't get a resolution, but then tore out of control again, directly in front of David McKay, who'd relied on there being a gap in front. The smallest car in the field was now blinding one of the largest.

'John wasn't hanging around, knowing that if we ever got near enough to see him we would get by,' McKay said. 'There was nothing we could do but to sweat it out. Without any breeze, his dust was hanging thickly down the track. I remember passing a pair of cars—one the Slotemaker DAF, and the other the Bengry Cortina—and we thought we must have been making good time, but the clock said otherwise and the points were piling up.

'We were running on the ragged edge, and it was only a question of time before the dust trapped us. We were motoring fairly briskly, around 140, when co-driver Liddle called left 120. There was no hope of making it, and the Monaro went off into the scrub. I could have wept as the cars we had fought so hard to pass went steaming by, for we would have to do it all again. Finally we caught up to a Porsche [Edgar Hermann], but unless he let us by there was nothing we could do short of running over the top of him.'

McKay dropped 26 points on the stage. It was doubly distressing because McKay's teammate, Eddie Perkins, driving these conditions like he was in his own backyard, went down just 4 points.

Perkins' drive into Lake King was one of the most outstanding performances of the marathon.

Barry Ferguson in the third Monaro dropped 15 on Lake King. 'This was undoubtedly the worst piece of rally road I've ever travelled on,' he said. 'There were holes of every type, trees of every size, stumps, washaways, rocky outcrops and boulders. The road deteriorated into two wheel tracks. Both sides of the track were lined with trees, and one mistake from the driver could write off the car for keeps.'

*   *   *

Lucien Bianchi and Jean-Claude Ogier had practised a very important routine for long straight roads. They would change places in the car on the move without losing valuable minutes stopping. They'd done it on the super highway across Iran, and now they were to do it again on the longest piece of straight road in Australia, the Eyre Highway across the Nullarbor Plain that linked the isolated West to the populated East. It's a misnomer that the Nullarbor is either straight or smooth. It is a deceptive piece of road that can easily catch out the unwary. In 1968, it was little more than a B-grade piece of dirt for about half its distance, full of potholes and populated by animals unwise in the way of the motor car. The number of burnt-out, wrecked cars at the side of the track bore testament to the need for maximum attention.

Weather forecasts for the 1442-kilometre run had been in excess of 40 degrees Celsius, but that was the week before. When the marathon passed through, the Nullarbor was on its best behaviour. Cars, crews and tyres ran cool. Bianchi, third on the road when they left the west, was two hours ahead of the field when they reached the east. He was running at ton-up, never stopping except halfway across at Eucla for fuel, and averaging a commendable 10 litres per 100 kilometres.

If only the Mercedes drivers and others had listened to Graham Hoinville. Desmo Praznovsky hit a wombat hole so deep that it could have been dug by Gelignite Jack's yowie. Before Norseman, he didn't see the hole until too late, braked hard and tore his radiator out. Four places in front on the road, Bill Bengry had done the same thing, bending his axle housing. He was limping to Norseman for repairs. Andrew Hedges in the disputed 'works' Benz saw Praznovsky parked at the side of the track, moved over to pass and hit the hole, too. At Norseman, the crew checked out the Benz but found nothing wrong.

Andrew Cowan said later that the hole was marked on his notes but that didn't stop his car from hitting it. With Colin Malkin at the wheel, the Hillman Hunter was launched into the air at what Andrew estimated to be 140 kilometres per hour. The three-point landing was something of which a pilot could be proud. 'If the Hunter had not been built so strongly, our marathon would have been over right there,' Cowan said.

Charging off onto the Eyre Highway, the Rootes team gave Cowan a chase car, another Hunter with no fewer than 16 sets of wheels and tyres mounted on the roof and in the car. The top-heavy Hillman bumped and thumped its way to South Australia and was never called on once. It did, however, create a dust storm, raising cries of discontent from competitors.

The Taylor–Ireland–Hedges car was having some difficulty living up to its amateur status. Mercedes had even turned on a light aircraft to provide service, joining a flight of some 25 planes chasing the marathon. On the Nullarbor, the cars were at least as fast as some of the aircraft. With Taylor at the wheel, the Mercedes began to lose power. Caught in the dust of a car in front, they'd not noticed the water temperature gauge go off the clock and then drop away to nothing, the sign of an engine about to blow. The Mercedes radiator had come loose. It was part of an epidemic affecting the cars of the three-pointed star, and this time it had been too late to stop it before the engine cooked.

But where was the plane? Bobby Buchanan-Michaelson was the team's immediate saviour. Along with David Seigle-Morris and Max Stahl, Bobby had bought a car in Perth when rental companies would not hire him one, and he pulled up on the Nullarbor with exactly the right expertise to help out. But not enough. The Benz mechanics arrived the next day. They'd been held up fixing Praznovsky's car. The six amateurs had spent a freezing cold night on the Nullarbor, hunting wildlife for food and using their only water to put out a scrub fire they'd started.

Two dozen people gathered at a service station at Ceduna on the eastern edge of the Nullarbor to wave the cars through. For Ceduna, it was a big crowd. They were enthusiasts, starved for accurate information. Lucien Bianchi and Harry Firth roared through, but there was no sign of the rally leader, Roger Clark. Even in such a small group, three different rumours were rife: Clark had rolled; his suspension had collapsed; he'd blown his engine. But none was true. Shortly after midday, they heard approaching engines, and Clark and Lampinen appeared side by side over a mound, as if in slow motion, large plumes of dust behind them and the bodywork shimmering in the heat. Clark peeled off into the service station; Lampinen powered straight on, the throb of his V6 purring nicely. Bruce Hodgson and Andrew Cowan followed soon after. The bigger touring cars with bigger engines had been expected to eat up the Nullarbor, but among them were Clark and Cowan. It was an incredible performance from both.

Ceduna saved Clark's teammates, Eric Jackson and Ken Chambers. They had four punctures across the Nullarbor. Their front suspension was splayed at such an angle it was wearing through tyres. Goodyear had laid down a minimalist cover in Ceduna, and they used all of it.

Nineteen crews lost points across the Nullarbor but, against expectation, 67 cars still remained mobile. There were now just 37 competitive hours left before Sydney. Fifteen stages remained. Twenty-two points covered the top ten in the field behind Clark and Andersson, who were still dominant. Ford, British Leyland, Hillman and the French Citroën were all in contention. As far as any observer in Ceduna was concerned, the elimination phase was over. The race was about to begin.

Ceduna to Quorn

Distance: 505 kilometres
Time allowed: 6 hours 18 minutes
Approximate average speed: 80 kilometres per hour

Quorn to Moralana Creek

Distance: 115 kilometres
Time allowed: 1 hour 17 minutes
Approximate average speed: 90 kilometres per hour

Moralana Creek to Brachina Gorge

Distance: 120 kilometres
Time allowed: 1 hour 30 minutes
Approximate average speed: 80 kilometres per hour

Brachina Gorge to Mingary

Distance: 336 kilometres
Time allowed: 4 hours 10 minutes
Approximate average speed: 80 kilometres per hour

Mingary to Menindee

Distance: 186 kilometres
Time allowed: 2 hours 12 minutes
Approximate average speed: 85 kilometres per hour

Menindee to Gunbar

Distance: 394 kilometres
Time allowed: 5 hours 18 minutes
Approximate average speed: 78 kilometres per hour

16

The Flinders Ranges

ROGER CLARK WAS OUT.

The news arrived at the tiny airport just as we were about to depart Ceduna—Clark was gone. Was it more rumour? Could it be fact? We were in a hurry to get going. There was a major service scheduled for Port Augusta on the shores of the Spencer Gulf. It was once the shipping lifeline for remote South Australia, north through the Flinders Ranges. Now it could become a life-saver for marathon competitors. We lined up, started rolling and then *bang*. A serious impact, a shudder, and the pilot came off the gas and onto the brakes. We were all out of the plane, looking for the damage. No roo. That was a relief—they're a menace at country airstrips. And then we found the nose luggage-hatch open. It hadn't been properly secured. The propeller, which the pilot feared had been bent by something being ejected, seemed straight and we assured him there was nothing missing. We took off tenuously, ready to pull back on the prop at any time and find a place for a soft landing. Pilots call it 'feathering'.

Clark and Andersson had feathered, too. It was at least 450 kilometres from Ceduna to Port Augusta and another 40 onto the control at the tiny bluestone township of Quorn at the doorstep of the Flinders. They were ahead of time, having survived the Nullarbor with a minimum of suspension damage, and they planned a major rebuild at Port Augusta to prepare for the special stages around Wilpena Pound, the natural amphitheatre that had served as a halfway house for the great Australian cattle drives almost a century before.

Every racing driver knows the feeling. You're in the lead, and things are going well, too well. You start to imagine noise, feel vibrations, you worry about things over which you have no control. You tell yourself you're a professional, just another component of the car. But you know you're more than that. You are the captain of the ship. You are the onboard monitoring system. Long before electronic control units, black boxes and plug-in diagnostics, 'seat of the pants' meant something. There was an instinct, a sixth sense that you developed. If you catch the problem in time, you just might save it from becoming a complete disaster.

Ove Andersson felt it coming. Just a hiccup, a slight catch in the engine's harmony. He threw it into neutral and got off the power just as the engine went *bang*, followed by a short clattering noise. Like Söderström and Palm, Smith and Pointet, the twin-cam Lotus Ford engine had dropped a valve and gone onto three cylinders. It was coming up to 11 p.m. They were 80 kilometres out of Port Augusta, and their only option was to limp in. Teammates

Ken Chambers and Eric Jackson caught them in the dust. There was nothing they could do, they decided, except speed ahead and warn Bill Barnett and the service team.

Lucien Bianchi arrived in Port Augusta for a full service. Simo Lampinen was so early he was able to have Jochen Neerpasch and the two Ford Germany mechanics change the suspension, complete with new, strong uprights, while he and Staepelaere went off for a meal, a shower and an hour's sleep. The sight of the current Le Mans winner on his back under a rally car in a paddlewheeler town was . . . unusual.

Ford had a problem, a big one. It seems extraordinary that they weren't prepared. They'd had sufficient warning of their cars' vulnerability. The timing chains on Lotus Cortinas were a known Achilles heel. And yet with Rosemary Smith's car already hinting at giving up again, they had no spare cylinder heads available in Port Augusta. If that turned out to be Clark's problem, they were without option. They did the maths. Minutes mattered. The only way they could win the marathon was to get Clark and Andersson to the Quorn control with an absolute minimum loss of points.

They needed a donor. If they were to strip Smith's car or that of the British Army Motoring Association of Harrison and Proudlock, they could get their Number One back in the event—but both were too far away. Jackson and Chambers were there. They were lying eleventh, down 47 points. Their known reliability was certain to advance them up the order, and they might even finish in the top five. But win? You could almost hear the dice turning over in the croupier's cup.

After the marathon, Ford liked to tell the story that Jackson and Chambers volunteered their cylinder head; that their selfless act of sacrifice provided Ford with their best shot at the main prize. Nick Brittan publicly said that Jackson stepped forward and said, 'Take the head off our car and give it to Roger,' followed by a hug from Clark. It may well have happened. But Brittan confirmed to me privately that Jackson was presented with the ultimatum earlier, before the wounded car had arrived. 'It's awfully hard to negotiate when you're standing naked in the shower.'

When Clark's Ford arrived in Port Augusta, it was like a serious Le Mans pit stop. The car pulled into the garage, and the shutter door slammed down behind it. The cylinder heads came off both cars, and the exchange was made while the crew was sent to refresh. Quorn control was 40 kilometres away along a dirt road in the middle of the night. Ford had allowed 30 minutes for Clark to bridge the gap if he was to arrive without points loss. Five minutes after that deadline, the Ford refused to start. They were now eating into their lead. They'd lost 11 points across half the world. Lampinen was down 20; Bianchi, 21. It was now a case of how much time they'd lose.

At two minutes to go before it needed to check in, the Cortina fired, reverse-spun out of the garage and took off into the night. Sixteen minutes later, it arrived at the control desk. Clark had averaged 156 kilometres per hour.

Fourteen minutes of late time took Clark and Andersson to a cumulative 25 total points, and they dropped to third.

For the first time since the marathon began, there was a new leader: Simo Lampinen and Gilbert Staepelaere (Ford Taunus V6) on 20, from Lucien Bianchi and Jean-Claude Ogier (Citroën DS 21) with 21, and Clark and Andersson (Lotus Cortina), 25. Next came Rauno Aaltonen, Henry Liddon and Paul Easter (Austin 1800), 31; Andrew Cowan, Brian Coyle and Colin Malkin (Hillman Hunter) and Evan Green, George Shepheard and Gelignite Jack Murray (Austin 1800) were tied on 32.

* * *

Evan Green changed the course of the marathon on the next stage with an act either of magnanimous sportsmanship or great foolishness. The jury is still out. In road order, Green was two behind Cowan, separated by Harry Firth's Falcon. Cowan plunged off the road.

'It was a hard left on the top of a crest,' George Shepheard recalled. 'Andrew was maybe 35 to 40 metres off the road. It appeared he didn't even try to make the corner because if he had he almost surely would have rolled. When we came across them, Evan pulled to a halt and asked if he could help. Suddenly I was out of our car, pushing and pulling.'

Shepheard remembered a tow rope was offered by Cowan, but Cowan denies this. 'We were beached. I hadn't given it enough oomph to get us over the dune on which we were stuck,' he said. 'It was a relatively simple matter to get us back on the road.' Incredibly, Green even let Cowan go first on the run into control.

Both made it without loss of points, but if Cowan had been left stranded it's a certainty he would have sacrificed time, perhaps even enough to determine the outcome of the marathon. The camps were divided then and remain so today.

'I didn't ask Evan to help,' Cowan recalls fifty years on with some embarrassment. 'He stopped and offered.'

George Shepheard, the last of the Austin 1800 crew still alive, disagreed with Green's decision. 'If they'd been in danger, it was the right thing to do. But there was no danger. We shouldn't have stopped.'

In control that day, Evan Green said to me, 'Hell, this is motor sport, not war.'

It was a spur-of-the-moment decision and, once started, was not able to be stopped. Given the outcome of the event, I often wondered if Evan had any regrets, but he never recanted.

The Moralana Creek Road at the base of Wilpena Pound is one of the most wonderful rally stages in the world—now. When the marathon surveyed it, there was little else but gibber rock to mark its path. It was then that Stewart McLeod had friends build a road through. It was his secret route. 'There are three ways of getting to Moralana Creek,' he told people on the *Chusan*. 'One will make everyone hopelessly late, another can just be cleaned, and anyone who uses my road will be in with time to spare.'

But the McLeod road, now famous and used by subsequent car rallies as a stage of rare beauty and challenge, had been discovered. When McLeod went north from his Adelaide home to cheer the marathon through, he found it covered with service crews. Competitors still needed to know how to find it, behind a gate guarded by a young man in a Morris 1100. There had been rumours of a British Leyland volunteer army of gate openers and closers, of false information given and people advised to go around by another route. David McKay ignored the gate man, charged through and made it to an astonished control official nine minutes ahead of Edgar Hermann's Porsche, which had left Quorn before him.

Competitors were arriving at control incensed. A bulldozer had been parked across a rally road; a young man had waved a marathon car to a halt and directed it a different way. Local car club officials, in a bid to be friendly, had placed bunting down the sides of creek crossings to show the best way through. For crews who had recced and believed they had an advantage, it seemed grossly unfair that knowledge was now being offered freely to all.

Fifty teams lost time through the two Flinders Ranges stages. Alec Gorshenin and Ian Bryson in the Mercedes-Benz 280 SL hit a rock and damaged their gearbox so badly they could not continue. At least it wasn't their radiator.

Andrew Cowan was in increasing trouble. On the 120-kilometre Moralana Creek to Brachina Gorge stage, he again ran off the road. 'The brake pedal went straight to the boards,' he said. 'I shot off the road into piles of soft sand.' They were near to control, so Colin Malkin ran ahead to get help and warn their service crew while spectators helped Cowan and Coyle back onto what was now a bitumen surface.

'We found a jet of fluid coming out of the brake pipe, and we feared the worst.'

Had it been cracked on the previous 'off'? How long would a repair take? They discovered a coupling between two pipes had simply come loose. It was quickly tightened, and they were away. A long way behind them on the road, the RAF Hillman Hunter of Carrington, Jones and King, their backup car, was having exactly the same problem.

Roger Clark and Ove Andersson were charging their way up through the field. They used the McLeod road and arrived at control sideways, Andersson flinging himself from the car to stamp his card. By the time they reached the end of the next stage into Brachina Gorge, they were back at first on the road, although third in the rally. They'd forced their way past both Lampinen and Bianchi. 'Bianchi gave me some trouble,' Clark said. 'But I pushed him out of the way.' It was language that Bianchi, the hardened professional racer, understood.

Lampinen tried to pass Bianchi as well but could not get close enough before he left the road. He'd been leading the marathon for just 180 kilometres.

'We were stuck in Bianchi's dust,' he told me in his small memorabilia-lined flat in Hamburg, where he and his wife, Milli, live to be near their airline pilot son and grandchildren. 'It wasn't just the dust but what the lack of visibility does to accurate note reading. Over a crest there was a deep rut, and I hit it at full speed. The rear axle went straight into it. Often it's better to go flat out over such an obstacle rather than try to slow down. The valves of the shock absorbers broke on both sides. So I had to drive all the way to control without shocks.'

Lampinen and Staepelaere dropped 8 minutes on the stage, falling back to third and advancing Clark and Andersson to second. The Taunus crew were the only ones of the top thirteen to drop points through the Flinders Ranges. The marathon had a new leader again—Bianchi and Ogier, still on 21 points, the ones they brought with them from Bombay. They were now the only crew to have clean-sheeted in Australia.

* * *

These days, the Barrier Highway from South Australia to Broken Hill is all bitumen. It is still extremely dangerous, especially in the twilight hours when local wildlife seeks the warmth of the road surface. In 1968, marathon officials and route charters rated the drive from Brachina Gorge to Mingary, a small community just inside the South Australian border and approximately 70 kilometres from Broken Hill, as the worst section of road in Australia. 'There is no asphalt, and the likelihood of breaking the car is very great. There are no fewer than 43 gates, which may have to be opened and closed. The dust is very bad, and there are many dips and gullies through dry riverbeds.'

It was 336 kilometres across and they'd allowed only 4 hours 10 minutes, an average speed of 80 kilometres per hour. One long night of hard-core special stage rallying was ahead in the Australian Alps. Despite the warning, it was hard not to think of this as a transport stage. Most Number One drivers handed over to their Number Twos, anxious to get some rest.

Evan Green, fifth-placed and heading for his home rally roads, was the first to strike major trouble. At Brachina Gorge, the British Leyland team had done a full spanner check. One of the crew had tightened the wheel bearings. There was a trick to that, and he didn't know it.

'We were about halfway across to Mingary when there was a big *bang*, followed by another,' George Shepheard recalled. 'The wheel bearing had exploded. It felt like a wheel had broken. The car fell right down on its suspension. I leapt out ready to change the wheel. But it was much worse than that. We needed an entirely new rear arm.'

Andrew Cowan came through and returned the Flinders favour. 'Tell the service crew up the road we need help,' Green said, and Cowan agreed. It was a huge mistake on Green's part.

Twenty kilometres further on, a British Leyland service crew were waiting at the happiest passage control of all. Passage controls are placed intermittently between full checkpoints. They exist to ensure teams are on the right road and to mark competing cars through. Curnamona Homestead had gone all out to welcome the marathon crews. There were welcome signs and barbecues and people had gathered from nearby stations, some in light aircraft. Stewart McLeod landed his plane there as well.

Andrew Cowan passed Green's message to the British Leyland crew, who acknowledged it but did nothing. At the outset of the marathon, British Leyland had laid down strict protocols. One said that any request for assistance had to come in writing. If it was verbal, ignore it. There would be disinformation about, and people were not to be blindsided by fake news. When Green's car did not turn up and still the British Leyland crew did nothing, the experienced Stewart McLeod, recognising that something must be wrong, took off in his plane to investigate. He found the Austin 1800 beside the track with a message spelled out in white stones. McLeod turned for Broken Hill, picked up a rear control arm and brought it back to Green, bypassing the service crew.

Green dropped 230 points, well out of contention but still in the marathon. While they'd been waiting, Green, Murray and Shepheard had held a conference—a quite acceptable process in a team run on bureaucratic discipline—and decided they would continue on the rally route no matter what. With Green's spirited driving through the Australian Alps, they'd finish the marathon in twenty-first position.

* * *

Photographer Ian Mainsbridge and I had flown to Broken Hill from Brachina Gorge, and our chief of staff, Ted Shiel, ordered us to travel 70 kilometres to Mingary against the direction of rally traffic while our colleagues stayed in Broken Hill filing copy. It was an interesting drive. Mainsbridge was no navigator. At Mingary, we found the *Telegraph* team leader's car battered on every panel with its right-hand window pillar crushed. George Reynolds had been at the wheel when it rolled in a sand dune, and the windscreen and pillar had given him a serious cut across the forehead.

The crew were anxious to keep going. Their plan was to speed into Broken Hill and fix the car. I would take Reynolds to hospital, get him stitched then deliver him back in time to get to the next control. Not even in our combined state of exhaustion did it seem like a good idea. But McKay would not be dissuaded. We hooked in behind, abandoning the Shiel instruction and sped at marathon pace back to Broken Hill. McKay was not going slowly, but at that moment he was no Roger Clark, either. The pace gave Mainsbridge some idea of what it takes to compete in, let alone win, a marathon.

McKay arrived at the Holden dealership like it was a pit stop in the Australian Grand Prix. David Liddle, Ian Mainsbridge and I gently lifted George Reynolds from the rear seat of the big coupe. He was semiconscious and disorientated, and any time we moved the dirty towel from his forehead the blood flow restarted. We drove him to hospital—nothing is too far from anywhere in Broken Hill—and met with an admission nurse who advised strongly against continuation.

'It is only when the end comes that one realises how wound up one gets with the desire to finish, and then the spring unwinds and one suddenly feels very old and tired. The great disappointment was almost too much to bear,' McKay wrote. 'I went up to see George in bed and give him his gear. He looked very small lying there and pale under his tan. He was obviously very sorry and distressed about the accident, for he realised that with him in hospital we were automatically disqualified.'

McKay's *Telegraph* teammate Barry Ferguson, lying tenth, was in trouble, too. In Perth, the Holdens had had new differentials fitted. Unknown to them, the originals were heavily reinforced Chevrolet units, while the replacements were standard. 'I was in the back seat,' David Johnson recalled. 'I looked out the window and saw our wheel travelling complete with axle alongside us.' They were near the passage control at Curnamona Homestead. Ford had flown in a huge contingent of dealers and media, and Holden supporters were thin on the ground. Johnson found one. He persuaded a policeman who was part of the welcoming party (because it was a party) to radio ahead to Broken Hill. The Holden dealer stripped a stock car and sent a new diff out to Mingary. They dropped 47 points with the slow drive into Mingary and handed a get-out-of-jail pass to the Falcon GTs, each of which cleaned the stage.

* * *

Broken Hill is about as historic and symbolically important as an outpost can get in Australia. The great mountain of iron ore that towers above the rural city stands for everything that is Australian—mateship, solidarity, mineral wealth. These days, the Miners Memorial atop the Line of Lode honours more than 700 people who have died working the site. The marathon did no more than pause in its headlong rush to the conclusion.

Sobieslaw Zasada paused, though, for exactly two minutes too long. The mighty Pole had been building up speed. In the race across Australia, he had been awe-inspiring, driving without notes, gaining confidence on every stage and pushing his Porsche to its very limits. Despite having the best roo bar of all, he never

Map 4: Map showing the race route through New South Wales and Victoria.

needed it. But he could have done with a clock. There is a small anomaly about Broken Hill. It is located in the state of New South Wales, but it works on South Australian time—and South Australia is half an hour behind New South Wales. Marek Wachowski did not know that, and Porsche apparently did not know it, either.

At Menindee on the other side of Broken Hill, the Porsche sat outside control waiting for the clock to count down so they could check in. And then they realised their mistake. They sped into control for the loss of 2 minutes—2 points. It was to be hugely significant. They were to lose third outright by 1 point.

Today Wachowski laughs about it. 'The atmosphere in the car was still normal,' he said. 'Von Hanstein said, "thank you" too.' But who was to blame? 'We are both in charge in the car,' Wachowski said. 'When I am awake, I am the boss. When Sobek [sic] is awake, he is the boss.'

John Sprinzel and Roy Fidler lost their chance of winning the Private Entrants Award on a transport stage. They had lost only 123 points and were neck and neck with Edgar Hermann's Porsche on 122. Midway between Menindee and Gunbar, a wheel tore off the tiny MG Midget. They'd broken a hub. Sprinzel sprinted back to Menindee with a spectator and sent a message to the British Leyland command post in Broken Hill. Although they were private entrants, Sprinzel and Fidler fell inside the cone of confidence that British Leyland had laid down for all its competitors. Command said they'd send a part immediately and dispatched it with Tony Fall, lying midfield in the Austin 1800. When it arrived, Sprinzel discovered it was for the right-hand side of the car; his damage was on the left. Once more he sprinted to Menindee. This time an Austin Healey Sprite in Broken Hill was stripped of parts, and the left-hand hub was sent with the *Telegraph*'s *Tortoise* team at the rear of the field. But the entire rescue took almost ten hours, and Sprinzel was out of time. He drove straight to the finish at Warwick Farm.

* * *

Gunbar in the Riverina district of New South Wales, on the wetlands of the Lachlan River, was home to a population of 37 people. It was in its heyday a hub that served the surrounding pastoral properties, most of them vast expanses and owned by international interests. On 16 December 1968, Gunbar became the venue of a most amazing and memorable meal. Andrew Cowan was due to meet his service crew in Gunbar but they weren't there, and as far as Cowan was concerned, they were officially missing. Cowan was on his own. He pulled up to the one lone petrol pump and was filling up when an Australian approached him. 'I'm the mayor,' he said, sweeping his arms across the vast emptiness around him. 'I'd like to invite you to a meal.'

On the side of the corrugated-iron community hall, under a peppercorn tree, someone had hand-painted the sign 'The Gunbar Hilton'. Inside was a long table at which was already seated almost everyone with whom he would be racing in the next 24 hours—the last day of the greatest road race on earth. Lucien Bianchi and Jean-Claude Ogier were there. The British Leyland team—Hopkirk and Aaltonen and their co-drivers— were there. The Ford team were not, but that was understandable because Clark and Andersson were under pressure. There was lamb on the menu. The farmers' wives had cooked it themselves. The meal could not last long; there was a marathon to complete. But, for just a few moments, in the midst of madness, there'd been a truce and a meeting, not of competitors but of respected and respectful colleagues.

Gunbar to Edi

Distance: 399 kilometres

Time allowed: 4 hours 26 minutes

Approximate average speed: 90 kilometres per hour

Edi to Brookside

Distance: 78 kilometres

Time allowed: 1 hour

Approximate average speed: 78 kilometres per hour

Brookside to Omeo

Distance: 155 kilometres

Time allowed: 1 hour 55 minutes

Approximate average speed: 82 kilometres per hour

Omeo to Murrindal

Distance: 158 kilometres

Time allowed: 2 hours 6 minutes

Approximate average speed: 75 kilometres per hour

Murrindal to Ingebyra

Distance: 129 kilometres

Time allowed: 1 hour 31 minutes

Approximate average speed: 85 kilometres per hour

17

The Greatest Road Race of All Time

WELCOME TO VICTORIA.

With one exceptional night of high-speed competition remaining and outright positions destined to change, police set up a speed trap on the way into one of the smallest towns on the entire route. Edi, on the King River, 35 kilometres south of Wangaratta and on the very first step of the Australian Alps, was nothing more than a single petrol station at the side of the road. Police pinged Simo Lampinen for 37 miles per hour in a 35-mile-per-hour zone (59 kilometres per hour instead of 56). Then they monstered him, threatening, he said, to have his car impounded. He had been in plenty of time to check in. Now he was two minutes late. Lampinen's penalty dropped him back within the clutches of fourth-placed Aaltonen, just 1 point behind, and it eased the pressure on Clark, now 5 points ahead. Every move in this chess game, no matter how small, was significant.

Huge controversy surrounded the police action. And it would intensify in the last eighteen hours of the marathon. There were two schools of thought. The marathon called it harassment. Things were said in the heat of the moment that would be actionable today. The Moskvitch team, booked earlier in Broken Hill, said they were treated worse by Australian police than they were by the Iron Curtain's military.

It was fuel for the media fire. Who was right and who was wrong? By any standard, speeding on the open road is illegal and arguably unsafe. The early Australian REDeX Trials had been beset by the same problem, and officials found it easier to work with authorities for mutual goodwill than to oppose the regime. Now it seemed the lessons of the REDeX had been forgotten by both sides. Much of the police action was nothing more than intimidation. It went way beyond the limits of right and wrong. Armed with authority, police were liberally interpreting its limits. Innes Ireland, out of contention and driving directly to Warwick Farm, reported in his own account of the marathon a policeman leaning on his car and 'speaking in the indulgent tones one might use to a wayward child'. In Cooma, at the end of the long night's competition, crews were greeted by a conga line of police cars, picking up each marathon competitor on the way into town and escorting it through—ready to pounce. It was unnecessary and unseemly.

But it wasn't totally wrong. Marathon bulletins warned of police activity. The event's regulations stipulated that 'being convicted of any driving offence during the event may be penalised by exclusion or by withdrawal of an award'. It was a nebulous threat and never put into action. But surely the marathon competitors should at the very least have treated the police as yet another hazard. Instead, there was resentment, even baiting.

Ireland again, on another police encounter: 'I've just timed you at 93 miles per hour [149 kilometres per hour]', the policeman said.

'Only 93?' came Andrew Hedges' voice from the back seat. 'Innes, we told you to keep it to the ton [161 kilometres per hour].' It was hardly good for relations.

* * *

At Wangaratta, heading towards Edi, Ian Tate, Harry Firth's loyal mechanic and 'the son he never had', begged Harry to change his differential. It was the final service before the last-night charge. Firth was lying sixth, the first of the Ford Falcon GTs, and he was only 4 points off a podium finish. But Firth would have none of it. Tate knew Firth would need all the help he could get on this last lunge. 'His eyesight wasn't what it had been, and his night driving wasn't as good as younger people. I wanted to make sure I'd given him the best possible tools for the job.'

Firth charged off. He knew these roads. He and Graham Hoinville had won Alpine rallies here. It was like driving in his own backyard.

Ford Germany mechanics were all over the rear of Lampinen's Taunus. The shock absorbers were replaced, again, but the service in no way made him late for the Edi check-in. He hadn't been speeding. He was adamant about that. The Ford GB team replaced the front struts in Roger Clark's car. The Australian corrugations had so attacked the fragile Fords that mechanics were now recycling used struts as best they could. Sobieslaw Zasada discarded every bit of weight he felt he could jettison from the Porsche. Zasada and Wachowski had always intended to sprint on the last night, but their marathon-winning game plan relied on more front-of-the-field retirements than had occurred. They were lying twelfth at Edi, too far back to win, but they'd never know if they didn't have one big go.

Andrew Cowan still could not find his service crew. There was no word of them. Both cars had been held up somewhere on the run from Broken Hill. It starkly highlighted the difference between a marathon car and a standard vehicle. Both of Cowan's support cars had broken down trying to keep up with the marathon. He was able to get tyre service, and he, Malkin and Coyle did their own spanner check. But on this last critical overnight elimination, they were on their own.

Edi to Brookside, the first Alpine stage, required 78 kilometres per hour, and the time allowed was exactly 1 hour. No one was expected to clean it. The road climbs through the Mount Buffalo National Park. The first half is extremely hilly, with ascents up to 800 metres through a pine forest. Then there is the plunge down to the Dandongadale River before hitting the ghost-gum forests rising up to 1700 metres into the snowline. The track is there only to service the powerlines. It's narrow, it's daunting and it's best done at night when you cannot see the obstacles off to the sides. Huge granite cliffs become sheer drops.

'It's time to find out who has the balls.' Hopkirk smiled straight down the barrel of the camera as he waited for the start.

At 11.05 p.m., Roger Clark and Ove Andersson sped off and were encircled by darkness. Three minutes later, Lampinen and Staepelaere followed. Back in thirteenth starting position,

Zasada patiently waited. When he dropped the clutch, it was as if the forest had come alight. There were few witnesses to the drive, but in the course of the next 60 minutes, the Pole mowed down the three cars in front of him, his lights urgently flashing for passage through. He reached Brookside control with a loss of just 1 minute—an average of 80 kilometres per hour—and he'd advanced to tenth in the field.

Paddy Hopkirk, brilliant, sensational, was next fastest, dropping 3 points. The next Austin 1800, Rauno Aaltonen, dropped 8. Hopkirk moved from seventh to tie with Aaltonen on fifth. He thought he should have been faster. He'd caught Lampinen but could not pass. 'I never rated him much as a driver,' he growled.

Roger Clark, expected to be fastest of all—as he'd been across Asia—dropped 4 minutes. Finally, the Lotus Cortina was starting to succumb to its punishment. It had been driven flat out all the way from London. Clark was going for the win—there was no use trying for second place now. The Cortina would either hold together or it would break. Which one would it be? The answer would be there for all to see in only an hour's time.

Bianchi dropped 6 points. That meant Clark had closed the gap on the marathon leader to just 2 points: 27 to 29. Lampinen also dropped 6. It was a disappointing run from the Flying Finn, who'd planned to use the stage to close in on the leadership. There'd been the lights from Hopkirk's car flashing behind him. He was now 7 marathon points behind Clark, two more than when he'd started.

Andrew Cowan had been held up in Aaltonen's dust. He couldn't get close enough to find a way through or even to demand the right to do so. He dropped 6 points, still enough to leapfrog into fourth ahead of Aaltonen. He'd had a problem, too. In the back seat,

Colin Malkin felt the underneath of the car getting very hot, so much so he could no longer sit down. Malkin tapped Coyle on the shoulder to alert him. Coyle was calling the shots, and the golden rule was not to disturb the driver or co-driver. But Cowan could not help being distracted. 'What the bloody hell are you doing?' he shouted, his mind momentarily off the road. None of the three knew what the problem was or whether the Hunter was about to explode when the heat hit the fuel tank. All they could do was press on, Malkin clinging to the roof grab handles for support. When they reached control, they found the exhaust had been forced up into the floor. It was an easy fix.

The biggest loser was Harry Firth. He dropped 10 points, moving from sixth to seventh, just in front of his two Ford team-mates. Ian Vaughan lost only 7 points; Bruce Hodgson, 8. Vaughan had been passed by Zasada. It prompted navigator Bob Forsyth to tell his driver to get moving. 'You think you're doing pretty well. Then someone like Zasada comes up behind you, and you know there's another level. You have to lift.'

Evan Green, just to make his presence felt, dropped 10, too, well out of outright contention but determined to display what could have been. Frankly, 10 points wouldn't do that. He needed to match-race Hopkirk.

In all great races, whether across the world or around a Formula One circuit, there inevitably comes a moment when all the planning, strategy and tactical execution fail in the face of human error. Brookside to Omeo—the middle leg of the overnight showdown—was British Leyland's moment of truth.

The stage, 155 kilometres, was double the distance of the first and almost double the allowable time at 1 hour 55 minutes, but still required an average of 82 kilometres per hour. For the first half, there was no straight more than 50 metres long. The road skirts around Bright, a glorious mountain town. The Great Alpine Road was dirt for the marathon. No one was expected to clean it, and no one did.

George Shepheard had discovered the road five years before the marathon. Young Shepheard's idea of fun was to go on long drives looking for great rally stages. He can lay claim to being one of the fathers of the high mountain ranges run. It sweeps and dips along craggy ridge lines and plunges into deep ravines, rimmed throughout by the great ghost gums that are so majestic in daylight and so eerily threatening at night, wraith-like and towering above the small ribbon of track.

In preparation for the marathon, Shepheard had been back to the road several times. 'Each time there was a locked gate at Dandongadale, and each time I could not get through,' he said. Dandongadale is nothing more than a waypoint on a trig map, but its ownership is shared by various authorities—national parks, local council, fire brigades and even local land users. As is so often the case in remote Australia, each has the right to apply its own access lock and then, illogically, they share keys with each other.

'There were six locks on the Dandongadale gate.' Shepheard could not get access to the full set of keys. And so, unlike the rest of Australia that fell under British Leyland's survey, it was never plotted in depth.

For British Leyland, it was a total disaster. Henry Liddon had surveyed the entire course, except for this stage. When he came through, it was deep under snow and impassable. On paper it looked easy, a chance to relax, and that's the way they set out to drive it.

Alec Poole, sitting alongside Paddy Hopkirk, was the first to catch on to the danger. In British Leyland's route charts, it had not been marked as anything threatening. 'We were driving along briskly but not flat out when I noticed that we were falling behind prescribed time,' Poole said. 'I was starting to get worried, and I said to Paddy that he better get stuck into it.' Hopkirk upped the pace—in fact, put himself close to being on maximum attack. Gradually, racing against the Speedpilot in his cockpit—the equivalent of ghost racing against yourself on modern-day wearable computers—he started to claw back lost time. But it was not enough. The damage had been done in the early few kilometres, and he finished the stage down 11 points.

The route chart wrong-call affected Aaltonen and, way back in the field, Tony Fall, who, after his problems in Europe, was lying 25th and with no hope of recovery. Both went down 24 points. Evan Green, more used to the area and aware of the changing nature of the road, dropped 15. 'I passed Rauno refuelling mid-stage,' Andrew Cowan said. 'I couldn't fathom why he was doing that.'

Cowan, also, had not surveyed the stage. Brian Coyle on his recce had been snowed out. But from the start, Cowan was on the pace. 'Because I didn't know the stage, I thought I had better keep up the speed from the start,' Cowan said. 'It was better to be safe, even if it meant going on attack when it might have turned out I didn't need to.' Cowan gave up 8 points to Hopkirk's 11. He lay fourth on 46, ahead of Hopkirk, 50.

It's impossible in circumstances like this to say: 'what if'. It's an abstract argument to speculate on what may have occurred if Hopkirk had been on it. Could he have been faster than Cowan; could the course of the marathon have changed right there and then? And could a changed order have imposed a different dynamic on the upcoming stages—forcing different decisions and altering outcomes? It's academic.

Zasada was fastest again, this time equalled by Lampinen. Both lost 4 points. The previous stage had been a wake-up call for the young Finn. He needed to get back onto RAC winning pace. Had he won only three weeks before? It seemed a lifetime ago. His reward at control was to see that he was now only 1 point behind Roger Clark in the race for the lead. And Clark was in trouble.

Mid-stage, the Lotus Cortina's differential was collapsing. Clark and Andersson maintained their dogged composure. Their job was to get to the end of the stage with a minimum loss of points, or to fail trying. Their second task was to find a solution. They dropped 10 points on the way into Omeo. Bianchi had lost 7. The gap between the leaders was now Bianchi, 34; Clark, 39; and Lampinen, 40.

Behind them there'd been changes in the order. Bob Neyret went off course. He lost 48 minutes. The second Citroën driver had been lying eleventh on 63 points, and on the previous stage he'd been only 1 minute slower than Bianchi. Now he was out of contention. Ian Vaughan had become the best of the Australian Fords, 1 point ahead of Harry Firth. He'd dropped only a brilliant 9 minutes on the stage, while Firth and Hodgson each went down 15. Vaughan skied in this area, and he regarded it as his own.

Desperation hung in the air like the night mist. Clark and Andersson needed a new differential, and they needed it fast. The next stage was a transport section, Omeo to Murrindal: 158 kilometres, 2 hours 6 minutes to make it, but it was bitumen all the way. Flat out, you could do it in an hour. There was no hope in sight at Omeo so they set off, as fast as they dared. Halfway to Murrindal they came to a small town, Bruthen, when with a *bang* their diff let go.

There was a spectator posse following the marathon. One of them was a Ford employee in a Cortina. Initial shock turned to willing assistance, and at 3 a.m., the Ford men swapped the standard axle into the Lotus Cortina. You never give up trying. Clark and Andersson accumulated 97 minutes of late time into Murrindal, the only one of the leaders not to clean the stage. They dropped from second to fourteenth.

Colin Malkin was at the wheel of the Hunter on the way to Murrindal when police pulled him over. Sometime after 3 a.m. they booked him for having no tail-lights on his car. It's an old rally trick; some might call it a dirty trick. You have a dashboard switch that disables your rear lights to make it more difficult for your competition to spot you in front. The police explained they'd also stopped Aaltonen and Hopkirk for the same defect. They'd turned theirs directly back on. The Hunter needed a quick rewiring fix at the next control.

Lucien Bianchi got a flat tyre. How fortunate to get it here and not on a totally competitive stage. Nerves were tightening. With Clark effectively eliminated, everyone had moved up a place behind Bianchi. His gap was now one more than he'd expected, five minutes in front of Lampinen. Only five? Simo thought he had that in him.

Of all the stages in this overnight marathon grand final, Murrindal to Ingebyra in New South Wales had the highest average. Over 129 kilometres, there was 1 hour 31 minutes allowed to complete it at an average of 85 kilometres per hour. This was a classic Alpine road. It wound through the Kosciuszko National

Park, leaving and rejoining a dirt track called the Barry Way. There were a lot of 90-degree bends, a lot of climbs and drop-aways, a lot of riverbeds. Banjo Paterson, Australia's most renowned bush balladeer, had written about this country in his seminal 'Man from Snowy River': 'Boys, go at them from the jump. No use to try for fancy riding now.'

It's as if Lampinen, a small, tightly wound enigma of a rally driver—a dour Finn as Finns are, but this one had soul—had read the poem. He cleaned the uncleanable stage. And as his V6 Taunus made the mountains ring with the whip crack of his exhaust, he brought others with him. Zasada cleaned it, too—no surprise there. The Pole was in a zone of his own. He was enjoying himself immensely and, without notes, so was Wachowski, sitting silently in the right-hand side, watching the trees flash by and ducking as the branches slammed into and then glanced off the roof-top roo bar. At least it was serving some purpose.

But then, among the strident sound of the sixes, there was the rumble of the V8s. Ian Vaughan and Bruce Hodgson both cleaned the stage, too. Firth dropped 3 minutes. Vaughan was now 4 points ahead of his team boss and, significantly, he was only 3 points behind Hopkirk, who'd lost 5. Zasada, who'd started the night twelfth, was now seventh, 1 point behind Firth.

Bianchi and Cowan both cleared the last mountain stage with a loss of 2 points. Had they backed off? With Clark gone, did Bianchi feel he had a lead he could control? It's a fine line. Jack Brabham, Australia's three-time Formula One world champion, always said, 'win at the slowest possible speed': that's okay in a motor race, where you have a visual reckoning and there are pit boards on every lap. Today in rallying there is onboard timing courtesy of GPS, telemetry and team radio. But not then. When you're on the limit, a loss of 2 minutes over 128 kilometres is a big lift. To deliberately wash off a second a kilometre, you make a conscious decision to back off, infinitesimally, where otherwise you'd stay flat. It's some- thing only a driver and, perhaps, his crew can feel. Sometimes, if a driver is falling off the absolute limit, it's up to the co-driver to act as manager–coach and spur them on. It's possible Bianchi and Ogier pulled back slightly. But they were as surprised as everyone else that four cars had cleaned the stage.

Cowan had entered the marathon to finish. With the best will in the world, he didn't expect to be first. But emerging from the mountains, after a night of 100 per cent effort, it appeared he was going to deliver Rootes a podium spot, and that was satisfying. Bianchi led the marathon on 36, from Lampinen (40) and Cowan (48). Hopkirk was back on 55 points from Vaughan, the first of the Australians, on 58.

What had happened to the Australian challenge? Everyone had said they would blow the Europeans away once they were on home soil. 'You're always faster on roads you know,' Ian Vaughan said, and that night he proved it. But there'd been a major miscalcula- tion. The European armada was simply more powerful. The drivers were consistently better, more resilient, more able to not only meet but lay on the pressure. They also had better service, more facilities and bigger budgets. There was a vast gap between the top works teams, the top drivers, and the rest of the field.

The marathon had split into cadres of competition. Behind the leading ten, a massive race within a race had broken out among four Australian crews vying to be the best of the rest. They would spend the last night carving each other up in their own backyard. Round Australia Trial winner, the already-veteran Ken Tubman, with fearless motorcycle ace Jack Forrest beside him, entered the last night in twelfth place in the Volvo 144 S. They were just 4 points clear of fellow Round Australia Trial winner, the even-more-veteran Eddie Perkins with three-time Australian Grand Prix winner Doug Whiteford beside him and Jim Hawker in the back in the Holden Monaro. Behind them, Gerry Lister and Andre Welinski (Volvo 144 S) and Barry Ferguson, David Johnson and Doug Chivas (Holden Monaro) were separated by 28 points. Ferguson was at the rear of the pack, on 120 points, almost double those of Tubman. All would attack, but by the end of the night Ferguson would have closed to throw out a huge challenge to the others on the event's final deciding stage.

It was an uneven and faltering contest, not like the race for the outright lead. With the exception of Ferguson, there was no consistency. Tubman lost twelfth place to Perkins at Brookside, then took it back again into Omeo. Ferguson was breathing down Lister's neck, just 2 points behind. Into Ingebyra, Ferguson gave it everything. Spurred on by Johnson, one of the most aggressive co-drivers in Australian rallying, a man not shy to berate his driver rather than cajole him to go faster, Ferguson flashed through Ingebyra with a loss of just 3 points. Tubman was next best with 11 points lost. As they emerged into the early morning light, Tubman had reclaimed twelfth place but by just 1 point from Perkins. Ferguson was now fourteenth, 7 points ahead of Lister, and was poised to attack his teammate.

Then came the private entrants—still murkily undefined by organisers: Edgar Hermann steadfastly laying down fast but safe times, followed by Captain Fred Barker, erratic and meteoric, throwing everything he could at the Porsche in front. Comparing the works cars to the private entrants was easy across the Australian Alps. Hermann and Hans Schuller (Porsche) were 12 minutes slower than Zasada over the 78 kilometres to Brookside: that's 10 seconds a kilometre off his pace.

The minor works teams were separated by skill, car condition and goals. Rob Slotemaker, the drift master, was having the time of his life. The clear direction from the DAF factory was to finish, to prove reliability, but it was as if Slotemaker was hard of hearing. He spent the night flinging the tiny DAF through the Alps. He started in a remarkable seventeenth position, into which he'd worked the belt-driven car, and he emerged with a cumulative loss of just 67 points to remain in the same position. He match-raced both the privateer entrants across the mountains and was faster than both Hermann's Porsche and Barker's Mercedes into Omeo by 7 minutes. It was an amazing, truly inspirational effort.

Slotemaker's teammate, David van Lennep, was dead last. All it takes is one broken sump in Erzincan. Van Lennep could not even hope to reclaim the 403 points he trailed behind Max Winkless' Volvo, so there was absolutely no incentive to go fast, except for his own natural competitive spirit, and he had to keep that in check. He'd been told to bring the DAF home no matter what, and that was what he was aiming to do. He would sacrifice 141 points through the mountains—a mobile chicane—more than double that of his teammate in a car that was arguably in the same condition.

The Russian Moskvitch team continued to carry each other home. Their performance had been remarkable. When one stopped, all stopped. They carried their entire support mechanism on board, even arc welders, and every one of the team had a specialty. Hauling a team of four across the world linked like a daisy chain was no easy matter. And yet on the final night, they lay from position 21 through 36. The top two, Tenishev–Kislyh and Aava–Lesovski, were so close they could have raced each other for position. But that was not the goal. In fact, it was forbidden. Their mission was to bring each other home. Into Ingebyra, the last stage of the night, the spread of time loss between the four was just 9 points. The top three were separated by just 4.

For the rest, it was as if there had been a collective agreement that, so close to home, it was important now not to fail. Overnight, charging through the Alps to determine the outright winner, not one of the 59 cars still left in the field would fail to complete the most challenging competitive stage of all. It said a lot about determination.

Max Winkless and John Keran had taken it upon themselves to shepherd the Elsie Gadd team home to a certain win in the Ladies class. They were doing well. The Gadd team were 2200 points ahead of Rosemary Smith and Lucette Pointet, and 5700 ahead of the *Telegraph*'s *Tortoise* team of Eileen Westley, Marion 'Minny' Macdonald and Jenny Gates. Even then, positions could change if someone went off or any one of the cars broke down. Max and John were determined that would not happen to 'their girls'. Hopelessly out of contention themselves, they turned Australia into a driving lesson for the Gadd team. 'They're doing very well,' a clearly satisfied Winkless said. 'They're actually pulling some really good times without taking risks, and they are learning the craft of rallying as well.' Winkless reached Edi with a loss of 22 points. The Gadd team dropped 21. To Brookside, Winkless sprinted ahead, opening 20 points on the Volvo station wagon, but recognising he'd pulled too big a gap, he dropped back and on the run into Omeo he gave back the 20-point deficit. Into Ingebyra, they dropped 17 points each. It was a grand effort, full of sportsmanship but also commercial imperative. It suited Winkless to see Volvo claim a major marathon prize—especially since, to his personal dismay, it wasn't going to be outright.

* * *

The mountains were over. A clear winner should have emerged. But experience told Jack Sears and Tommy Sopwith otherwise. Ten years before, they'd fought out the British Touring Car Championship in extra time. They knew that even their marathon could be decided by a tie break. So they'd built one final sting in the marathon's tail, an elimination stage. Crews, exhausted, their eyes on stalks after a night that rivalled the most savage of rally endings anywhere in the world—on top of more than 16,000 kilometres of competition—would face one final test.

* * *

Welcome to Cooma. As the sun came up on the last day of the greatest road race of all time, it went down on the reputation of the New South Wales police force. How Bob Askin, the premier, could turn up without shame at Warwick Farm racecourse hours later to greet the victors was beyond belief. Police treatment of the marathon in Cooma was the most disgraceful, most demeaning, most embarrassing and ultimately the most stressful way to bring the marathon towards conclusion. Every car driving into the Monaro High Plains township was 'greeted' with a police escort to shadow them through the city limits. It was a matter of attitude. Had the shepherding occurred with a smile and a wave, it would have been appreciated. But there was an air of menace about the entire affair. The international media was on to it. Even as they were celebrating the overnight leader and anticipating the showdown ahead, they were filing copy on police intimidation. It would become the story of the marathon, almost as big as the event itself. New South Wales had had the opportunity to turn Sir Frank Packer's event into a huge positive for state tourism. Instead, they'd blown it.

Ingebyra to Numeralla

Distance: 117 kilometres
Time allowed: 1 hour 29 minutes
Approximate average speed: 78 kilometres per hour

Numeralla to Hindmarsh Station

Distance: 57.5 kilometres
Time allowed: 42 minutes
Approximate average speed: 82 kilometres per hour

Hindmarsh Station to Nowra

Distance: 163 kilometres
Time allowed: 2 hours 1 minute
Approximate average speed: 82 kilometres per hour

Nowra to Warwick Farm

Distance: 178 kilometres
Time allowed: 3 hours 30 minutes
Approximate average speed: 51 kilometres per hour

18

The Sting in the Tail

SIMO LAMPINEN AND GILBERT STAEPELAERE were determined second was not enough. They were 4 points behind the lead. The final 'extra time' stage was 57.5 kilometres long. To pull back four minutes they would need to be better than 4 seconds a kilometre faster than Lucien Bianchi. They hadn't achieved that in the entire marathon. But what was there to be lost by trying? Bianchi was clearly under pressure. He'd just dropped two minutes on a stage he should have cleaned. Keep the pressure on. He might make a mistake.

Paddy Hopkirk adopted the same principle. He was 7 points down on Andrew Cowan. It was unconscionable. Cowan was a nice man, but seriously. Hopkirk was on another plane. Even Cowan recognised that 'I was just a small farmer,' he told me fifty years on.

'Paddy was a hero. It was almost: "Please Mr Hopkirk, may I speak to you?"' And now Cowan was leading Hopkirk. Hopkirk put it down to the misunderstanding in Omeo. He wasn't even thinking about the off at Lake King. Everything was focused on the here and now.

Harry Firth was focused on his differential. For the proud Firth, it was a moment of great embarrassment. On two occasions he'd told the young guns they were wrong. He'd knocked back Gowland and his mate Vaughan, who was now the lead Falcon GT, and he'd even had a blue with Tate, perhaps the only person, apart from himself, whom he trusted. But on the run-up to the start of the last special stage, the Number One Falcon—for that's how he thought of it—had developed a leak in an axle seal. He was lying sixth. He wanted fifth back from Vaughan.

A century before the marathon blasted through, Jinden Station in the shadow of Big Badja Mountain outside Braidwood in southern New South Wales was the scene of the massacre of four policemen by bushrangers Tom and John Clarke. The special constables were offered no mercy and no chance. They were buried on the property, near a bush track up the side of the Badja, before their bodies were exhumed and given respectful internment in Braidwood. The Clarkes were captured and executed by hanging six months later. When the Clarkes struck, John Hindmarsh's grandfather ran Jinden, a cattle and sheep property limited in its productivity by the dense scrub. In 1968, 30-year-old John was approached by Jack Sears to let the marathon pass through.

'There was a surveyors' track up the side of the Big Badja,' Hindmarsh, now 80, recalled from his bed of pain. He'd just crashed his four-wheel-drive farm bike and broken his collarbone, riding hard over the same terrain the marathon used. 'It was only 3 metres wide, not a lot of room for passing, and they said it was just what they were looking for.'

The road into the property was wider, with gates and cattle grids and room for the marathon cars to stretch their legs, but then there were the wetlands, bogs, creek crossings and rocks that could break a car. There were climbs with gradients so steep they needed four-wheel drive. But that was banned from the marathon. The marathon wanted an elimination section, and it couldn't have found a better one.

Hindmarsh and his family set about making Jinden marathon friendly. They opened their front paddock to the tent city that became an impromptu service area. 'British Leyland wanted exclusive use of our telephone—no one else was to use it—but I told them "no". It was a party line, and it had to stay open at all times.' The State Emergency Service was a big help. 'They brought in heaps of people and bunting to help keep the crowd back.' And the crowd: 'People came from everywhere to see the marathon.'

Hindmarsh helped officials set up a control point next to an old bullock cart at the side of the road, about 500 metres from the homestead. 'They wanted to see the cars coming, and give them plenty of time to stop.' In honour of Hindmarsh and his family, marathon organisers named the stage 'Hindmarsh Station', although no such location existed. Jinden disappeared from the lexicon, which is why, half a century on, it's difficult to trace the route. There is no Hindmarsh Station, and the Big Badja road—famous in later rallies—was constructed only in 1974. It's necessary to look at ordnance maps to a thin line called Jinden track to see where the marathon went.

Paddy Hopkirk was the fastest over Hindmarsh Station. He covered this impossible piece of ground in 42 minutes and 10 seconds. Allowed time was 42 minutes. The marathon, timed to the minute, always rounded up, so Hopkirk, who averaged 81.6 kilometres per hour, was penalised 1 minute.

Behind him but in front on the road, Roger Clark and Ove Andersson, running on a differential that was an odd fit in their Lotus Cortina and that had a final drive ratio unaligned with its gearing, lost 2 minutes. They were way out of contention, but they'd just confirmed eleventh position in the marathon and they'd restored some personal pride.

Lucien Bianchi was no fool. He was 4 minutes up on Lampinen. The German car could do no better than clean the stage. There were no bonus points for being early. So as long as Bianchi and Ogier lost no more than 4 minutes, they would retain their marathon lead. They lost 3 minutes. It was a controlled but nerve-racking drive. The cliché says 'to finish first, first you have to finish'. So many things could go wrong: a flat tyre, a breakage, a driver error. Bianchi had control over all three. He kept out of the potholes and on the road, and maintained pace.

Simo Lampinen crashed. He was on maximum attack. It's a phrase invented by the Finns and that only they truly understand. It's in their DNA: to go as fast as human and machine can possibly push and then lift again, to reach a level of concentration that is ephemeral, spiritual. For some, it's an out-of-body experience. You are going so fast that all mechanical functions become totally automatic, and you are in a state of suspension. Some say that the faster you go, the more your mind slows things down, that a moment in real time becomes an aeon of decision-making. Like a computer, your mind takes input—from what you see, hear and feel from the

G-forces of the car, which might not be exactly in tune with the G-forces on your body—puts it all together and serves it up as a solution to a situation that has occurred in an instant. And you are consciously part of it all.

'I came over a crest into a right-hand bend,' Simo recalled fifty years on. He is in turn sitting back in his easy chair and then thrusting forward. His foot, trapped in its Kevlar caliper, twitches with the nervous shock of reaction. 'The braking distance was not enough. The front wheel went into the gravel, and the car started to spin; I stayed on it, drifting it wide. Coming up was a cattle grid, and on each side of that was a fence post. In the RAC Rally I had seen these posts, and they were made of wood and they would easily break. By keeping on the power I was going to hit it, and I made the decision to strike it between my door and in front of the rear axle where it would do the least damage. The impact would straighten the car up. I had a nice slide on. I had set up the car nicely.'

But the fence post was metal, buried deep into the concrete surrounds of the cattle grid. 'I thought, "Bloody hell. Why didn't I let it go?"' The impact was immense. It spun the Taunus around and tore the steering arm away. 'My thoughts were now—"how can we get it going?"' Lampinen and Staepelaere had stripped the Taunus down to its bare essentials in Perth. They had virtually no recovery gear on board.

They drove the Taunus high up onto the embankment, creating a virtual inspection pit and, as the marathon roared past them, out of reach, they set to work. There were spectators at the grid, and they took Lampinen, complete with the broken arm and what tools he had, down to John Hindmarsh's work shed. And there he effected an amazing repair.

'I was pretty handy with a welder,' Simo said. He took each of his tools, spanners and the like, and used them as braces and welded them to the broken steering arm. Pretty soon he had a component, ugly looking, that he believed would get them to the finish. He shot back out to the car, fitted it up and drove into control 2 hours 46 minutes late. He had accumulated a total of 206 points and dropped to twelfth place. He'd had, in the Australian vernacular, a red-hot go. And it had not paid off—but 'Cologne was very happy'. The same car, with different pilots, went to the East African Safari the following year and won.

Harry Firth did his diff. The big Falcon ground to a halt. He needed parts to get going, and they were dropped, allegedly, by a Ford support aircraft. Firth, an excellent bush mechanic, effected the repair on the spot and dropped 52 points. Ian Vaughan and Bruce Hodgson both passed through the stage with a loss of 4 points. The three Falcons had claimed the coveted Teams Prize, but only because Firth, instead of giving up, had recognised his responsibility and pushed on. They would finish 302 points ahead of the British Leyland Number One team.

Andrew Cowan, Rauno Aaltonen and Sobieslaw Zasada each dropped 2 points. With Lampinen gone, Cowan moved into second place, 11 points behind Bianchi and 6 in front of Hopkirk. There were no more special stages to go—no more natural opportunities for driving brilliance to claim back a position. 'I kept hoping I'd see a Hillman Hunter at the side of the road with its axle hanging out,' Hopkirk said. But that was not to be.

Back on Jinden, John Hindmarsh was being kept busy. Rosemary Smith and Lucette Pointet, beset by the valve problems that had bedevilled Ford, were stuck on a steep incline. It must have been at least 20 per cent gradient. Smith had burnt out her clutch, stuffed first gear and, pointed upwards, there was no way she could even turn around to attempt reverse. 'There were spectators there but also an official who said I could not accept help,' Smith said. 'Another bastard.' Smith had not had a good marathon. She had to accept a missed-control penalty of 1440 points before John Hindmarsh was allowed to tow them up over the hill and send her on her way.

Media were fighting with British Leyland to use the party line. The greatest road race of all time had gone to a French car driven by a Frenchman and a Belgian. Behind them was a modest Scottish farmer in a Hillman Hunter, coincidentally a model just released in Australia, and they'd both outdriven the great Paddy Hopkirk—the first of the three who was truly known in Australia or, for that matter, in the UK. The first Australian entry was fourth, driven by Ian Vaughan, a young man who'd never won a championship, and then came the mighty Zasada—the name alone was evocative—and he'd raced up the leaderboard from twelfth to fifth. Rauno Aaltonen, who'd won the Bathurst 500 four years earlier, was sixth, ahead of Bruce Hodgson's Falcon GT and the silent achievers of the marathon, Herbert Kleint and Günther Klapproth for Ford Germany, who'd hovered at the back of the leaderboard for the whole marathon. Tenth place went to Bob Neyret and Jacques Terramorsi. The Citroëns were a perfect set of bookends. Over 17,000 kilometres, first to tenth were separated by just 86 minutes.

In eleventh, Roger Clark retreated behind his mirror-lens aviator glasses. 'How do you feel, Roger?' There's no such thing as a dumb question when a journalist is looking for a quote. 'Disappointed, wouldn't you be?' Clark responded and turned away. In the dying moments of the marathon—his marathon—Clark had fallen into the clutches of the also-rans. He was 21 points behind Neyret, a lifetime away, and just 2 in front of Ken Tubman.

Bianchi, with Ogier at the wheel, was cruising to victory.

* * *

Greg Stanton and Allan Chilcott never knew what hit them.

The two eighteen-year-olds were members of the CDMC, the Campbelltown District Motor Club. They'd both been students at Campbelltown High School and gone on to work at the only department store in the town, Downes. It was spread over three storeys, for its time an amazing emporium owned by local identity Rex Downes. Campbelltown was not a thriving metropolis. Some 60 kilometres south-west of Sydney, it was on a trunk road way off the main Sydney–Melbourne highways— the Hume, which went through rural Camden, and the Princes, which wound down the coastal escarpment past Wollongong and Nowra. Campbelltown's only claim to direct connectivity was the railway line, and each day the *Southern Highlands Express* hauled by a magnificent Garrett 38 steam locomotive would help people escape.

'Greg knocked on my door at about nine o'clock the night before the marathon was due down at Nowra,' Allan told me. 'He said we should go and have a look.'

This is the first time, ever, that Chilcott has spoken to a journalist about the crash that took out the marathon's leader. He had written a partial explanation for an enthusiast publication about ten years before, but this was different. 'Greg and I made a pact not to talk. It was better that way,' he said. Even when Andrew Cowan visited the CDMC on a PR visit a couple of years after the marathon, they maintained their vow of silence. 'We were intro-duced to him but never told him who we were.'

Stanton has passed away now, of an illness at age 61. Out of a sense of duty, Chilcott had protected his identity all these years. There'd been a bit of a falling-out. Wives had not gotten along, and the boys, now men, had drifted apart. Stanton went on to a career in electronics, working with an international conglomerate. Chilcott, a salesman at Downes, went into logistics for one of Australia's biggest freight companies and then for the large auto-motive bond store at Minto just up the road from Campbelltown where new cars are received from overseas, fitted with port instal-lations such as radios and sent on to their local distributors. He hasn't strayed too far from the district.

'When you were a kid, cars were your life,' Chilcott said. 'You couldn't afford both cars and girls, so cars won. Greg and I had been officials at CDMC events. We'd driven up to Oberon over the Blue Mountains and down the South Coast to work as control officials at overnight rallies. Rallies were navigational and held at night in those days. And you'd sit in your car all night, waiting to check cars through. We couldn't afford to compete, so it was the closest we'd get to competition.'

Allan Chilcott had a Morris 850, the basic Mini, and he'd occasionally participated in gymkhanas, the entry level of car-club competition that teaches car control. Stanton, an electrician at Downes, working in their basement electrical division, had saved like mad and bought a second-hand Mini Cooper S from Starline Motors on Sydney's Parramatta Road. It wasn't, Chilcott said, a former police car. The Mini Cooper S was the staple diet of police pursuit, but every eighteen-year-old enthusiast could spot one a mile off ('they were lowered, and there were telltale holes in the grill and dash where police gear was fitted'), and you avoided buying them second-hand for fear of getting a dud. Stanton had checked out the car thoroughly. 'He was a deep thinker, and he knew things. He was like the internet before we had the internet.' He'd had the car further repaired as part of the purchase agreement. It had new suspension, and the hydrolastic lines had been overhauled. And it had a genuine wood-rimmed steering wheel. These things mean a lot.

'We were keen to get to Nowra really early to see the cars come through, so we decided to go that night,' Chilcott said. 'We got our mothers to phone us in sick.' They agreed. The boys drove down and parked outside the control.

'There's stories we were drunk,' Chilcott said. 'It wasn't the case. Sure, we used to go to the pub after work. But we didn't drink that night, and there were no bottles in the car. There were no hotels near where we parked.'

The next morning, they turned up at control. '[It was] just a couple of tents at the side of the road and some soldiers with radios. The control officials couldn't tell us anything. One person was talking on a two-way radio, and we heard that "ETA is one hour". We understood that to mean at this location. We thought: "Let's go down to the creek crossing, about ten minutes away".' Chilcott is adamant that no one tried to stop them. They just drove off.

'We didn't see any cars on the road. Thinking back, instead of us it could just as easily have been a family going home.' Chilcott describes Stanton as a skilful driver. He claims speed was not a factor. 'The road was quite narrow. It would have been a single lane if it had been bitumen. There was a very distinctive curve on its crown. The last thing I remember is the Citroën coming towards us. I don't recall the crash at all.'

Stanton broke his right foot and suffered severe lacerations up his arms when the splintered wood-rimmed steering wheel cut into him. Chilcott banged his head hard on the Mini's B-pillar and had cuts to his legs from the parcel tray. Both had seatbelt burns. 'We were using three-point lap-sash belts and, as car-club members, we were early adopters of them.'

Chilcott denies they were wearing four-point harnesses as Jean-Claude Ogier suggested. 'We couldn't afford them,' he said. 'I remember being placed in the back seat of a Volvo, then being in Shoalhaven Hospital. There was a curtain in the emergency area, and Bianchi was on the other side, in the bed next to me. I heard French being spoken but didn't understand it. Nobody from that side came to see me.

'I remember they didn't give Greg anaesthetic when they put stitches in his arms. It hurt him a lot.'

Chilcott says he had a copy of the police record until a few years ago when he mislaid it. 'The only person who spoke to me was a sergeant. I remember he spelled the name of our car "Minnie".' The boys lay there all day. 'No one came to see us, no organisers, no press. We were offered no transport. That night, my parents came down and picked me up and drove me home.' Fake news had travelled fast. Chilcott's girlfriend had initially been told he'd been killed. The crash was all over the afternoon *Sun* newspaper that day.

Back at work, Chilcott and Stanton got nothing more than a 'stern look' from the boss at Downes. No action was taken against them. And it could have ended there—except for the insurance.

'Greg had insurance, and there was a concern that there'd be a claim made by Citroën against him. So the insurance person took us to the scene. They took measurements and notes and so there was a complete record of what happened.'

The motor-sport community had quickly spread the word that drunken yahoos, perhaps even off-duty police, had caused the crash. 'The insurance company was concerned about this. They insisted we defend ourselves because if we didn't, it could be construed that we somehow confirmed the allegations.' They hired a lawyer, took *Racing Car News* to court and, armed with the insurance evidence, won a settlement out of court. 'I got $800,' Chilcott said. It was worth about three months of wages.

Later they found the Mini in a wrecking yard at Grahams Hill, just outside Campbelltown. They hadn't seen it since the crash, and it was a sobering moment. They had escaped death.

Chilcott told me he is surprised by Ogier's accusations. Half a century on, he dismisses talk of sabotage and claims no knowledge of any betting syndicate that would want to influence the outcome of the marathon. 'We were just two kids from Campbelltown,' he said.

He remains a motoring enthusiast. He owns an MGB that he uses on vintage rallies. But for fifty years, the marathon 'has been a big thing on my mind'.

'One day, I was watching a replay on TV of the famous incident when Bathurst 1000 race leader Dick Johnson was eliminated by a rock that tumbled onto the track. I turned to my wife and said— "I know how the rock feels".'

* * *

'The police should have been there, not on the main roads.' Paddy Hopkirk was angry to the point of apoplexy. 'They are a bunch of twits, sitting in cars instead of getting out on their feet, controlling traffic.' And then he wound up: 'Oh God, don't talk to me about your police. They're a bunch of SS men. There were seven cars and a motorbike behind us all the way up from Nowra—just keeping an eye on marathon drivers, but where were they when Bianchi was hurt? If they had been controlling intersections and danger spots, the accident probably wouldn't have happened.'

Barry Ferguson joined the outrage: 'We had fantastic cooperation from police everywhere we went except in New South Wales. At one stage, we had a Rambler in front of us and a Mini behind us, both watching us like hawks. We saw something like 60 police vehicles from the time we hit Nowra. They overdid it.'

Only Rosemary Smith, always on the hunt for a headline, took the opposing view. 'I met an ever-so-sweet policeman. He told me I was exceeding the speed limit. I gave him a nice smile, and he was ever so sweet. He even showed me the way to Warwick Farm.'

Bianchi's crash changed the marathon in more ways than the lead. Like normal motorists at the scene of an accident, crews stopped to look, creating a traffic jam and adding to the chaos. The marathon was no different, perhaps worse, because people who'd bonded, no matter how slightly, since Crystal Palace were in shock. It was devastating. There'd been other crashes over the course of the marathon, but none like this, in full view. Everyone had to pass it. In the manner of cars of their time, both vehicles were twisted sheets of metal, their front ends torn away. Perhaps it was fatigue, perhaps the shock, perhaps people regarded the marathon as now over, but no fewer than 26 teams, almost half the surviving field, relinquished points on what was supposed to be a transport stage. None of the professionals went down. Even Hopkirk, so tied up in the rescue, recognised that the marathon offered no force majeure, no compassionate relief, for stopping at the scene of an accident, and so he'd sprinted to the Nowra control, leaving Bianchi, as he cemented his own place in marathon history.

Which is why it is so perplexing, even now, to note that the two Holden teammates, Ferguson and Whiteford, traded places on the transport stage. Ferguson had been fourteenth after Hindmarsh Station and advanced to twelfth with a loss of 9 points on the way into Nowra. Whiteford dropped a massive 24 and fell behind his teammate and the Lister–Welinski Volvo. 'I know we stopped at Bianchi's accident, and we were there for some time helping out,' Ferguson said. 'And I know we lost points but I have no idea what happened to Doug [Whiteford], Eddie [Perkins] and Jim [Hawker].'

At the time, the Bianchi crash and the Cowan victory were all-consuming news stories. No one in the press corps had the inclination to look back through the field. And then, suddenly, everyone had dispersed and there was no opportunity. In the grand scheme, who came twelfth and fourteenth in the London–Sydney Marathon is of little consequence. And yet, the fact that the only two crew members of either Holden who remain alive, Ferguson and Johnson, whose memories are so sharp in every other area, have no recollection of this important moment remains a loose end.

* * *

Warwick Farm was the last time control of the marathon. Built by the Australian Jockey Club nine years before to encircle its horseracing track, as did the combined car and racehorse complex Aintree in England, the Farm was already on shaky ground. Like

London's suburban Crystal Palace, it was falling victim to the urban sprawl, limited in its use by the whim of councils and the protests of residents. Sir Frank Packer was on the committee of the Australian Jockey Club and, although he professed no love of car racing, he was still part of the slender majority that kept the Farm operating as a motor-racing venue.

For the marathon, it was neither an inspirational nor particularly accessible venue, a long way from the city. Next day, the marathon would make a triumphal parade into the Sydney CBD to arrive at Hyde Park, right opposite the headquarters of Packer's Australian Consolidated Press. Show business had not yet touched Sydney. The power of its harbour as a tourist magnet had not been realised. The Sydney Harbour Bridge was never envisaged by marathon organisers as a symbolic closure, and the Sydney Opera House, the city's second icon, had not been built. Compared to the drive-by of Big Ben at the start, the arrival in Sydney was a bit of a damp squib.

Paddy Hopkirk was the first to arrive at the gates of Warwick Farm, and he parked to one side to allow Andrew Cowan the right to enter first. Cowan had had a nightmare of a trip on the 178-kilometre drive from Nowra. Chrysler Australia had sent a follow-me car to Nowra, and they insisted that Cowan, Coyle and Malkin should fall into convoy behind them. 'We had more trouble with them than anyone else on the entire marathon,' Cowan recalled. 'I was quite upset with them.'

After you've been on your own recognisance, the last thing you need is someone telling you what to do, especially while you're still on the clock. 'If we'd overtaken inappropriately, gone the wrong way, or been led astray, we could have still gone down. Our lead was only 6 minutes.' At 12.35 p.m. on a sweltering hot early summer's day, the Hillman Hunter arrived, solo, at Warwick Farm to be greeted by Premier Bob Askin, who dropped an Australian flag over its bonnet. Cameraman Rob McAuley was an uninvited but welcome passenger, riding on the boot lid, filming as the car drove in.

More than 10,000 people had flooded the Farm, and Cowan and his crew took to the roof of their car. In the manner of the day, they popped champagne. Deliciously and ironically, it was French. But rather than spraying it, a spontaneous reaction by American Dan Gurney at the Le Mans 24 Hour two years before, they poured it into a champagne coupe—not flute—and sipped politely from it. 'I'd rather have a beer,' Malkin said, and was given one.

It took eleven hours for the field to make it in from Nowra. The last car—the *Telegraph*'s *Tortoise*—rolled in at 11.35 p.m. By then, Cowan, Coyle and Malkin were in their hotel, the Travelodge at Rushcutters Bay. They'd been greeted there by the taciturn Des O'Dell who, true to the Rootes Group's rigid schedule, had not gone to Warwick Farm and so had missed the moment of triumph.

If Cowan was expecting a hero's welcome from the boss, he was to be disappointed. 'He just looked at me and said: "So? That's why we came here." Coming from him, it was as big a compliment as you could expect.' Cowan asked the switchboard to hold all his calls and went to sleep for three hours. It was all the time he could spare.

* * *

On Wednesday, 18 December, 56 winners and survivors of the London–Sydney Marathon drove in triumphant convoy to Hyde

Park in the middle of Sydney. The streets were lined with people: impossible to say how many—not as many as London's farewell— but still more than a hundred thousand. Not bad for a weekday. The crowds spilt onto the roads, waving banners and flags. King Street, one of the main city thoroughfares, was closed to traffic to give the marathon free rein, and the sound of air horns split the air and echoed off the tall buildings. Paddy Hopkirk created titillation by occasionally moving up on and ramming Andrew Cowan's Hillman Hunter in front of him. It was dismissed as light-hearted fun, but some read it as more—a last gasp of frustration over what might have been. 'He's a wild man, that Paddy,' Andrew said, his teeth clenched.

'This makes it all worthwhile,' homecoming Barry Ferguson said from the seat of his twelfth-placed Monaro. 'All the tension and struggling and the times you wondered what you were doing in the marathon at all.' No one wanted it to end. The rush was too great, and it washed away the exhaustion.

The Daily Telegraph exalted the winners, applauded the participants and announced a fund to help Lucien Bianchi. With donations limited to $5, the first day raised $1300.

The next evening, marathon crews attended the official prize giving at Sydney's Trocadero Ballroom. It should have been a grand affair, but the 'Troc', home to so many end-of-year school formals, was a tired old thing, and its drabness drew criticism from marathon participants who thought they deserved better. Maybe the adrenalin was wearing off. But it shouldn't have. The achievement had been immense—never to be repeated.

Sir Roden Cutler, VC, war hero and New South Wales state governor, told them that night: 'The winners are men who have broken the restrictive bonds of caution. They have sparked into a flame the embers of a forlorn chance and captured the world's interest in sporting challenges.'

Andrew Cowan, marathon hero, said: 'When you do an event like this, there's got to be a lot of luck in it. But as far as I'm concerned, it wasn't luck that won it. It was bad luck that lost it.'

Even as Cowan was speaking, the UK House of Commons was passing a resolution: 'that this House notes with pride the success of British drivers and British cars in the London–Sydney Marathon and congratulates the teams taking part on their skill and endurance, the organisers and supporters for their enterprise and efficiency and the British Motor Manufacturing Industry for making the best cars in the world.'

19

The Curse of the Bianchis

ON 30 MARCH 1969, three months and fourteen days after his marathon crash, Lucien Bianchi, still recovering from his injuries, was strapped into a 3-litre Autodelta V8 Alfa Romeo 33/3 proto-type for the second day of testing for the Le Mans 24 Hour race. He was defending his title not in the Ford GT 40 with which he'd won the previous year but in the first monocoque version of the Alfa. Bianchi had competed in thirteen successive Le Mans races, more than any but three other drivers, all of them heroes, and his victory meant the world to him.

Bianchi had experienced difficulty with the rear bodywork on the 750-kilogram Alfa. It wasn't sealing properly and air was getting underneath it, affecting the handling. Approaching the end of the Les Hunaudières straight, the fastest part of the circuit where speeds are well above 300 kilometres per hour, it was reported that his right-hand indicator began flashing, but he did not slow. The car touched the soft right-hand verge, then spun back to the left, impacting a telegraph pole and disintegrating. Bianchi, 34, died instantly.

His brother, Mauro, seriously burned at Le Mans the previous year, called a halt to the Bianchi family's direct involvement in motor racing. The ban held for one generation. His son, Philippe, ran a go-kart school for young hopefuls, and one of its graduates was Mauro's grandson, Lucien's grand-nephew, Jules. In 2014, Jules, a promising young Formula One driver and a member of Ferrari's elite Driver Academy, was killed in the Japanese Grand Prix.

* * *

In the afterglow of their success, Sir Max Aitken and Sir Frank Packer speculated on the potential for a second London–Sydney Marathon in 1972 to coincide with the Olympic year. It never happened.

Events overtook them. Sir Frank sold his beloved *Telegraph* to Rupert Murdoch's News Limited. Murdoch's tabloids hounded Sir Max's broadsheet in the UK, and with circulation dropping he did not have the appetite to go it alone.

An Australian impresario, Wylton Dickson, not a motor-sport enthusiast, took the germ of an idea, abandoned the Olympics and inserted the FIFA World Cup. In 1970, he promoted the London to Mexico World Cup Rally over 25,000 kilometres. He got works entries from Ford, British Leyland and Moskvitch.

In 1974, he did it again—the London to Munich World Cup Rally. Entries were down to 70, and no works teams competed.

A massive navigational error in the middle of the Sahara put lives at risk, including that of Stirling Moss, finally competing, who was stranded without water in Algiers.

In 1977, Dickson ran his last event—a re-run of the London–Sydney Marathon, except this one was billed as 30,000 kilometres over 30 days. Transport difficulties, a result of poor organisation, made it longer: 45 days in total.

All three of Dickson's events were won by people who'd contested the original London–Sydney Marathon and been infatuated by the challenge.

Gunnar Palm, who did not get out of Europe at his first attempt, won the London–Mexico partnering Hannu Mikkola in a works Ford Escort 1850 GT.

Ken Tubman and Andre Welinski invited Jim Reddiex into their Citroën DS 23 to win the London–Munich by a massive 28-hour margin.

Andrew Cowan made peace with Colin Malkin and, in the absence of Brian Coyle, who was no longer his brother-in-law, invited Mike Broad to make up a threesome. Cowan won his second London–Sydney marathon in succession in 1977, this time driving for the works Mercedes-Benz team.

Nick and Jenny Brittan turned marathoning into their life's work. They formed a company, Trans World Events, and over twelve years from 1993 ran eight well-organised, self-funded events for amateurs who wanted to live the dream. Two of those went from London to Sydney. The last was in 2004. Nick Brittan died two years later as a consequence of stress. Jenny Brittan followed a decade later, of cancer.

Each event, in its own way, was sensational. Each of Dickson's events challenged teams to perform accelerating feats of endurance, but escalation of that magnitude was not sustainable, especially in a shrinking world with increasing restrictions. The Brittans' events were also afflicted. Their organisation was stronger, their control tighter, but the cost of those services was skyrocketing. Fewer people could afford to pay. The scale was all wrong.

There is a lot of reason to be thankful to the Sirs, Max Aitken and Frank Packer, and to Tommy Sopwith and Jocelyn Stevens. The 1968 London–Sydney Marathon was not only the first of all the ultra-marathons, it was also the pinnacle.

Acknowledgements

The London–Sydney Marathon was a major influence on everyone who competed and participated in it. For some, it was a life changer—evidenced by their passionate recollections and the spirited debate those memories have sparked even half a century on.

Was Andrew Cowan 'gifted' the race win, and was Lucien Bianchi the moral victor? That was the conclusion of this author's first book on the marathon, *The Bright Eyes of Danger*, co-written with David McKay in 1969. Andrew, naturally, took an opposing view in his book *Why Finish Last?* With the benefit of a lifetime of reflection, it's finally possible to bring context to the polarised positions. No doubt Lucien was cruelly denied victory, but Andrew's preparation, determination and raw speed when it counted delivered him a deserved first place. Were he with us today, it's most likely David McKay, as a racer, would still defend his original point of view.

To a degree, we all underestimated the lasting contribution and vast influence of the marathon when it occurred. We were so focused on moving this great race across the world at breakneck speed that we hardly noticed the impact it was creating or the barriers it was breaking just to exist. It's been a pleasure, in this retrospective, to expose more deeply the motivations that made it possible and the ambitions that drove its success.

That the British motor industry failed to capitalise more fully on the opportunity can be sheeted down to factors far beyond the reach of a mere car race, but it remains all these years later an open wound of frustration to those who competed that their efforts were not better rewarded with more, not less, emphasis on motor sport as a showroom sales tool. The marathon sapped resources, and for those who didn't win it was hard to post-justify. The Hillman Hunter, though, happily and coincidentally launched simultaneously with its marathon victory, was an unexpected sales success.

The joy of writing *Race across the World* has been reconnecting with the greats of the marathon and of the genre of long-distance competition. They are a special breed, and I was fortunate to meet with many, sifting perhaps for the first—and last—time the facts from the fiction that is the stock in trade of any racer's public recall of a recent competition.

I'm particularly grateful for the time and effort given by Andrew Cowan, Paddy Hopkirk and Ian Vaughan, the three podium place getters. And also to Jean-Claude Ogier, who still views the Nowra Road incident as something that might have happened just yesterday, so raw are his memories. Competitors, participants and media who brought fresh perspective include Rauno Aaltonen, Bob Bottom OAM, Barry Ferguson, John Gowland, Bob Holden, John Hartigan, David Liddle, Simo Lampinen, Rob McAuley, Ian Morton, the late Russell McPhedran, Ken Murden, Shirley Morton (Bell), Lucette Ogier (Pointet), Alec Poole, Michel Parot, Bill Price, Jim Reddiex, George Shepheard, Rosemary Smith, Max Stahl, Ian Tate, Stuart Turner, Marek Wachowski and Sobieslaw Zasada. A very special mention must go to David Johnson, one of the most outstanding 'high-speed office managers' in the business, who guided the recounting of this story stage by stage and obstacle by obstacle.

Doors were opened, lost contacts regained and additional insights were obtained through the help of Ray Berghouse; Mike Breen; Garry Connelly AM; Chris Curry; Rene de Boer; Bill Forsyth; John and Janette Hindmarsh of Jinden Station; Ray Kennedy; Dr Carl Le; Patricia Lodge of the UK Guild of Motoring Writers; Roger Parsons; Andrew, Kate, Karen, Cameron and Matilda Smailes; Lisa Smith; Bruce Thomas; Dan and Rosemary White; and Janek Zdzarski. The mystery of the Nowra crash was illuminated for the first time thanks to the gracious cooperation of the Mini Cooper's passenger, Allan Chilcott, and Jason Stanton, son of the Mini driver the late Greg Stanton.

I acknowledge the works of those who wrote marathon books at the time—Paddy Hopkirk, Innes Ireland and Andrew Cowan— and one completed more recently by enthusiast Robert Connor. Each has helped confirm (or deny) my notes of fifty years ago and my recent interviews. In that respect, I'm grateful also to friends and colleagues who have passed on: Mike Kable, doyen motoring editor of *The Australian* newspaper; Nick Brittan and his wife, Jenny, with whom I spent several days comparing notes after the marathon for the books we both wrote; and Ove Andersson, another 'moral victor' with whom I enjoyed friendship right up to his death in an historic rally in South Africa.

The marathon changed my young life, and my never-ending gratitude goes to *The Daily Telegraph* stalwarts David McNicoll CBE, Ted Shiel and motoring writer and hero David McKay, who persuaded Sir Frank Packer to 'let the young bloke go' in the face of spirited competition from perhaps more qualified reporters.

Race across the World is my latest association with Allen & Unwin, and my thanks go to publishing director Tom Gilliatt, always challenging senior editor Samantha Kent, copyeditor Susan Keogh, the positive-pedant, and cover designer Luke Causby. It's been a grand partnership.

* * *

It was 9 p.m. on a cold, raining, dismal winter night in Sydney—summer in Brighton, UK—when executive assistant Elisha Pople got her boss on the phone after months of persuasion. Tommy Sopwith had been strangely reluctant to engage. But that night the barriers came down, and he was enthusiastic and enlightening. As a reporter, I've always believed in the Japanese edict of *genchi genbutsu*—go to the source. The story of how the great race across the world was conceived is so fanciful as to be unbelievable except in folklore. With steadfast modesty, and perhaps more than a little pride, Tommy confirmed it all—and more. It's quite a story.

Marathon Facts
and Figures

The Entrants

ENTRANT	COUNTRY	CAR	CREW
1. RTS Motorway Remoulds	UK	Ford Cortina GT	B. Bengry/A. Brick/ J. Preddy
2. Ford Motor Co., Australia	Australia	Ford Falcon GT	H. Firth/G. Hoinville/ G. Chapman
3. Avon/RAF	UK	Ford Cortina GT	F/O N. Coleman/ Flt. Lt. A. Dalgleish/ Flt. Lt. P.S. Moloney
4. British Leyland	UK	BMC Austin 1800	T. Fall/M. Wood/ B. Culcheth
5. R. Lewis	UK	Chrysler Valiant Estate	P. Lumsden/P. Sargent/ R. Lewis/J. Fenton
6. Combined Insurance Co. of America	Australia	Ford Fairmont XP	C. Hodgins/D. Wait/ B. Lawler

ENTRANT	COUNTRY	CAR	CREW
7. Avtoexport	USSR	Moskvitch 408	A. Ipatenko/A. Terehin/ E. Bazhenov
8. AMOCO Aust. Pty Ltd	Australia	Volvo 144 S	P.H. Winkless/J. Keran
9. A.A. Bombelli	Switzerland	Ford Cortina Lotus	A. Bombelli/T. Belso
10. Royal Green Jackets	UK	Porsche 911 T	G. Yannaghas/ Lt. J. Dill
11. Blick Racing Team	Switzerland	Renault 16TS	F. Reust/P. Gratzer/ A. Béguin
12. TVW Ch. 7, Daily News, Perth	Australia	Volvo 144 S	K. Tubman/J. Forrest
13. J.G. Tallis	UK	Volvo 123 GT	J. Tallis/P. Coltelloni
14. Ford Deutschland	West Germany	Ford Taunus 20 MRS	D. Glemser/M. Braungart
15. G.P. Franklin	Australia	Ford Cortina GT	G. Franklin/A. Brassington
16. D.A. Corbett	UK	BMC Austin 1800	D. Corbett/G. Mabbs/T. Fisk
17. Royal Navy	UK	BMC Austin 1800	Capt. J. Hans Hamilton/ Capt. I. Lees-Spalding/ Cmdr. P. Stearns
18. M.A. Colvill	UK	Ford Cortina	M. Greenwood/D. Aldridge
19. Avtoexport	USSR	Moskvitch 408	S. Tenishev/V. Kislyh
20. Avtoexport	USSR	Moskvitch 408	V. Schavelev/E. Lifshits/ V. Shirotchenkov
21. Hillcrest Motor Co.	UK	BMC Austin 1800	B. Williams/M. Thomas/ B. Hughes
22. G. Baghetti	Italy	Lancia Fulvia 1.3 HF	G. Baghetti/G. Bassi
23. P.R.H. Wilson	UK	Ford Corsair 2000E	P. Wilson/I. Mackelden/ K. Dwyer/D. Maxwell
24. Ford Motor Co., Australia	Australia	Ford Falcon GT	I. Vaughan/R. Forsyth/ J. Ellis

ENTRANT	COUNTRY	CAR	CREW
25. Chesson, Lydden Circuit/La Trobe Brafield Stad.	UK	Volvo 122 S	J. La Trobe/W. Chesson/ G. Warner
26. M.J.C. Taylor	UK	Mercedes-Benz 280 SE	M. Taylor/I. Ireland/ A. Hedges
27. F. Goulden	UK	Triumph 2000	F. Goulden/B. Goulden/ J. Goulden
28. A.N. Gorshenin	Australia	Mercedes-Benz 280 SL	A. Gorshenin/I. Bryson
29. Ford Motor Co., Australia	Australia	Ford Falcon GT	B. Hodgson/D. Rutherford
30. Dutch National Team	The Netherlands	DAF 55	R. Slotemaker/R. Janssen
31. BMC Aust.	Australia	BMC Austin 1800	E. Green/J. Murray/ G. Shepheard
32. Capt. F. Barker	UK	Mercedes-Benz 280 S	Capt. F. Barker/Capt. D. Dollar/Capt. J. Lewis
33. Miss E. Gadd	UK	Volvo 145 S Estate	Miss E. Gadd/Miss J. Tudor-Owen/Miss S. Kemp/ Miss A. Castell
34. K. Brierley	UK	Ford Cortina Lotus	K. Brierley/D. Skittrall
35. R.A. Buchanan-Michaelson	UK	Mercedes-Benz 280 SE	R. Buchanan-Michaelson/ D. Seigle-Morris/M. Stahl
36. Sydney Telegraph 1	Australia	Holden Monaro GTS	D. McKay/G. Reynolds/ D. Liddle
37. W.D. Cresdee	UK	BMC Austin 1300	W.D. Cresdee/B. Freeborough/J. Syer
38. Ford Motor Company	UK	Ford Cortina Lotus	B. Söderström/G. Palm
39. Addison Motors	Australia	Alfa Romeo 1750	S. McLeod/C.J. Lock/ T. Theiler
40. Jim Russell Racing Drivers' School	UK	Vauxhall Ventora	D. Walker/B. Jones/ D. Morris

ENTRANT	COUNTRY	CAR	CREW
41. Sydney Telegraph 4	Australia	Morris 1100	Miss E. Westley/Miss M. Macdonald/Miss J. Gates
42. P.G. Graham	UK	Ford Cortina Savage V6	P. Graham/Dr. L. Morrish/ M. Wooley
43. AMOCO Aust. Pty Ltd	Australia	Volvo 144 S	A. Welinski/G. Lister
44. British Army Motoring Assoc.	UK	Rover 2000 TC	Maj. M. Bailey/ Maj. F. Preston
45. RAF Motor Sports Assoc.	UK	Hillman Hunter	Flt. Lt. D. Carrington/Sqdn. Ldr. A. King/Flt. Lt. J. Jones
46. Simca Motors Team 1	France	Simca 1100	B. Heu/J. Syda
47. Nova Magazine	UK	MGB	Mrs. J. Denton/T. Boyce
48. Ford Motor Company	UK	Ford Cortina Lotus	R. Clark/O. Andersson
49. Major P.S. Ekholdt	Norway	SAAB 96 VA	DID NOT START
50. Ford Motor Company	UK	Ford Cortina Lotus	N. Brittan/Mrs. J. Brittan
51. British Leyland	UK	BMC Austin 1800	P. Hopkirk/T. Nash/A. Poole
52. J. Sprinzel	UK	MG Midget	J. Sprinzel/R. Fidler
53. S.H. Dickson	USA	Rambler American	S. Dickson/J. Saladin/J. Sims
54. British Army Motoring Assoc.	UK	Rover 2000 TC	Maj. J. Hemsley/ WO1 F. Webber
55. E.G. Hermann	Kenya	Porsche 911 T	E. Hermann/H. Schuller
56. A.J. Percy	UK	SAAB 95 Estate	A. Percy/J. Delmar-Morgan
57. Ford Deutschland	West Germany	Ford Taunus 20 MRS	G. Staepelaere/S. Lampinen
58. S. Zasada	Poland	Porsche 911 S	S. Zasada/M. Wachowski
59. Porsche Cars GB Ltd	UK	Porsche 911 S	T. Hunter/J. Davenport

ENTRANT	COUNTRY	CAR	CREW
60. Terry-Thomas Team	UK	Ford Cortina 1600 E	P. Capelin/A. Pargeter/ T. Baker
61. British Leyland	UK	BMC Austin 1800	R. Aaltonen/H. Liddon/ P. Easter
62. D. Praznovsky	Australia	Mercedes-Benz 200 D	D. Praznovsky/S. Zovko/ I. Inglis
63. AMOCO Aust. Pty Ltd	Australia	Volvo 142 S	R. Holden/L. Graham
64. Flt. Lt. J.T. Kingsley/Evan Cook Ltd	UK	BMC Austin 1800	Flt. Lt. J.T. Kingsley/Flt. Lt. D. Bell/Flt. Lt. P. Evans
65. Hydraulic Machinery (GB)	UK	BMC Austin 1800	G. White/J. Jeffcoat/ D. Dunnell
66. T.E. Buckingham	UK	Ford Cortina GT	T. Buckingham/J. Lloyd/ D. Hackleton
67. C.J. Woodley	UK	Vauxhall Ventora	C. Woodley/S. Green/ R. Cullingford
68. Sydney Telegraph 3	Australia	Holden Monaro GTS	D. Whiteford/E. Perkins/ J. Hawker
69. Dutch National Team	The Netherlands	DAF 55	D. van Lennep/P. Hissink
70. Wilson's Motor Caravan Centre	UK	BMC Austin 1800	A. Wilson/F. McDonnell/ C. Taylor
71. Vantona Everwear Ltd	UK	BMC Austin 1800	B. Field/R.D. Tilley/D. Jones
72. E. McMillen	UK	Ford Cortina Lotus	E. McMillen/J. L'Amie/ I. Drysdale
73. Ford Motor Company	UK	Ford Cortina Lotus	E. Jackson/K. Chambers
74. R. Neyret	France	Citroën DS 21	R. Neyret/L.J. Terramorsi
75. Rootes Motors	UK	Hillman Hunter	A. Cowan/B. Coyle/ C. Malkin
76. Sydney Telegraph 2	Australia	Holden Monaro GTS	B. Ferguson/D. Chivas/ D. Johnson

ENTRANT	COUNTRY	CAR	CREW
77. Big 'N' Cash & Carry Group	UK	BMC Austin 1800	R. Eaves/J. Vipond/ F. Bainbridge
78. Supersport Engines Ltd	UK	Ford Escort GT	J. Gavin/J. Maclay/ R.M. Maudling
79. P.A. Downs	UK	VW 1200	P. Downs/A. Downs
80. I.M. Large	UK	BMW 2000	DID NOT START
81. Dr. B. Wadia	India	Ford Cortina Lotus	Dr. B. Wadia/K. Tarmaster/F. Kaka
82. D.G. Bray	UK	Ford Cortina Lotus	D. Bray/S. Sladen/P. Sugden
83. Kentredder (Ireland) Ltd	Eire	Peugeot 404 Inj.	J. Cotton/Miss S. Kay/ P. McClintock
84. C.K.W. Schellenberg	UK	Bentley 1930 Sports Tourer	K. Schellenberg/N. Barclay/ Hon. P. Lindsay
85. Tecalemit Ltd	UK	Ford Cortina Lotus	P. Harper/D. Pollard
86. Pan Aust. Unit Trust/S. Cross Management	UK	BMW 2000	C. Forsyth/R. Uniacke/ J. Rich
87. Citroën Cars Ltd	France	Citroën DS 21	L. Bianchi/J-C. Ogier
88. Simca Motors Team 2	France	Simca 1100	R. Masson/J. Py
89. Longlife Group	UK	Ford Cortina	R. Clark/M. Pearson/P. Hall
90. British Army Motoring Assoc.	UK	Ford Cortina Lotus	Capt. D. Harrison/ Lt. M. Proudlock
91. Maitland Motors	Australia	Holden HK Automatic	B. Madden/J. Murray/ J. Bryson
92. Ford Deutschland	West Germany	Ford Taunus 20 MRS	H. Kleint/G. Klapproth
93. Henry Ford & Son	UK	Ford Cortina Lotus	Miss R. Smith/ Miss L. Pointet
94. Automobile Club de France	France	Citroën DS 21	J-L. Lemerle/O. Turcat/ P. Vanson

ENTRANT	COUNTRY	CAR	CREW
95. N. Koga	Japan	Vauxhall Viva GT	N. Koga/Y. Terada/ K. Mitsumoto
96. R. Rogers	UK	Ford Cortina 1600 E	R. Rogers/A. Sheppard
97. Lunwin Products Pty Ltd	Australia	Ford Falcon GT	R. Lunn/C. Tippett/J. Hall
98. Avtoexport	USSR	Moskvitch 408	U. Aava/J. Lesovski
99. 17/21st Lancers	UK	Land Rover 2WD	Lt. M.G. Thompson/ Lt. C. Marriott/ Cpl. C. Skelton/ Tpr. M. Lewis
100. Simca Motors Team 3	France	Simca 1100	P. Boucher/G. Houel

Outright Positions

First place: *The Daily Express* trophy:
Car 75 (Hillman Hunter), Andrew Cowan, Brian Coyle, Colin Malkin (Rootes Motors)

Second place: *The Daily Telegraph* prize:
Car 51 (BMC Austin 1800), Paddy Hopkirk, Tony Nash, Alec Poole (British Leyland Motor Corporation)

Third place: *The Daily Telegraph* prize:
Car 24 (Ford Falcon GT), Ian Vaughan, Bob Forsyth, Jack Ellis (Ford Motor Company, Australia)

Special Awards

First in General Classification at Bombay, Carreras Guards trophy:
Car 48 (Ford Cortina Lotus), Roger Clark, Ove Andersson (Ford Motor Company, UK)

Best performance by an Australian crew, *The Daily Telegraph* prize:
Car 24 (Ford Falcon GT), Ian Vaughan, Bob Forsyth, Jack Ellis (Ford Motor Company, Australia)

Best performance by a team of three cars of any one make, Ladbroke's prize:
Cars 2, 24 and 29 (Ford Falcon GTs), Harry Firth, Ian Vaughan, Bruce Hodgson (Ford Motor Company, Australia)

Best performance by a private entrant, *The Evening Standard* trophy:
Car 55 (Porsche 911), Edgar Hermann, Hans Schuller (E.G. Hermann)

Best performance by an all-woman crew, Cibie Prize:
Car 33 (Volvo 145 S Estate), Miss Elsie Gadd, Miss Jennifer Tudor-Owen, Miss Sheila Kemp, Miss Anthea Castell (Miss E. Gadd)

The Results

PLACE	1	2	3	4	5	6	7	8	9	10	11	12	13	14	15	16	17	18	19	20
CAR	75	51	24	58	61	29	92	2	74	48	12	76	43	68	55	57	30	32	64	19
CONTROL																				
PARIS	0	0	0	0	0	0	0	0	0	0	0	0	0	0	0	0	0	0	0	0
TURIN	0	0	0	0	0	0	0	0	0	0	0	0	0	0	0	0	0	0	0	0
BELGRADE	0	0	0	0	0	0	0	0	0	0	0	0	0	0	0	0	0	0	0	0
ISTANBUL	0	0	0	0	0	0	0	0	0	0	0	0	0	0	0	0	0	0	0	0
SIVAS	0	0	0	0	0	0	0	0	0	0	0	0	0	0	0	0	0	0	0	0
ERZINCAN	21	17	25	28	17	18	32	20	36	6	29	26	39	42	58	14	46	60	67	46
TEHRAN	21	17	25	28	17	18	32	20	36	6	29	26	39	42	58	14	46	60	67	46
KABUL	21	17	25	28	17	18	32	20	36	6	29	26	39	42	58	14	46	60	67	46
SAROBI	27	22	37	40	24	36	44	29	42	11	47	37	56	53	71	20	69	79	94	73
DELHI	27	22	37	40	24	36	44	29	42	11	47	37	56	53	71	20	69	79	94	73
BOMBAY	27	22	37	40	24	36	44	29	42	11	47	37	56	53	71	20	69	79	94	73
POSITION LEG 1	6	4	=11	13	5	10	15	7	14	1	=17	=11	21	20	27	2	=25	29	32	28
YOUANMI	27	22	37	40	24	36	44	29	42	11	47	37	56	53	71	20	69	79	94	73
MARVEL LOCH	27	22	37	40	24	36	44	29	42	11	47	37	67	64	83	20	84	99	110	106
LAKE KING	32	36	42	54	31	43	55	34	52	11	63	52	87	68	106	20	119	116	134	136
CEDUNA	32	36	42	54	31	43	55	34	52	11	63	52	87	68	106	20	119	116	134	136
QUORN	32	36	42	54	31	43	55	34	52	25	63	52	87	68	106	20	119	116	134	136
MORALANA	32	36	42	54	31	43	55	34	52	25	63	52	87	68	106	20	119	116	134	137
BRACHINA	32	36	42	54	31	43	55	34	52	25	64	52	92	68	111	28	128	129	140	158
MINGARY	32	36	42	54	31	43	55	34	52	25	64	99	92	68	111	28	130	176	159	183
MENINDEE	32	36	42	56	31	43	55	34	52	25	64	120	92	68	124	28	130	176	159	183
GUNBAR	32	36	42	56	31	43	55	34	52	25	64	120	92	68	124	28	130	176	159	183
EDI	32	36	49	57	39	51	66	44	59	29	95	131	108	86	137	30	130	176	159	183
BROOKSIDE	38	39	49	57	39	51	66	44	59	29	95	131	108	86	137	36	149	193	181	203
OMEO	46	50	58	61	63	66	79	59	107	39	125	153	151	120	170	40	175	227	227	238
MURRINDAL	46	50	58	61	63	66	79	59	107	136	125	153	151	120	175	40	175	227	227	238
INGEBYRA	48	55	58	61	66	66	85	62	116	142	136	156	163	137	185	40	188	250	249	259
NUMERALLA	48	55	58	61	66	66	85	62	116	142	136	156	163	137	186	40	197	250	249	259
HINDMARSH	50	56	62	63	68	70	91	114	121	144	146	160	171	147	195	206	208	264	265	269
NOWRA	50	56	62	63	68	70	91	114	121	144	146	169	171	173	195	206	208	264	266	269
WARWICK FARM	50	56	62	63	68	70	91	114	121	144	146	169	171	173	195	206	208	264	266	269
POSITION FINISH	1	2	3	4	5	6	7	8	9	10	11	12	13	14	15	16	17	18	19	20

PLACE	21	22	23	24	25	26	27	28	29	30	31	32	33	34	=35	=35	37	38	39	40
CAR	31	98	1	4	56	62	83	71	72	90	17	45	7	70	60	77	54	20	18	46
CONTROL																				
PARIS	0	0	0	0	0	0	0	0	0	0	0	0	0	0	0	0	0	0	0	0
TURIN	0	24	0	0	0	0	0	0	0	0	0	0	0	0	0	6	0	0	0	0
BELGRADE	0	24	0	0	0	0	0	0	0	0	0	0	0	0	3	6	0	0	0	0
ISTANBUL	0	24	0	0	0	0	0	0	0	0	0	0	0	0	3	6	0	0	0	0
SIVAS	0	24	0	0	0	0	0	0	0	0	0	0	0	0	3	6	0	0	0	0
ERZINCAN	22	91	38	20	49	43	61	58	115	48	73	38	69	74	107	60	173	47	74	76
TEHRAN	22	91	38	20	49	43	61	58	115	48	73	38	69	74	107	60	173	47	74	76
KABUL	22	135	38	324	49	43	129	183	258	254	205	38	211	272	283	572	263	437	285	661
SAROBI	30	151	47	344	69	59	153	215	289	271	254	227	250	291	309	602	287	476	345	690
DELHI	30	151	47	344	69	59	153	215	289	271	254	227	250	311	309	602	287	476	494	690
BOMBAY	30	151	47	344	69	59	153	215	289	299	254	482	250	311	309	602	287	476	494	1101
POSITION LEG 1	8	33	=17	50	=25	23	34	37	43	45	41	53	40	48	47	56	42	52	54	59
YOUANMI	30	151	47	344	69	59	153	215	289	299	254	482	250	311	309	602	287	476	494	1101
MARVEL LOCH	30	181	65	369	88	65	198	233	326	303	319	514	299	343	346	622	326	527	539	1130
LAKE KING	32	220	88	383	130	88	243	250	343	323	369	536	341	378	431	645	372	612	602	1176
CEDUNA	32	220	90	383	153	219	315	250	343	323	369	536	341	378	532	645	372	612	624	1176
QUORN	32	220	90	383	267	293	315	250	343	323	369	536	341	439	532	645	372	612	624	1176
MORALANA	32	234	91	383	267	303	330	250	400	323	370	536	413	378	543	648	379	662	671	1183
BRACHINA	32	243	104	383	284	303	343	257	408	477	390	547	437	443	564	712	403	704	704	1210
MINGARY	262	261	134	383	318	376	369	478	420	477	449	622	623	467	652	714	464	767	791	1393
MENINDEE	291	261	134	383	318	376	380	478	420	506	449	622	623	569	652	777	519	767	791	1505
GUNBAR	291	261	134	383	318	376	380	478	420	506	449	622	623	591	681	777	519	767	791	1505
EDI	291	261	134	383	318	376	401	478	420	519	463	642	623	591	682	777	519	785	885	1546
BROOKSIDE	301	284	150	393	346	397	401	506	486	546	492	664	659	621	743	794	554	814	929	1570
OMEO	316	322	181	417	377	419	440	539	554	583	533	686	705	726	788	819	600	873	996	1609
MURRINDAL	318	322	322	417	377	419	440	539	554	583	545	686	705	743	788	833	675	873	998	1611
INGEBYRA	325	342	351	424	399	441	457	558	573	603	573	703	735	773	829	859	705	897	1025	1634
NUMERALLA	325	342	351	424	399	441	457	558	575	603	585	703	735	783	829	859	718	897	1025	1634
HINDMARSH	332	358	360	430	416	455	470	570	587	619	615	714	757	799	845	873	834	917	1057	1653
NOWRA	332	358	360	430	438	455	470	570	587	623	656	715	776	816	873	873	894	942	1075	1658
WARWICK FARM	332	358	360	430	438	455	470	570	587	623	656	715	776	816	873	873	894	942	1075	1658
POSITION FINISH	21	22	23	24	25	26	27	28	29	30	31	32	33	34	=35	=35	37	38	39	40

PLACE	41	42	43	44	45	46	47	48	49	50	51	52	53	54	55	56	DNF	DNF	DNF	DNF
CAR	33	47	11	44	78	53	42	93	99	41	79	40	82	91	8	69	87	89	52	36
CONTROL																				
PARIS	6	0	0	0	0	0	0	0	0	12	0	0	0	0	0	0	0	0	0	0
TURIN	6	0	0	0	0	0	0	0	0	12	0	0	0	0	0	0	0	0	0	0
BELGRADE	6	0	0	0	0	0	0	0	0	12	0	0	0	0	0	0	0	0	0	0
ISTANBUL	6	0	0	0	0	0	0	0	0	12	0	0	0	0	1440	0	0	0	0	0
SIVAS	6	0	0	0	0	0	0	0	38	12	0	0	0	0	2880	0	0	0	0	0
ERZINCAN	68	67	153	39	117	157	69	45	269	207	424	117	239	34	3320	1440	16	58	46	66
TEHRAN	68	67	153	39	117	157	69	45	269	207	424	1557	257	34	5760	2880	16	58	46	66
KABUL	351	274	528	713	259	157	645	242	1709	4527	1864	7317	6017	4354	10080	8640	16	155	46	66
SAROBI	410	319	570	752	295	1597	2085	1682	3149	5967	3304	8757	7457	5794	10098	8640	21	175	66	86
DELHI	452	319	570	804	295	1597	3525	1682	3336	6047	4744	9255	8897	7234	10098	10719	21	175	66	86
BOMBAY	452	319	570	804	295	1782	5623	4253	3384	6154	5992	9255	10990	8657	10098	10719	21	175	66	86
POSITION LEG 1	51	49	55	58	44	61	65	64	63	67	66	69	72	68	70	71	3	36	24	30
YOUANMI	452	319	608	804	295	1873	5623	4253	339	7594	6105	9255	10990	10097	11538	10719	21	175	66	86
MARVEL LOCH	507	407	684	836	305	1943	5653	4271	3456	7594	6161	9269	11050	10097	11538	10737	21	215	78	86
LAKE KING	569	457	2124	2276	384	3383	5733	4297	4896	7663	7601	9363	11095	10114	11554	12177	21	233	106	112
CEDUNA	569	652	2124	2427	384	3383	5733	4297	4959	7692	7652	9363	11160	10114	11554	12177	21	299	106	112
QUORN	675	652	2124	2427	384	3383	5733	4297	4959	7692	7652	9363	11160	10114	11626	12177	21	299	106	112
MORALANA	700	666	2147	2431	422	3419	5743	4297	5000	7702	7695	9388	11174	10114	11650	12177	21	299	106	113
BRACHINA	2140	2106	2159	2470	1867	3453	5764	4307	6440	7751	9135	9388	11209	11554	13090	13617	21	315	117	113
MINGARY	2234	2158	2228	2492	1952	3549	5825	4350	6493	7908	9578	9578	11286	11559	13184	13617	21	524	123	127
MENINDEE	2242	2160	2228	2537	1965	3549	5825	4380	6493	7917	9283	9686	11299	11559	13192	13617	21	1964	1563	RTD
GUNBAR	2242	2160	2228	2537	1965	3555	5825	4380	6522	7917	9311	9686	11299	11559	13192	13617	21	1964	RTD	
EDI	2263	2290	2284	2537	2024	3555	5831	4482	6574	7917	9334	9686	11299	11559	13214	13617	21	1964		
BROOKSIDE	2295	2328	2331	2556	2072	3589	5862	4449	6618	7961	9380	9708	11333	11581	13246	13636	21	2103		
OMEO	2331	2365	2364	2600	2120	3642	5889	4476	6675	8024	9432	9737	11388	11609	13282	13725	34	2153		
MURRINDAL	2331	2365	2364	2657	2120	3651	5889	4476	6675	8024	9466	9737	11388	11609	13282	13725	34	2153		
INGEBYRA	2348	2389	2385	2680	2158	3697	5907	4493	6740	8065	9517	9761	11421	11627	13299	13758	36	2179		
NUMERALLA	2349	2389	2385	2722	2159	3701	5907	4505	6752	8065	9517	9761	11421	11627	13300	13758	36	2179		
HINDMARSH	2370	2408	2427	2754	3599	3722	5917	4699	6773	8090	9549	9775	11444	11642	13326	13777	39	RTD		
NOWRA	2399	2408	2491	2848	3665	3746	5925	6139	6787	8111	9603	9775	11465	11646	13350	13790	RTD			
WARWICK FARM	2399	2408	2491	2848	3665	3746	5925	6139	6787	8111	9603	9775	11465	11646	13350	13790				
POSITION FINISH	41	42	43	44	45	46	47	48	49	50	51	52	53	54	55	56				

PLACE	DNF 94	DNF 10	DNF 3	DNF 95	DNF 28	DNF 100	DNF 27	DNF 73	DNF 26	DNF 13	DNF 25	DNF 6	DNF 88	DNF 9	DNF 34	DNF 63	DNF 96	DNF 66	DNF 14	DNF 39
CONTROL																				
PARIS	0	0	0	0	0	0	0	0	0	0	0	0	0	0	0	0	0	0	0	0
TURIN	0	0	0	0	0	0	0	0	0	0	0	0	0	0	0	0	0	0	0	0
BELGRADE	0	21	0	0	0	0	0	0	0	0	0	0	0	0	0	0	0	0	0	0
ISTANBUL	0	21	0	0	0	0	0	0	0	0	0	0	0	0	0	0	0	0	0	0
SIVAS	0	21	0	212	0	0	0	0	0	0	0	0	0	0	0	0	0	0	0	0
ERZINCAN	36	89	119	345	60	68	168	22	32	38	53	98	76	163	49	25	85	261	17	26
TEHRAN	36	89	119	345	60	68	168	22	32	38	53	98	76	163	49	25	85	375	17	26
KABUL	36	205	460	1785	60	147	761	22	32	38	205	269	159	4483	5809	25	262	3255	RTD	RTD
SAROBI	46	249	507	2042	89	162	1034	31	50	57	229	308	418	4666	6480	34	290	RTD	RTD	
DELHI	46	249	801	2042	89	162	1034	31	50	57	229	308	418	6106	7920	RTD	RTD			
BOMBAY	46	249	801	2042	89	162	1500	31	50	57	229	308	RTD	RTD	RTD					
POSITION LEG 1	16	39	57	62	31	35	60	9	19	22	38	46								
YOUANMI	46	249	801	2187	89	217	1524	31	50	57	229	308								
MARVEL LOCH	46	364	917	3627	128	255	1584	31	65	1497	1669	1748								
LAKE KING	56	1804	2357	3760	153	313	3024	47	96	RTD	RTD	RTD								
CEDUNA	56	1804	2423	3760	185	1753	4464	47	1536											
QUORN	56	1805	2442	3856	185	3193	4464	RTD	RTD											
MORALANA	56	1827	2460	3856	191	RTD	RTD													
BRACHINA	58	1858	2484	RTD	RTD															
MINGARY	RTD	RTD	RTD																	
MENINDEE																				
GUNBAR																				
EDI																				
BROOKSIDE																				
OMEO																				
MURRINDAL																				
INGEBYRA																				
NUMERALLA																				
HINDMARSH																				
NOWRA																				
WARWICK FARM																				
POSITION FINISH																				

338

PLACE CAR	DNF 59	DNF 22	DNF 21	DNF 86	DNF 23	DNF 35	DNF 81	DNF 50	DNF 97	DNF 15	DNF 65	DNF 84	DNF 5	DNF 37	DNF 38	DNF 85	DNF 16	DNF 67	DNS 49	DNS 80
CONTROL																				
PARIS	0	0	0	0	0	0	0	0	0	0	0	0	0	0	0	0	0	0	DNS	DNS
TURIN	0	0	0	0	0	0	0	0	0	0	0	0	0	0	0	0	0	0		
BELGRADE	0	0	0	0	0	0	0	0	0	1	0	0	0	0	0	1440	RTD	RTD		
ISTANBUL	0	0	0	0	0	0	0	0	0	1	0	0	0	0	0	2880				
SIVAS	0	0	0	0	0	0	0	0	0	1	0	223	RTD	RTD	RTD	RTD				
ERZINCAN	32	43	84	93	101	480	100	132	33	67	98	RTD								
TEHRAN	32	43	84	93	101	1920	1540	1572	RTD	RTD	RTD									
KABUL	RTD	RTD	RTD	RTD	RTD	RTD	RTD	RTD												
SAROBI																				
DELHI																				
BOMBAY																				
POSITION LEG 1																				
YOUANMI																				
MARVEL LOCH																				
LAKE KING																				
CEDUNA																				
QUORN																				
MORALANA																				
BRACHINA																				
MINGARY																				
MENINDEE																				
GUNBAR																				
EDI																				
BROOKSIDE																				
OMEO																				
MURRINDAL																				
INGEBYRA																				
NUMERALLA																				
HINDMARSH																				
NOWRA																				
WARWICK FARM																				
POSITION FINISH																				

Index